This timely, rich study explores the complex journeys of young Arab–Australian men who pursue creative vocational aspirations as they juggle the competing forces of peers, family, and community. Using a life-history narrative analysis approach the book offers new insights into the enduring significance of class, place, gender, and ethnicity. In imagining their vocational futures they seek to belong to a broader creative community, building identities that go beyond shared migrant experience.

Professor Johanna Wyn, *Director of the Youth Research Centre, University of Melbourne, Australia*

Young Migrant Identities

In this day and age, much has been discussed as to what it means 'to be an Arab'. However, this enlightening volume seeks instead to invite us deeper into young Arab–Australian men's lives as we explore their vocational aspirations and working experiences within highly racialised and hierarchical industries.

Young Migrant Identities is an in-depth exploration into the lives of Arab–Australian young men living in Western Sydney with creative career aspirations. Indeed, not only does Idriss explore how these men develop interests in fields such as music, filmmaking, and design, but she also examines the multilinear routes that they take to turn these interests into vocational identities. However, in the local migrant communities in which these young men live, creative identities are seen to compromise individual and familial prospects for social mobility, and artistic interests tend to go unsupported. Thus, this book also strives to offer new insights about how notions of gender, ethnicity, and social class are experienced because of these young men's 'risky' career ambitions.

A timely volume, *Young Migrant Identities* draws together a range of theoretical issues and debates, engaging with sociological approaches to race and social class, creative and cultural economies, and studies on youth. It will particularly appeal to post-graduate students and post-doctoral researchers interested in fields such as Youth Studies, Ethnicity Studies, Cultural Economy, and Migration Studies.

Sherene Idriss is an Adjunct Fellow at the School of Social Sciences and Psychology (Religion and Society Research Cluster), Western Sydney University.

Youth, Young Adulthood and Society
Series editor: Andy Furlong
University of Glasgow, UK / Andy.Furlong@glasgow.ac.uk

The **Youth, Young Adulthood and Society** series brings together social scientists from many disciplines to present research monographs and collections, seeking to further research into youth in our changing societies around the world today. The books in this series advance the field of youth studies by presenting original, exciting research, with strongly theoretically- and empirically-grounded analysis.

www.routledge.com/Youth-Young-Adulthood-and-Society/book-series/YYAS

Published:

The Subcultural Imagination
Theory, Research and Reflexivity in Contemporary Youth Cultures
Edited by Shane Blackman and Michelle Kempson

Muslim Youth in the Diaspora
Challenging Extremism through Popular Culture
Pam Nilan

Young People in the Labour Market
Past, Present, Future
Andy Furlong, John Goodwin, Sarah Hadfield, Stuart Hall, Kevin Lowden and Henrietta O'Connor

Young Migrant Identities
Creativity and Masculinity
Sherene Idriss

Forthcoming:

Identities, Inequalities and Social Change
David Farrugia

Rethinking Young People's Marginalisation
Beyond Neo-Liberal Futures?
Perri Campbell, Lyn Harrison, Chris Hickey and Peter Kelly

Youth, Class and Everyday Struggles
Steven Threadgold

Young Migrant Identities

Creativity and Masculinity

Sherene Idriss

Routledge
Taylor & Francis Group
LONDON AND NEW YORK

First published 2018
by Routledge
2 Park Square, Milton Park, Abingdon, Oxon OX14 4RN

and by Routledge
711 Third Avenue, New York, NY 10017

Routledge is an imprint of the Taylor & Francis Group, an informa business

British Library Cataloguing in Publication Data
A catalogue record for this book is available from the British Library

Library of Congress Cataloging in Publication Data
A catalog record for this book has been requested

ISBN: 978-1-138-23404-8 (hbk)
ISBN: 978-1-315-30815-9 (ebk)

Typeset in Times New Roman
by Deanta Global Publishing Services, Chennai, India

Contents

Introduction

Edward Said, one of the most prominent scholars of postcolonialism and celebrated Arab intellectual, had a daughter, Najla. She was born and raised in the United States and attended Chapin, a prestigious school for girls in Manhattan, New York. As a young girl she was painfully shy so her mother enrolled her in acting lessons to boost her confidence. Years later, while studying literature at Brown University, Najla decided to pursue acting as a career and says her parents 'indulged' her in this aspiration. Even without financial constraints or familial disapproval, she found herself struggling with intense racial prejudice as she attempted to turn her childhood hobby into a profession. In her memoir she writes,

> I ventured out into the commercial world with the name Najla Said. I was repeatedly and constantly described by casting directors and agents as 'ethnic' and then just as often rejected with, 'No! You're like a Jewish Italian girl from New York. You're too white to be ethnic'. I struggled to figure out which I was. I refused to change my name. I had no deep attachment to my culture, but I felt very strongly that I should not have to do something so arcane to be seen for all that I was. I felt that deep painful racist punch in my stomach every time I even considered the idea of becoming 'Nancy Smith' so that I could get a job. I pressed on. My [non-Arab] friends began to succeed.
>
> (Said 2013: 201)

Najla came from wealth and a highly educated, cosmopolitan family. But in the world of acting, she was still treated as 'Other', as defined by and stereotyped because of her inescapable brownness. Indeed, it was repeatedly suggested to her by casting agents that she ought to find herself a niche, perhaps emphasise her 'exotic' difference. Although she had been well versed in Orientalist thought, it did not change the fact that even Edward Said's daughter remained vulnerable to the racial prejudice facing Arab youth living in the West who aspire to make their living as creative people.

Creative forms of labour, in fields such as film, music, and design, have become increasingly popular vocational pathways among young people in contemporary society (Haukka 2011; McRobbie 2004). They seemingly offer a chance for young people to engage in authentic forms of self-expression, to work in collaborative environments and perhaps avoid the monotony of older, traditional forms of labour. Often, creative work is highly romanticised by young people who have yet to venture into formal employment. Recent studies have exposed systemic issues such as precarious employment agreements (Ross 2008; Morgan *et al.* 2013), unequal forms of access to particular creative sectors depending on pre-existing social networks (Blair 2009), and gendered forms of exploitation (Gill and Pratt 2008; Christopherson 2009). Less remains known about how creative aspirations play out in particular social milieus among different groups of young people, or how aspirations develop over time according to the intersections between one's gendered, classed, and ethnicised identities (one exception is Taylor and Littleton 2012). Mainly, this is because studies of creative workers are treated as a cohesive group with fully formed vocational identities competing for the same interests.

The post 9/11 hybridised Arab

In her memoir, Najla Said reflects on how her Arabness shaped and was shaped by her attachment to a creative vocational aspiration. She notes that as an aspiring actor, her ethnicity and gender became incredibly politicised especially in a post 9/11 climate. The pressure to fit into a stereotypical character as the 'exotic Other' was something she resisted entirely, saying,

> I don't feel entirely American, never have, but it's not because I don't want to or because I don't seem it – I do want to, I do seem it. I don't feel entirely Arab either, for the same reasons. But I also certainly don't feel like any *combination of the two.*
>
> (Said 2013: 217)

Such ambivalence led to a re-evaluation of her original creative vocational aspirations. The frustration experienced by Arab artists living in the diaspora is that they exist in a double bind whereby they cannot escape their Arabness – heightened especially in a climate of rising anti-immigration sentiments and rampant xenophobia across the West – but refuse to reduce their entire creative identities into narrow and simplistic categories of Otherness.[1] This book is inspired by those artists who have to continually renegotiate their creative aspirations on the basis of racial, class, and gendered prejudice as well as communal obligation and expectations. As such, the book challenges the myths of inclusivity of creative labour by documenting the complicated, multifarious ways that young men of ethnic minority backgrounds develop creative identities. It is specifically concerned with the intersections between ethnicity, gender, social class, and the ways that processes of racialisation shape creative aspirations.

Situated specifically within the Australian context, I examined how Arab–Australian young men develop creative vocational aspirations in the context of competing forces, including family, community and individual agency. I conducted life-history interviews with young Arab–Australian men who wanted to be musicians, actors, filmmakers, writers, work in web design and animation. Unlike Najla, these young men came from socio-economic disadvantage as they grew up in Bankstown, in the South-West of Sydney, in families where parents spoke little English and where they attended under-resourced schools in the local area. This region of Sydney has the highest concentration of all Arab–Australian migrants in Australia with 21 per cent of the total Bankstown population speaking Arabic at home[2] and it has been negatively portrayed as an 'ethnic ghetto' (Al-Natour 2010). Unlike Najla, the parents of these Arab–Australian young men did not indulge their creative interests; instead this book will explore how creativity was actively negotiated within family and communal dynamics wherein creative identities are more often than not treated as problematic.

Further, unlike Najla, these informants' families were invested in projects of social mobility, as so many migrants of non-English speaking backgrounds are, by encouraging their children to study at university in order to become stable professionals like lawyers, doctors or teachers. As such, this book investigates how creativity and individual pursuits of creative vocational trajectories, which are so often vaguely defined, multilinear and not necessarily well paid, complicate the process of migrant aspirations for social mobility.

In addition to closely examining the familial and communal dynamics that inform personal creative aspirations, the book also pays close attention to the processes of racialisation that produce additional burdens and roadblocks to vocational ambitions. In the Australian context, moral panic about Arab youth emerged in the late 1990s when fears erupted over the use of firearms among rival ethnic-based bikie gangs; the use of such weapons was represented by the media as a failure of allowing migration from the Middle East to Australia.[3] Additionally, the criminalisation of all Arab–Australian men as sexual predators became intensified during the early 2000s when a group of Lebanese–Australian teenage boys, led by ringleader Bilal Skaf, gang raped two Anglo–Australian girls in a public park in Greenacre, a suburb that falls within the Bankstown City Council region (Dagistanli 2007). This association between ethnicity and sexual violence has persisted fifteen years on. In 2015, the *Sydney Morning Herald* published an article by well-known journalist Paul Sheehan in which he claimed that a homeless Anglo–Australian woman 'Louise' was gang raped by 'carloads' of Muslim men and the police never investigated the case or charged any of the perpetrators.[4] Neither Sheehan nor his editors at the *Sydney Morning Herald* actually checked the claims made by Louise. It turned out that she had fabricated the entire tale and had used it in a speech she gave a month prior at a Reclaim Australia[5] protest as propaganda to galvanise the far-right supporters against the governments' migration laws.

The *Sydney Morning Herald* retracted the story immediately. In spite of such a retraction, it is impossible to ignore the fact that such 'reporting' of the connection between ethnicity and sexual violence can be made freely in national newspapers. In Lentin's (2015) discussion of 'what race does' she outlines that race governs, orders and structures individuals into hierarchies leaving some disempowered; race-thinking is how racism remains sustained in the everyday governance of 'post-racial' societies. The inevitable conclusion for Sheehan and his editors then is that claims presented by 'Louise' need not be interrogated because *of course* a Middle Eastern man *would* commit such a crime against women.

It is in this context that my book examines the ways that Arab–Australian young men with creative aspirations traverse various employment fields and their experiences of, as Najla had felt, the deep painful racist 'punch in their stomach' as they are faced with structural inequalities. In a post 9/11 climate, where Arabness and Islam are demonised in the rhetoric of the global 'war on terror' and where Arabs are generally grossly misrepresented and stereotyped in Western works of art (Said 1997; Shaheen 2001), young people of Arab–Australian backgrounds seeking to participate in creative industries are offered marginal spaces in which they can express themselves. Of course, this position of marginality is one that has plagued so many other ethnic minority groups in the West, as Hall (1997) and Hutnyk (2000) have demonstrated. Postcolonial writers like Gloria Anzaldua (1999) and Mae Henderson (1990) have eloquently explored the inner dialogue that takes place when one exists at the border, the violence that takes place when the voices of black and female artists and intellectuals are sidelined and subsumed within white, male hegemonic literary traditions. This book seeks to contribute to these debates by examining a group of young migrants who have never been researched in relation to their creative and artistic life aspirations and who find their voices sidelined and discounted.

In the Australian context, the Arab youth in my research were not simply marginalised because of their ethnicity, but also because ethnic hierarchies and urban locales often operate in the public consciousness as metonyms for social class. This book adopts an intersectional and cultural framework for understanding class that moves away from rigid Marxist definitions and considers, in addition to income and employment type, a host of social relations and symbolic markers (Anthias 2012). Even when the informants in my study are unable to articulate their own social class positions, often the case for young people from all walks of life, it remains generally the case that Arab–Australian young men who live in and around Bankstown are perceived, in certain circumstances, as lacking the right economic, social and cultural resources to fully participate in mainstream creative industries.

Thus, Arab–Australian young men with creative vocational aspirations who come from socio-economic disadvantage, from migrant backgrounds and as 'demonized' young people, do not simply pursue creative aspirations without engaging, to varying degrees, with questions of ethnicity, masculinity and social class. Do the challenges around access to creative industries sway or change their vocational aspirations? Does their membership in an Arab–Australian community lead to a reshaping of their creative passions and aspirations? Do personal creative vocational aspirations result in this cohort of young people becoming ambivalent and insecure in their membership of something called an Arab–Australian community?

Creative industries and risky societies: A short overview

This book examines the discursive strategies employed by these young men in the course of their life-history narratives to negotiate these challenges and issues. I follow the lead of Ganguly (1992) in her study of Indian immigrants who suggests that

> Recollections of the past serve as the active ideological terrain on which people represent themselves to themselves. The past acquires a more marked salience with subjects for whom categories of the present have been made unusually unstable or unpredictable, as a consequence of the displacement enforced by postcolonial and migrant circumstances.
>
> (Ganguly 1992: 29)

By analysing the ways that Arab–Australian young men recount important life-history moments, I aim to capture detailed, complex and highly personalised conceptualisations of creativity that emerge in particular local contexts. These definitions of creativity, as we will see in Chapters 1–5 continually shift according to the ways in which these young people reconstruct their past and imagine their future selves. Such definitions engage with, but are distinct from, the broader ways in which we have come to understand creativity as it relates to craft, skill, and, more recently, employment and industry.

The creative and cultural industries are growing employment sectors in Australia (Higgs *et al.* 2007; Hartley 2005). This is partly due to globalisation, rapid technological advancements and new labour markets opening up while primary industries, such as manufacturing, are rapidly declining in Australia and moving offshore. Government bodies are making substantial investments to support these sectors based on the premise that in a knowledge society, creative work is integral for economic growth (Pratt and Jeffcutt 2009). Indeed, creative and cultural industries are now "emblematic of a new economic order and a key growth sector" (Allen and Hollingsworth 2013: 499). In 2013, it was reported that the creative industries contributed "around $90.19 billion to the national economy annually in turnover. It adds almost $45.89 billion in gross domestic product (GDP) and helps generate exports of $3.2 billion dollars annually" (Creative Industries Innovation centre, 2013: 62).

These changes to the labour market have a longer history that is important to briefly note. During the 1950s and 1960s, much employment was in manufacturing and manual labour; it was a time when workers were de-skilled and subject to strict hierarchical structures of management (Sabel 1994). The most significant change since then has been what Garnham (2005) calls the "Thatcherite version" of post–Fordism whereby cultural and media institutions became deregulated, niche markets and technological innovation flourished, entrepreneurship was heavily supported while the old style of centralised hierarchical management slowly dissipated. These policy changes, which were accelerated in Australia under the Keating government, contributed to, and were simultaneously a reflection of, a new "compulsion of consumption that now so energises human need, pleasure and identity" (Amin and Thrift 2007: 147). In fact, "making money out of culture, consumption and spectacle are all now assumed to be the staples of a knowledge intensive post-industrial economy" (Amin and Thrift 2007: 151).

Creative industries then are at the centre of our knowledge economy. But it is not only the case that people want to make money out of culture and creativity, but also that there has been a collective shift in our approach to work in which creativity plays a pivotal role. Cohen (2006), for instance, conceptualises the new work ethic as a synthesis of creativity, communication and collaboration. Young people from all socio-economic backgrounds are driven by the intrinsic benefits and personal satisfaction of work alongside monetary incentives while also remaining realistic about their prospects in an unstable marketplace that disproportionately exploits young people (Allen and Hollingworth 2013).

The risk society thesis reveals a concurrent trend to the rise of creativity (Beck 2000), one that has heavily influenced the work of youth sociologists in Australia (Woodman and Wyn 2006; 2013). Despite coming from different sides of the theoretical spectrum, these authors all suggest that risk has now become institutionalised in our contemporary society. The importance of tradition is said to be all but diminished and the comfort gained from rites of passage relating to marriage and family has weakened. In their place, work – not family – becomes the primary institution where individuals are said to achieve self-actualisation; especially as more people in Western societies spend more of their day working, travelling to and from work and taking up courses and further training to prepare themselves for work. We can understand the importance young people place on finding paid employment that resonates with their creative interests within this broader context.

Additionally, creativity has become a policy buzzword that seems to be characteristic of the 'soft' skills, in tandem with other characteristics such as flexibility, risk-taking, mobility and individualism, that more young people are encouraged to possess in order to increase their chances of employability (Morgan 2006; Atkinson 2010). This character trait, being 'creative', is one that is sought after across a range of employment sectors, not just in the creative and cultural arena, signalling broader changes to our labour market. With the decline of industrial labour in Australia and the increased numbers of young people with higher education qualifications (Norton 2012), employers take seriously these skills of 'creativity' to distinguish between candidates who are all highly qualified and experienced.

Studies show that more young people now aspire to work in creative fields because it is sold to them as exciting, sexy, and fun (McRobbie 2002; Gill 2002; Neff *et al.* 2005). An array of new courses and degrees have been introduced across Australian universities, colleges, and schools (Graham 2005) where one can now undertake study programs to specifically gain the skills required to become what is called a 'creative worker'. For example, the Queensland University of Technology offers a degree called Bachelor of Creative Industries where expected career destinations include – advertising professional, art project manager, art writer, arts administrator, fashion professional, and internet professional.[6] As indicated by this list, the definition of creativity has broadened beyond traditional notions of fine arts so as to include work in visual and performing arts, museums, and galleries but also broadcasting, film, publishing, recorded music (Galloway and Dunlop 2007: 18). Thus, when we talk of the rising popularity of creative industries, there are a wide variety of employment fields made up of music and performing arts, film, television and radio, advertising, software development, writing and print media, design and visual arts, and architecture (Creative Industries Innovation Centre 2013).

The 'creative industries' are distinguishable from other employment fields such as law, medicine, teaching, accountancy, and engineering in that irrespective of one's qualifications and educational background, aspirants can, like Edward Said's daughter was, still be openly judged on visibly non-white identity markers. There is little to no protection from such prejudice in these industries unlike the legal safeguards in place in traditional employment markets. Such insecurity is compounded for young people who make up a large part of these creative industries; we cannot ignore the youth-centred nature of fashion and music sectors for example.

Economic and urban policymakers use loose, vague definitions of creativity to encourage young people to join the supposedly exciting and fun 'creative class' (Gill 2002; Banks and Hesmondhalgh 2009). In reality, the daily tasks required of many creative workers might bear closer resemblance to business administration but in new fields that have opened up due to technological advancement such as multimedia or film editing (Gill 2002; Banks and Hesmondhalgh 2009). The mismatch between the myth of the creatives' lifestyle and reality has been critiqued by Ross (2007) who suggests that there are major problems to come from uncritically embracing creativity into the ethos of contemporary working life.

> The kind of development embraced by policymakers seems guaranteed merely to elevate this traditionally unstable work profile into an inspirational model for youth looking to make an adventure out of their entry into the contingent labour force. If the creative industries are the ones to follow, all kinds of work, in short, may well look more and more like musicians gigs: nice work if you can get it.
>
> (Ross 2007: 18)

Ross suggests that creative work is scarce, not often well paid, and difficult to sustain over the course of one's life. His remarks echo the key concerns of others who have researched creative-based working practices (Gill and Pratt 2008). Individuals working in these fields are often exploited, agreeing to work for free because they simply have the passion for their craft.They are expected to network constantly in order to remain up to date about upcoming jobs and there is often no formalised support system available during what can be extended periods of unemployment (Murray and Gollmitzer 2012). While this book does not extensively investigate working practices, I was interested in the awareness levels among Arab–Australian young men about these realities. Further, I aim in this book to explore how socio-economic background, gendered performativities, and ethnic ties produce particular attitudes towards the challenges of creative work.

Following on from Ross's critique, that applying the doctrines of creative work across employment fields increases instability and risk, it is important to situate my interest in creativity and creative vocational aspirations within what Beck (2000) calls a "risk society", Bauman (2000) "liquid modernity" and Giddens (2003) the "post-traditional order". There are many attributes and characteristics to each of these accounts of contemporary society that I explore over the course of this book as I aim to situate narratives of youthful vocational aspirations within local and global contexts. Briefly though, each of these conceptualisations of the self – from Beck, Bauman and Giddens – suggests there is no likelihood of a return to a stable, linear development of one's biography under postmodern structures and conditions. There are fewer templates available to individuals about how to navigate through youth to adulthood as a multitude of vocational, and also lifestyle, pathways are presented to them. Where in the past, workers may have been promised a 'job for life' or remained in one employment field with very little disruption, young people today are susceptible to rapid fluctuations of a deregulated market (Wyn 2005). Young people today are expected to complete post-compulsory education with few guarantees of a job at the end, and when they enter the employment market they are required to continually re-skill and retrain in order to remain competitive. As Roberts (2009) has claimed, "today's young people are neither surprised nor alarmed that they cannot step straight into jobs for life at sixteen. Most are comfortable with uncertainty" (Roberts 2009: 362).

While critics of contemporary labour conditions, especially those investigating creative labour, generally call for employers to offer more security and for lawmakers to implement safeguards to protect freelancers from exploitative working conditions (Morgan *et al.* 2013), postcolonial theorists and those working with intersectional frames of analysis are much more sceptical. Mitropolous (2011), for example, warns that critiques of cultural and creative labour that call for a return to the stability offered under Fordist regimes of production are short-sighted and blind to historical racial and gender inequality and exclusion. She suggests instead that "regular, full time and secure work, where it did exist, depended upon organisation and maintenance of precarious conditions for the vast majority of the world's populations" (Mitropolous 2011). The stability offered to working-class families living in the West under Fordism was thus at the expense of those on the periphery, such as unpaid domestic labour offered by women, and those in the global South. The working lives of the fathers and grandfathers of the young men in this study have always been inherently precarious, not least of all due to the upheaval of the migration process. These are important considerations that distinguish my research from existing studies about young people experiencing difficulties adapting to contemporary working conditions.

In spite of the structural conditions working against young people, the public discourse remains that if young people are passionate, ambitious, tenacious, and individualistic, 'anything is possible' (Roberts 2009). There are concerns for current generations of youth in this globalised, technologically-advanced society, because their expectation for endless possibilities has arguably resulted in an 'agency overloaded' sense of self (Skeggs 2005). Young people today are less likely to adopt a fatalistic approach to life and career as compared to earlier generations of youth, partially out of the fear of retrenchment and partially because, as I noted earlier, they view work as a way to express an authentic identity; working identities thus act as an extension of the self (Woodman and Wyn 2006). Further, young people have generally internalised the neoliberal rhetoric that those who are fatalistic, who simply accept their socio-economic conditions, are likely to end up as the 'losers' of our society (Sennett 1998). These facets of youth transitions are not specific to creative vocational identities, but they shape the ways that young people approach working life.

Masculinity and creativity: What is at stake?

This book takes an intersectional approach to understanding the entanglement between creativity, youth, gender, ethnicity, and social class. A main concern of the research was how Arab–Australian young men negotiate the templates of masculinity that are available to them in their local ethnic communities as well as within global youth cultures more generally. In Arab–Australian communities there has been, until very recently[7], almost complete silence from emerging artists and especially from male artists. This is partly due to the ways in which the arts are perceived as feminine and controversial; two characteristics that the socially mobile migrant family seeks to avoid at all costs for their male sons. Thus, a central question of my research is how does the investment in a creative identity produce new ways of performing masculinity within the migrant community when so much is at stake? This was never assumed to be separate from discussions of ethnicity or class but always treated as an intersecting process of identification following the methodological approaches of other youth researchers in local spaces such as Back (1996) and Nayak and Kehily (2008).

Several studies have looked at how working-class or socio-economically disadvantaged young men have had to respond to the structural changes in the world of work (McDowell 2003; Nixon 2009; Kenway *et al.* 2006; Nayak 2006). This body of work has revealed that working-class young men have inherited attitudes towards work and vocational dispositions that are ill suited to the demands of the service and knowledge economy. McDowell (2003), in her study of white working-class young men in two UK cities, Cambridge and Sheffield, found that they experience difficulty in their post-schooling transitions and pathways to employment because "traditional ways of becoming a man are increasingly less available" (McDowell 2003: 4). These young men were not likely to pursue further education because they hoped to replicate their father's 'masculine' occupational identities and yet the car and steel industry that many of the Sheffield young men aspired to work in were downsizing. When some of her informants attempted to work in retail and service roles, they became overwhelmed by having to work alongside girls, most of whom could easily adopt the right sensibilities needed for customer service. Similarly, Nixon (2006) in his study of working class men in the service industry found that, because "orientations to manual work develop from a young age, stem from educational failure and are embedded in an adherence to a particular form of working class 'embodied' masculinity, they cannot be reconstructed as easily as theories of post and reflexive modernity imply" (Nixon 2006: 202).

These studies follow in the tradition of Willis' (1977) ethnographic, in-depth study of working-class youthful masculinity. In his study, the young working-class men he interviewed displayed "general and personalised opposition to authority" (Willis 1977: 11), particularly towards teachers. They expressed that within a manual labour environment, the power imbalance between employer and employee is less felt than in the school environment in relation to their teachers. Manual labour is therefore articulated as the "resistance to mental work" they feel forced to do within the classroom (Willis 1977: 103). For the "lads" in that study, "physical labouring stands for and expresses most importantly, a kind of masculinity and ... aggressiveness, a degree of sharpness and wit ... an obvious kind of solidarity" (Willis 1977: 104). The young men prefer manual jobs for its association with the "social superiority of masculinity" whereas academia is associated with femininity.

In this book, I situate Arab–Australian young men's individual life-history narratives within this body of literature. To complement this set of the literature, I also draw on the work of Poynting *et al.* (2003) who look at how Lebanese–Australian young men display what they call 'protest masculinity'. This is explored in further detail in Chapter 2. Protest masculinity refers to the ways that young migrant men in Western Sydney, in Bankstown, resort to physical intimidation, exaggerated masculine traits of sporting prowess and performances of hyper-sexuality. They do this, on the one hand simply because of their youth, as they develop their identities, and on the other hand as a strategy to deal with racism within broader Australian society. The authors treat these particular performances of masculinity as therefore intimately tied into their *Lebaneseness* and as strategies to reclaim the 'respect' lost by being blamed for the social ills of Australian society. Similar arguments are made in relation to 'chavs' in the UK context whereby, as Nayak suggests, young men adopt specific street style, engaging in "the body reflexive technique of 'hard' masculinity", to overturn the class derision directed towards them (Nayak 2006: 822).

According to Poynting *et al.* (2003), young Lebanese–Australian boys in their study resist authority, treat 'femininity' as an inferior identity position and thus invest their time and energy towards developing 'hard' masculine identities which can only be fully understood in the context of their local areas and their migrant backgrounds. Following their findings, we see that the hegemonic masculinity identities of Arab–Australian Western Sydney youth run counter to creativity because creative self-expression is perceived as feminine. Several studies have looked at the entanglement between youth subcultural practices and creative expression (Thornton 1995; Hutnyk 2000; Hyder 2004). In light of the findings by Poynting *et al.*, my research takes a different approach by asking how young men who belong to an ethnic minority community in which creative expression is restricted and the cultivation of quirky subcultural personal style is generally met with disapproval, negotiate their sense of masculinity and develop personal aspirations?

Overview of the study: Methodological considerations

At this juncture it is necessary to note my own position as a member of the Lebanese/Syrian–Australian community. I was born in Australia to a Muslim family and grew up in various suburbs of South-West Sydney. Like my informants, my father and extended family members spoke little or broken English and I thus enjoyed life in a bilingual household although my Arabic dialect, like most children of Arab migrants in the West, grew to become some hybrid form we call 'Arabish'. While I can identify with my informants in many ways and their stories were by and large familiar to me, my research was not auto-ethnographic in any sense. This book was also not designed to tell us 'what it means to be an Arab–Australian'. In a similar vein to Ramy Aly's (2015) recent work on the ethnic performativity of Arabs in London, I too am sceptical of research that seeks to offer neat solutions or answers about 'being' of a particular ethnic or religious category. It is much more useful, I would contend, to consider how Arab–Australianness, gender and social class are 'performed' in light of creative aspirations.

Thus, my research is a qualitative study based primarily on life-history interviews. To recruit participants, I approached several youth-based arts organisations in Bankstown in order to gather an impression about the kinds of young people that were mostly accessing their services. One organisation runs creative writing workshops, filmmaking classes, and photography lessons as well as regularly holding showcases and participates in state-wide writing festivals. One of the staff members was a Lebanese–Australian young man and so, in addition to helping me meet with some of the creative aspirants he taught, I also interviewed him in his capacity as an artist/community arts worker. Over a 12-month period, I regularly attended creative writing workshops at the invitation of the community arts worker; some were held at local high schools and some were run at the centre. I was interested to see how the participants of these workshops and programs were taught creative skills, a discussion of which takes place in Chapter 5. For the most part though, the young men with whom I conducted interviews were not engaged in any current community arts workshops. They may have done so in the past but I learned that these programs are targeted towards much younger students (usually up to age fourteen, although this is not strictly regulated). The community arts organisation in Bankstown helped me locate some of these past members and this was the primary way in which I was able to access creative aspirants – whose creative interests ranged from writing to film, performing arts and design.

Each of the informants in this study are between eighteen to thirty years old and live in and around Bankstown; most were second-generation Lebanese–Australians, but some were a mix of Syrian, Iraqi and Palestinian. Of course, each of these specific ethnic groups have differentiated histories of migration to Australia but what makes them comparable is their common experience of being of Arabic-speaking background and the fact that their parents relocated to Australia as a result of civil strife in their homelands, as quasi-refugees without higher levels of education or Australian recognised tertiary credentials, a finding that is consistent with older research on Arabic speaking diasporas in Australia (Petty 1985). Some informants had travelled back to their parents' homelands and some had even lived there for a time but all completed their education in Australia. The label 'second generation' is a problematic one as Skrbis *et al.* (2007) have already noted. The label carries implications that these youth are locked into the category of 'non-white', it can also serve to reinforce ethnic hierarchies and finally, it prompts the question – when do you stop being from elsewhere? Despite these flaws, I use the term in this book to simply denote the children of parents born overseas, which all of these young men are. In the final chapter, I critically examine how labels around ethnicity are both fluid and sticky and frame the kinds of working lives some of these young men eventually have.

Almost all of the creative aspirants reported that their parents work in manual labour based jobs, in factory work, or are self-employed small business owners –usually of the corner store variety which demands quite a lot of physical labour. Apart from one informant, all the young men lived at home with their parents and most of them contribute very little of their earnings to the bills of the family home and as such they are dependent on their parents' economic situation. Additionally, all informants explained that their parent's English skills were weak and this created intergenerational conflict, a theme explored in some depth in Chapter 1. There is considerable evidence to suggest that proficiency in the English language in Australia is central to social mobility and increased working opportunities (Burnley *et al.* 1985; Jupp 1989). In this book I focus less on the improved life conditions that stem from English proficiency and more on the intergenerational conflict about the value of creative self-expression in itself.

The 20 face-to-face life-history interviews I conducted lasted approximately one hour, sometimes slightly longer, and the scope of questioning was left to be rather broad. There were overarching themes that I aimed to cover, such as childhood memories, school experiences, and of course future vocational aspirations, but beyond some basic questions the interviews remained fairly flexible in order to allow the informants to discuss their creative interests and anything associated with those interests as much, or as little, as they liked. We usually met in a café in Bankstown. The location of the interviews was significant because all around us were landmarks and sites that triggered memories for these young people who had spent most of their lives in the neighbourhood. They would point to the McDonalds, for instance, and mention how they spent most of their time there after school when they were younger.

Narrative, according to Zigon (2008) refers to the

> stories persons tell one another (or themselves) in order to create and maintain meaning and order in one's or a community's life. These narratives are limited by certain socio-historic cultural expectations and understandings of, among other things, what constitutes a story and how and to whom it can be told.
>
> (Zigon 2008: 146)

In this book, I adopt this branch of psycho-social narrative analysis to the interview material I collected. Following Mishler (1999), I examine how informants structure and organise key moments of their lives within the interview process, the particular linguistic codes they use to relay their life histories, as well as how those stories shed light on the intersections between their ethnic, class, and gendered identities and the particular outcomes that emerge from such intersections within specific social contexts at a given moment in their adolescence and early adulthood.

Thus, life-history narratives are often contradictory, incomplete, and messy. In this book, I aim to capture some of this messiness and avoid employing older notions of hybridity, of claiming that Arab–Australian youth live out a combination of two distinct cultures, something Najla Said explains she never really felt despite the external pressure to fit into essentialised, pre-existing categories for identification. The life-history narrative analysis approach aims to avoid a reading of these young men's lives whereby personal events or utterances are given too much weight as indicative of cultural and religious difference in an attempt to provide a cohesive portrait of various ethnic and religious groups.

Leila Abu-Lughod (1991) suggests that one powerful tool for "subverting the process of 'othering' it entails is to write 'ethnographies of the particular'" (Abu-Lughod 1991: 149). In her ethnography of Bedouin women's lives she says,

> Societies of the circum-Mediterranean have often been characterised as 'honour and shame' societies. What if one asked how an Egyptian schoolgirl waiting for her marriage to be arranged by an important family in the 1980s lived in this 'cultural' complex? By stressing the particularity of that girl's experiences or of that single marriage and by building a picture of polygyny or honour from individuals' discussions, recollections disagreements, and actions, one could make tangible and several larger theoretical points.
>
> (Abu-Lughod 2008: 13–14)

Abu-Lughod's approach has not only been influential in the way I analyse the data I have collected, it has also shaped the way I conceived of my research aims and questions. When I started conducting life-history interviews with young men of Arab–Australian backgrounds, I was guided by the belief that they would articulate their lives and their identities in ways that go beyond positioning themselves as ethnic subjects or as victims of discrimination and prejudice. Indeed, like many young people in western societies, Arab–Australian young men are deeply anxious about their career goals and aspirations. They continually ask themselves, what kind of job would best suit me? Should I go to university? What degree or course should I choose? Are there any consequences of choosing one career path over another? There exists a complicated relationship between identity-making processes and vocational aspirations as they appear in different moments of the life-history narratives.

Narrative analysis is also critical for understanding the ways that creativity is appropriated and mobilised by these young men for specific purposes at different moments in their lives. I will explore, for instance, how creativity operates as a floating signifier within the interview material. For example, creativity will be shown to stand for social mobility at particular moments, as indicative of an authentic Bankstown or working-class identity at others, as constitutive of these young men's intellectual capacity, and even as a sign that they imagine themselves to be more assimilated and integrated into broader Australian society than other members of their migrant communities. As such, I use this methodological approach to show how creative identities emerge from the interplay of how informants perceive themselves within their local working class communities, their youthful leisure practices, the specific ways they aimed to achieve social mobility, and the ambivalent relationships they had with their ethnic heritage and local communities.

Outline of the book

Over the course of each chapter, the aim is to trace how creative biographies unfold across key moments in these young men's life histories. While the book is structured sequentially over the key moments of informants' lives, this structure is not intended to suggest that young people experience the youth to adulthood transition in any linear fashion. Of course, there is no timetable to govern young people's transitions through life. As Price *et al.* (2011) explain, "youth transitions are shaped by theses of individualisation and detraditionalism – each young person must consciously tailor his or her own life trajectory" (Price *et al.* 2001: 70). Thus, the chapters are organised to explore the messiness involved in the youth experience during what were once thought of as neatly contained life 'stages' in the lead up to adulthood.

By doing so, I explore a number of interrelated themes such as the ways that creative practices are always contested and negotiated within families, how creative talent often goes unrecognised within the social networks of these young men, and how creative aspirations represent a break from communal traditions and norms. These themes, I will suggest, are specific to these young men's membership in an Arab–Australian local community wherein intergenerational conflict occurs around gender roles, individual youthful expression, and expectations around the transition from adolescence to adulthood, all of which are critical to the formation of their creative biographies.

In Chapter 1, I examine the role that families play in the narratives detailing the formation of creative aspirations provided by young people from Arab–Australian backgrounds. Existing literature (Poynting *et al.* 2003) reiterates the importance of the family and the local community in the socialisation process of young Arab–Australian men. I will look at how the immediate and extended families play central roles in shaping these youth's career aspirations. In this chapter, I investigate informants' use of the language of passion, looking at how they use this concept within the context of their interpersonal relationships. By doing this, I aim to highlight the ways that passion is constructed in oppositional terms to the idea of 'profession' in ways that parallel the disjuncture between informants and their parents at the particular moment in which these biographical narratives were collected.

Chapter 2 looks at the how creativity is appropriated by these informants when they reflected on their secondary schooling experiences. Specifically, I argue creativity becomes the key way in which these young men construct boundaries between self and other. The 'other' according to these informants is the other Arab–Australian boys in their school who belonged to what I call an ethnic-based local subculture called the 'Lebs'. During this phase of compulsory schooling, informants claim that their creative identities left them feeling as outsiders among their co-ethnic peers. The data analysed in this chapter reveals the uneasy relationship between young men's creative interests and their place as members of their local ethnic communities but also argues that the way they define themselves in relation to 'Leb' style, is an integral part of these informants' broader projects for upward social mobility.

Most informants were enrolled in or had completed further study. This was a carefully considered choice among this cohort and one that most of their parents heavily encouraged. In Chapter 3, I examine the themes that emerged when informants reflected on their higher education experiences. Higher education acted as a testing ground for working in the creative industries which, up to this point, many informants had little experience in. Informants were shocked by what they found to be 'weird' subcultural scenes in inner Sydney; they felt disconnected from their authentic sense of self (Lawler 1999; Archer 2012) and disillusioned with their vocational choices. These higher educational experiences transform the aspirations these informants once had to work in the creative industries because it leaves them questioning whether they will be accepted or whether their minority status and their lack of cultural capital will leave them on the fringes of their chosen employment sector.

There are certain ways to perform creativity that will be perceived to be more credible than others (Adkins and Lury 1999; Banks and Milestone 2011). Informants in this study tend to associate creative careers with degrees and educational achievements, whereas most existing research shows that those who are successful as creative workers are so because of the ways they are immersed in city-based, creative lifestyles and subcultural scenes and their abilities to effectively network (Banks and Milestone 2011). Thus, in Chapter 4 I look at informants' discomfort to enter what they see as the individualistic, bohemian lifestyle of the creative precariat who are likely to work in bars and as waiters to make ends meet. It specifically deals with the ways that issues of masculinity and 'respectability' appear in the rationale offered by these informants for their decision to become self-employed business owners.

Finally, in Chapter 5, I return to themes of authenticity to argue that there are marginal spaces in which young Arab–Australian men can become artists. For many, the most obvious pathway becomes community or multicultural arts. This chapter asks what kinds of consequences occur when young people from ethnic minority backgrounds are encouraged to develop their creative working identities in ways that largely speak to their position in ethnic minority communities. By the same token, it uses concepts of racialisation to argue that these community arts workers are restricted in their capacity to work outside the parameters of multicultural arts scenes. As such, an 'authentic' portrayal of the Bankstown-based, Arab–Australian youthful experience is always politicized.

Najla Said found comfort when she connected with a group of American–Arab writers and actors who, in a post 9/11 world, had something political and important to say to the world. Finally, in her late twenties, she felt she belonged somewhere and embraced her newly hyphenated identity. In Bankstown, where Arab–Australian young men are never too far from people who look like them, who speak in their parent's language and who share an unspoken solidarity, there may be a sense of familiarity and comfort, but no real advantages are to be gained from other people identifying them as Arab–Australian or from Bankstown. This book will show how the personal investments these young men make in a creative passion reflect their projects of social mobility and how the development of creative identities is part of their aspirations to undo the disadvantages associated with their hyphenated titles.

Notes

1 http://www.dazeddigital.com/artsandculture/article/24579/1/how-a-new-wave-of-poc-artists-are-challenging-britishness
2 http://profile.id.com.au/bankstown/highlights
3 http://www.dailytelegraph.com.au/middle-eastern-crime-connections/story-fn2mt2ft-1225851600458
4 The article has since been removed.
5 Reclaim Australia is a far right movement whose main grievance with the Australian government is that they have been too liberal in allowing Muslims to establish their own places of worship and enjoy freedom of religion. Like other far-right movements in the UK, they call for a ban on mosque development and a 'return' to British Christian values. http://theaimn.com/an-open-letter-to-reclaim-australia/
6 http://www.qut.edu.au/creative-industries/courses-and-study/undergraduate-courses
7 The Lebanese Muslim Association has recently branched out from providing basic services to the community to incorporating arts programs for Lebanese and Muslim youth; Bankstown Poetry Slam has also emerged in 2015–2016 as a popular space for local spoken word poets of Lebanese and Muslim backgrounds to share personal experiences with a wider audience.

References

Abu-Lughod, L. (1991) 'Writing against culture', in *Recapturing Anthropology: Working in the Present*, Ed. R. Fox, Santa Fe, University of Washington Press.

Adkins, L. and C. Lury (1999) 'The labour of identity: Performing identities, performing economies', *Economy and Society*, 28(4): 598–614.

Al-Natour, R. (2010) 'Racism, ragheads and rednecks', *Nebula: Journal of Multidisciplinary Scholarship*, 7.1(June 2010): 1–22.

Allen, K. and S. Hollingworth (2013) '"Sticky subjects" or "cosmopolitan creatives"? Aspirations for work in the knowledge economy', *Urban Studies*, 50(3): 499–517.

Aly, R. (2015) *Becoming Arab in London*, London, Pluto Press.

Amin, A. and N. Thrift (2007) 'Cultural-economy and cities', *Progress in Human Geography*, 31(2): 143–161.

Anthias, F. (2012) 'Hierarchies of social location, class and intersectionality: Towards a translocational frame', *International Sociology*, 28(1): 121–138.

Anzaldua, G. (1999) 'How to tame a wild tongue', in *Borderlands/La Frontera*, San Fransisco, Aunt Lute Books, pp. 75–86.

Archer, L. (2012) 'Between authenticity and pretension: Parents', pupils' and young professionals' negotiations of minority ethnic middle-class identity', *The Sociological Review*, 60(1): 129–148.

Atkinson, W. (2010a) *Class, Individualization and Late Modernity: In Search of the Reflexive Worker*, London, Palgrave Macmillan.

Back, L. (1996) *New Ethnicities and Urban Culture: Racisms and Multiculture in Young Lives*, London, Routledge.

Banks, M. and D. Hesmondhalgh (2009) 'Looking for work in creative industries policy', *International Journal of Cultural Policy*, 15(4): 415–430.

Banks, M. and K. Milestone (2011) 'Individualization, gender and cultural work', *Gender, Work & Organization*, 18(1): 73–89.

Bauman, Z. (2000) *Liquid Modernity*, Cambridge, Polity Press.

Beck, U. (2000) *Risk Society: Towards a New Modernity*, London, Sage Publications.

Blair, H. (2009) 'Active Networking: Action, social structure and the process of networking', in*Creative Labour: Working in the Creative Industries*, Eds. A. McKinlay and C. Smith, New York, Palgrave MacMillan, pp. 116–134.

Burnley, I., S. Encel, G. McCall (1985) *Immigration and Ethnicity in the 1980's*, Sydney Longman, Cheshire.

Christopherson, S. (2009) 'Working in the creative economy: Risk, adaptation, and the persistence of exclusionary networks', in *Creative Labour: Working in the Creative Industries*, Eds. A. McKinlay and C. Smith, Basingstoke, Palgrave Macmillan, pp. 72–91.

Cohen, P. (2006) 'Re-doing the knowledge: Labour, learning and life stories in transit', *Journal of Education and Work*, 19(2): 109–120.

Creative Industries Innovation Centre (2013) *Valuing Australia's Creative Industries: Final Report December 2013*, Retrieved from http://www.creativeinnovation.net.au/ce_report/webapp/static/pdfs/CIIC-Valuing-Australias-Creative-Industries-2013.pdf

Dagistanli, S. (2007) '"Like a pack of wild animals": Moral panics around 'ethnic' gang rape in Sydney', in *Outrageous! Moral Panics in Australia*, Eds. S. Poynting and G. Morgan, Hobart, ACYS Publishing, pp. 181–197.

Galloway, S. and S. Dunlop (2007) 'A critique of definitions of the cultural and creative industries in public policy', *International Journal of Cultural Policy*, 13(1): 17–31.

Ganguly, K. (1992) 'Migrant identities: Personal memory and the construction of selfhood', *Cultural Studies*, 6(1): 27–50.

Garnham, N. (2005) 'From cultural to creative industries: An analysis of the implications of the "creative industries" approach to arts and media policy making in the United Kingdom', *International Journal of Cultural Policy*, 11(1): 15–29.

Giddens, A. (2003) *Runaway World: How Globalisation is Reshaping Our Lives*, New York, Routledge.

Gill, R. (2002) 'Cool, creative and egalitarian? Exploring gender in project-based new media work in euro', *Information, Communication and Society*, 5(1): 70–89.

Gill, R. and A. Pratt (2008) 'In the social factory? Immaterial labour, precariousness and cultural Work', *Theory, Culture and Society*, 25(7-8): 1–30.

Graham, C. (2005) *Enterprise Education: Connecting Schools with the Creative Knowledge Economy*, Frenchs Forest, Pearson SprintPrint.

Hall, S. (1997) *Representation: Cultural Representations and Signifying Practices*, London, Sage in association with The Open University.

Hartley, J. (2005) *Creative Industries*, Malden, Mass, Blackwell Publishers.

Haukka, S. (2011) 'Education-to-work transitions of aspiring creatives', *Cultural Trends*, 20(1): 41–64.

Henderson, M. G. (1990) 'Speaking in tongues: Dialogics, dialectics, and the black woman writer's literary tradition', *The Scholar and Feminist XXX: Past Controversies, Present Challenges, Future Feminisms.*

Higgs, P., S. Cunningham, J. Pagan (2007) 'Australia's creative economy: Basic evidence on size, growth, income and employment', *QUT*, pp. 1–50.

Hutnyk, J. (2000) *Critique of Exotica: Music, Politics, and the Culture Industry*, London, Pluto Press.

Hyder, R. (2004) *Brimful of Asia: Negotiating Ethnicity on the UK Music Scene*, Aldershot, Ashgate.

Jupp, J. (1989) *The Challenge of Diversity: Policy Options for a Multicultural Australia*, Canberra, Australian Government Publishing Service.

Kenway, J., A. Kraack, Hickey-Moody, A. (2006) *Masculinity Beyond the Metropolis*, Basingstoke, Palgrave Macmillan.

Lawler, S. (1999) '"Getting out and getting away": Women's narratives of class mobility', *Feminist Review* 63: 3–24.

Lentin, A. (2015) 'What does race do?', *Ethnic and Racial Studies*, 38(8): 1401–1406.

McDowell, L. (2003) *Redundant masculinities?: Employment change and white working class youth*, Malden, MA, Blackwell Publishers.

McRobbie, A. (2002) 'Clubs to companies: Notes on the decline of political culture in speeded up creative worlds', *Cultural Studies*, 16(4): 516–531.

McRobbie, A. (2004) 'Creative London-creative Berlin: Notes on making a living in the new cultural economy', in *Atelier Europe: Creative Labour in New Cultural Economies* Munich, pp. 1–22.

Mishler, E. G. (1999) *Storylines: Craft artists narratives of identity*, London, Harvard University Press.

Mitropolous, A. (2011) From precariousness to risk management and beyond, *EIPCP: European Institute for Progressive Cultural Policies*. Available at: http://eipcp.net/transversal/0811/mitropoulos/en [Accessed July 5, 2016].

Morgan, G. (2006) 'Work in progress: Narratives of aspiration from the new economy', *Journal of Education and Work*, 19(2): 141–151.

Morgan, G., J. Wood, P. Nelligan (2013) 'Beyond the vocational fragments: Creative work, precarious labour and the idea of "Flexploitation"', *Economic and Labour Relations*, Review 24(3): 397–415.

Murray, C. and M. Gollmitzer (2012) 'Escaping the precarity trap: A call for creative labour policy', *International Journal of Cultural Policy*, 184: 419–438.

Nayak, A. (2006) 'Displaced masculinities: Chavs, youth and class in the post-industrial city', *Sociology*, 40(5): 813–831.

Nayak, A. and M. Kehily (2008) *Gender, Youth and Culture: Young Masculinities and Femininities*, New York, Palgrave Macmillan.

Neff, G., E. Wissinger and S. Zukin (2005) 'Entrepreneurial labor among cultural producers: "Cool" jobs in "hot" industries', *Social Semiotics*, 15(3): 307–334.

Nixon, D. (2006) '"I Just like working with my hands": Employment aspirations and the meaning of work for low-skilled unemployed men in Britain's service economy', *Journal of Education and Work* 19(2): 201–217.

Nixon, D. (2009) '"I can't put a smiley face on": Working class masculinity, emotional labour and service work in the new economy', *Gender, Work and Organisation* 16(3): 300–321.

Norton, A. (2012) *Mapping Australian Higher Education*, Grattan Institute, Melbourne.

Petty, M. (1985) 'The transition from school to work, or employment of Lebanese youth in Sydney', in *Immigration and Ethnicity in the 1980s*, Eds. I. Burnley, S. Encel and G. McCall, Melbourne, Longman Cheshire, pp. 143–151.

Poynting, S., G. Noble and Tabar, P. (2003) 'Protest masculinity and Lebanese youth in Western Sydney', in *Male Trouble*, Eds. M. Donaldson and S. Tomsen, Sydney, Pluto Press, pp. 132–155.

Pratt, A. and P. Jeffcutt (2009) 'Introduction', in *Creativity, Innovation and the Cultural Economy*, Eds. A. Pratt and P. Jeffcutt, New York, Routledge.

Price, R., P. McDonald, J. Bailey and B. Pini, Eds. (2011) *Young People and Work*, Surrey, Ashgate.

Roberts, K. (2009) 'Opportunities structures then and now', *Journal of Education and Work*, 22(5): 355–368.

Ross, A. (2007) 'Nice work if you can get it: the mercurial career of creative industries policy', *My Creativity Reader: A Critique of Creative Industries*, Eds. G. Lovink and N. Rossiter, Amsterdam, Institute of Network cultures, pp. 17–39.

Ross, A. (2008) 'The new geography of work: Power to the precarious?', *Theory, Culture & Society*, 25(7–8): 31–49.

Sabel, C. (1994) 'Flexible specialisation and the re-emergence of regional economies', *Post-Fordism: A Reader*, Ed. A. Amin, Oxford, Blackwell, pp. 101–156.

Said, E. W. (1997) *Covering Islam: How the Media and the Experts Determine How We See the Rest of the World*, New York, Vintage Books.

Said, N. (2013) *Looking for Palestine: Growing Up Confused in an Arab–American Family* New York, Riverhead Books.

Sennett, R. (1998) *The Corrosion of Character: The Personal Consequences of Work in the New Capitalism*, New York, Norton.

Sennett, R. (2001) 'Street and office: Two sources of identity', *On the Edge: Living with Global Capitalism*, Eds. W. Hutton and A. Giddens, London, Vintage.

Shaheen, J. G. (2001) *Reel Bad Arabs: How Hollywood Vilifies a People*, New York, Olive Branch Press.

Skeggs, B. (2005) 'Exchange, value and affect: Bourdieu and "the self"', *The Sociological Review*, 52(s2): 75–95.

Skrbis, Z., Baldassar, L. and Poynting, S. (2007) 'Introduction – negotiating belonging: Migration and generations,' *Journal of Intercultural Studies*, 28(5): 261–269.

Taylor, S. and K. Littleton (2012) *Contemporary Identities of Creativity and Creative Work*, Surrey, Ashgate Publishing.

Thornton, S. (1995) *Club Cultures: Music, Media and Subcultural Capital*, Cambridge, Polity Press.

Willis, P. E. (1977) *Learning to Labour: How Working Class Kids Get Working Class Jobs*, Farnborough, England, Saxon House.

Woodman, D. and J. Wyn (2006) 'Generation, youth and social change in Australia', *Journal of Youth Studies*, 9(5): 495–514.

Woodman, D. and J. Wyn (2013) 'Youth policy and generations: Why youth policy needs to 'rethink youth'', *Social Policy and Society* 12(2): 265–275.

Wyn, J. (2005) 'Youth, risk and education', in *No Time to Lose: The Well-being of Australia's Children*, Eds. S. Richardson and M. R. Prior. Carlton, Vic, Melbourne University Publishing, pp. 255–280.

Zigon, J. (2008) *Morality: An Anthropological Perspective*, Oxford, Berg.

1 Shu Hal Ayb!

The moral implications of creative passions in Arab–Australian families

We have very limited quantitative data on the number of artists and creative aspirants enrolled in training programs who come from Arab and/or Middle Eastern backgrounds or from ethnic minority backgrounds more generally. However, in a study of culturally and linguistically diverse (CALD) artists in Western Australia, it was revealed that out of the seven categories of migrants (European, African, The Americas, the United Kingdom and Ireland, Asia), migrants born in the Middle East had the lowest rates of participation across all creative sectors (Rentschler *et al.* 2008). This finding is consistent with my own experience living in a Lebanese/Syrian–Australian community in which almost no one I knew personally in my ethnic networks worked in the arts, especially not those of the generation born overseas. Thus, in order to understand the kinds of challenges Arab–Australian young men face when they formulate creative identities, it is first necessary to examine how creativity is perceived within Arab–Australian communities. This chapter discusses the ways that, in the context of these communities, it can be risky to have a creative passion.

Giddens (1990; 1991; 2003), Beck (2000; 2007), and Bauman (2000) deploy concepts of risk in a similar way, as at the core of the postmodern condition. This chapter will evaluate these debates but present life histories that offer alternative ways to understand risk as individuals who feel stifled and stigmatised in their traditional familial and ethnic networks. The investment in a creative identity may inadvertently disrupt normative gender expectations, unsettle communally defined values, and challenge the social mobility pathways that are typically open to young men of ethnic minority backgrounds.

This chapter is organised according to the three main ways that informants view creative passions to be risky. The first is that creative activities, such as singing, acting, or creative writing are measured by their ethnic communities on moral grounds; that is, such leisure interests and the prospective vocational pathways that can ensue, are perceived to be 'bad' and are thus less likely to be encouraged. I look at the kinds of strategies informants undertake to overcome these negative perceptions. The second way that creativity is understood as risky is in relation to familial social mobility aspirations. Parental aspirations for the young men in this study involve particular educational choices and careers that can offer financial success, thereby earning them respect within their communities, for example in medicine, law, or small business ownership.[1] This is a commonly cited experience among the children of migrants of other ethnic backgrounds (Noble 2007; Pasztor 2012). By contrast, I examine how the Arab–Australian young men view paid work as an extension of their creative passions, and as a way to achieve self-actualisation, as do most creative people (Du Gay 1996; McRobbie 2002). It is difficult for these migrant parents to understand the relevance of passion to working identities, and as such, the chapter examines how familial relationships become transformed as a result of these differing perspectives.

Where passion is central to the development of the creative biography, the notion of profession is central to informants' transitions to adulthood. The idea of profession is also central to their status within their local community. Thus, in the final section of this chapter I show how informants are torn by divergent logics and examine the balancing act that they feel they must do between their creative passions and communal ideals around particular professional titles as they try to 'hold it all together' (Archer 2012). This theme, which emerged strongly across many of the interviews, has broader implications for the ways we understand discourses of choice and agency in youth transitions which, in post-industrial societies, are represented as increasingly self-directed (Heinz 2009).

Conceptualising risk

The de-standardisation of labour, the reconfiguration of gender roles, and the spread of globalisation aided by rapid technological advancement support Lash's (1996) suggestion that "we now live in a post-traditional order" (Lash 1996: 250). The social and economic policies of governments in the West, with the privatisation of public services and incremental restrictions on social welfare since the 1980s seems to also reflect a shift from a traditional to a 'liquid modernity' (Bauman 2000), a 'de-traditionalised modernity' (Lash 1996), a 'reflexive modernity' (Beck and Beck-Gernsheim 2002), and a 'risk society' (Beck 2000). All facets of life according to these theorists are now characterised by risk and fluidity rather than stability and predictability.

The risk society model is a recent phenomenon according to Beck; it is a model that has emerged rapidly, globally, and singularly transformed every aspect of life from work to family life, to leisure activities and consumption. The permeation of 'risk' beyond the public sphere and into the realm of domestic life is central to his arguments; he names 'risk' as the unifying feature of twenty-first-century life (Beck 2000;2007). Beck suggests that all people are affected by the risks associated with rapid modernisation and globalisation, albeit to differing degrees depending on their socio-economic status (Beck 1992:21). Because de-industrialisation has resulted in more people working in knowledge-based roles and information industries, "a process of individualization has taken place" whereby, for the "sake of economic survival" (Beck 1992: 92), individuals must place their interests at the centre of all decisions. Accordingly, individuals' lives become de-traditionalised, they rely less on family and community networks for social, moral, and financial support as identities become shaped and reshaped according to one's vocational trajectory. This process of individualisation has resulted in a shift in the way people relate to one another according to Bauman (2007). He says,

> Interhuman bonds, once woven into a security net worthy of a large and continuous investment of time and effort, and worth the sacrifice of immediate individual interests…have become increasingly frail and admitted to the temporary.
>
> (Bauman 2007: 2)

The frailties of communal ties seem apparent at various moments in the biographical interviews of these Arab–Australian young men. Whether this frailty is indicative of the loss of traditional commitments and supportive relationships is a central question of this chapter and indeed the book more generally.

Beck (2007) claims that people no longer identify with 'normal families' because the end of the 1960s signalled the demise of the 'normal family'. He does not deny the existence of family units but that the levels of attachment one has to such structures are based on personal choice, part of the broader project of 'institutionalized individualisation'. Bauman concurs with Beck's suggestion that the importance of categories of family and more broadly class, gender, and ethnicity are declining (Bauman 1998; 2001). Bauman sees this structural shift in somewhat positive terms because in bygone eras

> Class and gender hung heavily over the individual range of choices; to escape their constraint was not much easier than to contest one's place in the 'divine chain of being'. To all intents and purposes, class and gender were 'facts of nature' and the task left to the self-assertion of most individuals was to 'fit in' – that is, fit into the allocated niche by behaving as other occupants did.
>
> (Bauman 2002: xvi)

In a similar vein, Thompson (1996) suggests that the "development of modern societies is accompanied by an irreversible decline in the role of tradition" (Thompson 1996:89). The traditions associated with one's particular class background and social status, gender roles, and families thus become increasingly 'fragile'. More pressing, according to Beck (2007), is "the ethic of self-fulfilment and achievement", which is arguably, "the most powerful current in modern society" (Beck 2007:22). Ultimately, he argues that "the choosing, deciding, shaping human being who aspires to be the author of his or her own life, the creator of an individual identity, is the central character of our time" (Beck 2007:22–23).

Writers across various academic disciplines grappling with the risk society thesis have concentrated on how institutionalised risk results in youth inequalities (Raffo and Reeves 2000; Devadason 2007; Furlong *et al.* 2011), new working conditions and experiences (Christopherson 2009; Atkinson 2010), or the globalisation phenomenon itself (Appadurai 2001). They reach varying conclusions about the impact risk has on individuals but are in agreement that ethnicity, class, and gender, and the intersections that occur between those identity positions are not, for the most part, redundant, especially in the case of youth and young adults. Anthias (2006), for example, says our attachments to various social structures and institutions are not often freely made choices and that "identities cannot be thought of as cloaks to put on at will or to discard when they no longer fit or please" (Anthias 2006:20). Rather, individuals become 'disposed' towards particular ideas and values; habits develop incrementally over time (Bourdieu 1973; 2005) and, most importantly, personal values and ideas as well as life experiences and life chances are differentiated according to the specific intersections between ethnicity, gender, and social class among other identity positions (Anthias 2006).

Taking an intersectional approach, this chapter will examine how individual identities can be very difficult to realise for Arab–Australian young men in the context of their local migrant communities. The conditions in which these Arab–Australian young men live generally do not assist them in turning their beliefs and dreams into realities.

Familial obligation and hidden talents

In this study, informants developed creative identities in spite of the fact that many of their parents, and the wider ethnic public, perceived creativity to be something that could jeopardise their sense of morality or religiosity. This was not exclusive to any one religious group, but was a theme that emerged across many informants' life histories whether Muslim or Christian. Ibrahim, a thirty-year-old self-employed film editor from a conservative Islamic family, considered how creativity is undervalued among Arab–Australians and within Bankstown more broadly. He said,

> I think that there is so much talent in the Islamic community and in the Middle Eastern community especially. But it's not pursued because of, (sighs), I've seen what parents do and a lot of it [creativity] is not encouraged. I used to know two other people who were great artists and now they're doing things that are totally unrelated to that. And mainly the problem is that this is not the right nurturing environment. I mean, I don't know, there's got to be work for these young people who are creative … Right now, I think it is important to start redefining what the arts are about in the community. Because there is literally no support in the Arabic community in terms of artistic support, and I hate to generalise but I think it's true. And then in the Islamic community there are all these other issues … drawing, painting, sculpture; it creates all these added issues on top of that. So you get the deterrents, but it need not be that way. If you're a young creative person, even though it's hard, you just got to get yourself educated and see what all the [Islamic] rules and restrictions are and make a decision.

Some broader clarification about the rules around art in Islam is needed here. The production of figural art, that is, representations of living subjects, has been hotly contested among Islamic scholars for hundreds of years. In conservative circles, Islamic aniconism refers to a prohibition of images based on the premise that representations of living subjects could then be idolised and worshipped over Allah (Ramadan, 2006). Islamic scholars associate figural art with Paganism and this is why images of Prophets and God more generally are deeply offensive to Muslims, as we witnessed in the Danish cartoon scandal of 2005 and the *Charlie Hebdo* magazine covers in 2015.[2] There are other Islamic scholars, however, who suggest that representations of figures, such as people or animals, are only prohibited within the category of Islamic art and the ruling does not apply to secular art (Soganci 2004). Therefore, when Ibrahim says Islam poses a deterrent to "drawing, painting, sculpture", he is referring to his inner turmoil at potentially engaging in practices that compromise his religious identity, which he revealed over the course of our interview to be incredibly important to him in how he navigates through major life decisions.

Bauman (2000) and Giddens (2003) have argued that the templates for life prescribed by tightly bound communities have less sway in a post-industrial, 'liquid modernity' as individuals become invested in consumption and leisure-based lifestyles. These arguments are sustained by Ibrahim's decision to pursue creative interests despite community disapproval. But the alternative is not to simply develop an individualised lifestyle that best fits one's authentic sense of self as Bauman (1993) has argued, but actively to work against residual communal constraints, among other conditions, that repress the emergence of a creative identity in the first place. Where Beck and Beck-Gernsheim (2002) argue that class and gender no longer hang over people's shoulders, restricting them in their life choices, the reverse is true in Ibrahim's description of how artistic inclinations are developed in an Arab–Australian family and community. His experiences reveal that communal moral norms do in fact constrain the life decisions of young Arab–Australian men living in Bankstown, evident where Ibrahim says, "even though it's hard, you just got to get yourself educated and see what all the [Islamic] rules and restrictions are and make a decision". He feels that although there is "no artistic support" in the community, young people from Arab–Australian backgrounds should persevere with their ambitions anyway but, importantly, within the guidelines of Islam so as not to break entirely with one's religious values.

Thus, while Ibrahim wants to show his community that 'the arts' are valuable, he still feels he needs to justify this in line with normative communal values. For example, Ibrahim has played an instrumental role in developing two Islamic music festivals and much of his work is based in the Bankstown area, predominantly dealing with community organisations. Both his parents and the religious clerics he mentions in the excerpt I detailed earlier approve of his activities. His role is unusual in the sense that he has been able to take an artistic interest and develop this into a creative career that is understood as valuable in the broader Arab–Australian and Muslim community. As such, we see that the traditions found in families and in local communities continue to shape the life decisions of Arab–Australian youth with creative aspirations. However, Ibrahim's account reveals how traditions become renegotiated in light of his creative interests.

It is this continual renegotiation process of what is 'normal' and 'acceptable' that interests me most in this chapter.

Hamid, a twenty-five-year-old writer, actor, and community arts worker from Bankstown describes how youthful creative practices are often unsupported within Arab–Australian communities. Hamid went to great lengths to explain how creative leisure interests were atypical among the young boys in his local area, many of them being of Arab–Australian backgrounds, saying,

> I was twelve years old and John* came to my high school and showed us a book. He goes, 'who would like their story to be published in it?' and there was only one person in that class that wanted their story published and that was me. So I sent in a story and a year later it got published. So that's how I got my first fifteen minutes of fame and that's what triggered my passion for writing. I can honestly say it started with John coming in to my classroom that day. That's the story of how my career took off.

There are several overlapping themes contained here. First, Hamid establishes his identity as unusual within Bankstown as a young boy who had creative writing inclinations where noone else did; as he says, "only one person wanted their story published". He frames this as risky, mainly because of the ridicule that could face him among his peers. In Chapter 2, I look more closely at how creative identities are developed in light of the youth subcultural groups in high school, where creative young men are often ridiculed and bullied for their unorthodox interests. Notably, we can see that Hamid's family and his extended Lebanese–Australian networks are absent from his earliest memory of what 'triggered' his 'passion for writing'; the opportunity to develop this interest only became available through the intervention of a third party, John from the local community arts centre. I return to this theme, about how the creative interests of Arab–Australian young men require external affirmation to become legitimate identity positions, later on in the chapter.

Hamid told me that he was initially interested in becoming an actor but felt, even as a teenager, that acting was "just unrealistic" as a career path because of the high levels of competition in that field. Nonetheless, he convinced his father to pay for weekend acting classes but found them to be quite intimidating as there were students from much wealthier, privileged backgrounds in his class leaving him feeling "out of [his] league". I asked why he found acting to be an unviable career option, to which he said

> Well, you know, in our [Lebanese, Muslim] community, acting is immediately looked down on because they think sex scenes. You know, when you say you're an actor, they immediately think you're on *Neighbours* getting on to some white chick.

Hamid and I come from the same minority within the larger Australian–Muslim community. We knew each other through mutual friends before the interview and as such, when he says "our community" he is referring to a Lebanese/Syrian–Australian, Muslim community. The local geography, Bankstown and Western Sydney, is less important to this particular construction of community though he is mostly referring to a set of social networks based in Western Sydney (and some parts of the city's inner west such as Marrickville). Like Ibrahim, he is essentially claiming that creative vocations pull these young men too far outside the moral codes of the community; that creative leisure interests go unsupported by families because later in life they can result in promiscuity, evidenced in the concern his parents have that he will be "getting on to some white chick" as part of his acting roles.

Later in our interview, Hamid explained how he directed his attention towards writing instead of acting, not only because of the improbability of an acting career, but also because he came to realise that writing activities tend to fly under the radar within his family and the broader ethnic community. He makes this point emphatically, saying, "I come from a line of peasants; they don't read. You could have a book that I wrote, sitting right in front of them and they won't pick it up". By gravitating towards writing instead of acting, the negative perceptions the community has of particular creative interests and creative vocations are actively negotiated, rather than simply abandoned, by Hamid in the context of his life-history interview. In turn, this means that individuals are not always 'embedded' or 'disembedded' from interpersonal, local networks, as has been argued by Bauman and Beck. The creative passion and how these young men negotiate what this means in a local setting reveals that these young men sit, uncomfortably, between being a 'reflexive, choosing, deciding author of his life' and being someone who 'fits in' with the ethno-religious migrant group.

These brief interview moments from Ibrahim and Hamid show how the associations to community have not become 'unstuck', as Beck and Beck-Gernsheim (2002) have claimed. The process of developing a creative passion is messy and complicated by the fact that individuals have differing degrees of attachment to specific aspects of their local communities. They attempt to balance this with their personal interests which are ultimately perceived to be unorthodox within their interpersonal networks. In what follows, I examine how the narrative of passion does not only produce inner turmoil but also creates familial tensions. Parents have particular kinds of aspirations for their children and these informants' attachment to a creative passion undermines them.

Although the interviews I conducted were mostly directed by the informants in terms of how they wanted to narrate their life histories, one of the questions I asked all informants was, "what are your earliest memories of being creative?" I imagined responses to this would allow me to gauge how closely their contemporary working lives aligned with their earlier leisure interests or aspirations. Some informants did in fact answer this question by linking childhood creative or art-based hobbies to their current professions or current vocational aspirations, as we saw in Hamid's case. On the whole though, this question allowed informants to reflect on their family relationships and their communities' attitudes towards creativity more than at any other moment during our interview.

Bashir was nineteen when we spoke. He came from a Lebanese–Maronite family and had grown up in Bankstown. His father, a carpenter by trade, had his own cabinet-making company that Bashir worked at in his free time but when asked what he thought about pursuing carpentry as a career option, he rejects it saying he would be "so bored". Bashir was completing a bachelor of arts and psychology at university and while he calls himself a creative person, with a "passion for reading and writing", he had no plans to pursue writing full time preferring to establish himself professionally and financially as a psychologist before returning to his original creative interest. He was one of the many informants who reflected on his childhood memories of being creative as a secret, hidden pleasure and something that disconnected him from the rest of his family.

He said,

> For the longest time, I would write and read like crazy … it's my hobby it's what I do; umm, as a kid I used to read a lot. Fantasy books were my favourite … I started reading them when I was in year one or two. It was very impressive to everyone around me. The thing is I kept reading the same books over and over and over again to the point where my parents were like, they got to the point where they started hiding the books from me. Yeah 'cause they were like, "you should be reading stuff on, err you know science or maths you know get better at those things 'cause nobody gets, you know, anywhere in the world on English" or something like that, you know. It was typical sort of Lebo-ish ideology at the time. But I didn't care. From kindergarten to about year five I spent essentially every day umm in the library. Every day. Every lunch, every recess I was in the library. I made real good friends with the librarians, you know, I could take whatever book I wanted and I read a lot, I was a very enthusiastic reader. So I grew up like that and umm every year my parents would push me towards maths and science and stuff like that but I would be good at English and terrible at Arabic and okay at maths and not much science, didn't really know much about science. And I would write. I used to write a lot. I still, I don't write as much pen and paper, definitely not now because I have terrible handwriting so definitely not and ahh I have a whole bunch of characters sitting in my head pretty much all the time.

Bashir invokes creative writing as a solitary activity; this fits in neatly for the reasons he gives about feeling excluded in high school, a theme that is explored in the next chapter. More importantly, despite his 'enthusiasm' for reading, this was an activity that his parents found troubling. Bashir also situates his creative passion as conflicting with the 'Lebo-ish ideology' that permeated across his family and extended social networks. What he calls an 'ideology' basically refers to the ways that math and science are seen by parents as legitimate and suitable interests and skills for boys, whereas creative writing is deemed feminine and thus rejected by the parents. Further, as migrants with high hopes for their children, Bashir's parents see creativity as financially risky. There are no clear formulas on how to turn a passion for reading and writing into a viable, secure career path. Becoming better at math or science on the other hand can lead to career paths that make sense to Bashir's parents; these subjects appear to translate better to the world of business or finance, for example.

As we see, Bashir rejects his parents' views, which results in some intergenerational tensions. If being creative goes against what Bashir sees as a 'Lebo-ish ideology', then his interest in writing and reading becomes something he has to either justify to his family members or keep secret from them in order avoid further conflict. He chose to mostly keep quiet about his writing saying,

Bashir: I wrote but I couldn't show anyone.
Sherene: Just anyone in your family or anyone at all?
Bashir: Well, no I mean, I've submitted poems and writing, short stories, every now and again to different places. I've won a few awards and whatever … some money.
Sherene: And do your parents know about this, do they know that you are a published writer?
Bashir: I'm not sure they do. Wow. [Pauses] I never thought about it. I won money, they know I won money, I'm not sure they know I got published.

Here, we see that even accomplishments, when they are based on creative skills, are ones to be hidden from the family out of fear that they will not be supportive. Bashir, like other informants in this study, thus make claims to having a creative passion and, later, a creative identity without ever receiving any validation or recognition from their families or their immediate social networks. This kind of validation comes from outside of the ethnic community because, as I noted earlier, creative interests are usually unsupported by the broader ethnic community.

I interviewed Adam, a nineteen-year-old design student with 'a passion for drawing, sketching and lifedrawing'; he was very clear that his creative interests were a major source of conflict in his family. Adam's father ran his own company, delivering imported small goods to local convenience stores and restaurants. As he was getting older and looking to retire, Adam felt pressured to work for the family business and eventually 'inherit' the company. Despite saying his parents, especially his mother, were always very supportive of his interests as a child, he says that his artistic inclinations made him feel incredibly guilty as he got older because of the unspoken pressure to take on the family business.

Sherene: What did your parents think about those art subjects you were doing (in high school)?
Adam: Mum was really supportive of it.She was just like, as long as you're getting through school it's alright. Umm dad didn't really respond but you could tell what he was thinking.
Sherene: What do you think he was thinking?
Adam: Like I could, like just once he asked me, "what subject are you doing?" and I said drama and he just sighed and … (pause)

Sherene: So what do you think the sigh meant?
Adam: It pulled me down a bit … yeah I barely have any real conversations with him. There is barely anything in common so that's sort of like… get pulled down about that and I think how am I meant to get this bond?

Earlier, I noted how creative passions are seen to subvert normative gender expectations within Arab–Australian communities. Hibbins and Pease (2009) explain that masculinity is constructed in relation to one's migrant background, class position, and other factors such as geography but add that "little is known about the influence of the diaspora on constructions of male gender identities in Australia" (Hibbins and Pease 2009:11). The work of Connell (2005) has shown how gender is not evenly experienced, but that variables such as education, class, ethnicity, and racial hierarchies produce different versions of masculine identities. In the case of my informants, young men's attachments to notions of art and creativity unsettle Arab–Australian gendered and cultural expectations. In this interview moment, Adam positions his creative interests as causing his strained relationship with his father. His mother appears to act as an intermediary between traditional migrant ideas of masculinity and potentially new gender constructions that emerge from participating in art cultures and studying art subjects.

It is interesting how powerful something as subtle as a sigh can be for this young person and how it makes him view his creative identity; as something that causes problems for him in his interpersonal relationships. Other informants often spoke of the difficulties of translating their degrees or their vocational titles from English to Arabic. But the way Adam describes this exchange with his father does not reveal intergenerational misunderstandings or language barriers, between English and Arabic, about what is involved in drama as a final year elective subject. Rather, the sigh, and Adam's strong instincts about what this means, reveals that there are previously established and culturally shared views about art and creativity within his family and in his social networks. In short, drama appears to be an unsuitable subject for Adam. While his parents were generally supportive of his childhood interests in drawing and sketching, they were less supportive of the decision to complete a fine arts degree. This choice, what Giddens might call 'active risk-taking', reflects the ways that Adam prioritises his own personal interests over a sense of familial duty.

In another part our interview, he told me that his oldest sister is an artist but that her career choice did not present any problems in the family even though she has had to rely on her parents for financial support at times when she was unemployed for long periods at a time. According to Adam, her relationship with her father was not altered because of her creative work. So perhaps 'the sigh' was not an outright rejection of drama or art entirely, but specifically related to the fact that Adam was a young man and that there are gender expectations about careers. We might see choosing 'art subjects' as an act of rebellion against those expectations.

The narratives of creative passions that appear in Adam's interview are characterised by an obvious sense of guilt. This is sharply contrasted with the excerpts presented from Hamid's interview earlier, where his attitude towards creative passion is one of indignation and anger. Hamid appears to be saying, "why shouldn't I be able to be an actor or a writer? Why should this be risky?" On the other hand, Adam accepts that there are consequences for his choices and actions and understands why creative passions are both problematic and something he must strategically manage within his family.

The association between gender and creativity, whereby creative passions are seen as feminine and thus seen as unsuitable for young Arab–Australian males appeared at other moments in my interview with Adam, and thus the stigma associated with creative interests is of a different nature to Ibrahim's references to religious doctrine. Eventually, he accepted a place in a design course at university instead of in a business degree but explains how this was met with negative responses from family members and friends within the community. He said,

> It was hard and it was a lot of pressure. Especially when I started my course there was a lot of pressure coming from my relatives, coming from a very strong Lebanese family um they do put a lot of pressure on you. And like when I told my relatives I'm doing a Bachelor of Design they kind of did a head flick and then just like you think to yourself "what are they thinking?" Like I don't understand, am I meant to be in business? Like I don't know … a lot of relatives will like, well one of my aunties came up to me once and she's just like "you're studying design. Are you gay?" and I just thought if that's going to be the reaction of my family then why I am doing this?

In a similar sense to Bashir, Adam presents his vocational choices and creative leisure interests to be mediated by the presence of a 'very strong Lebanese family' though he stops short of calling this an 'ideology'. Although he does appear to be engaging in a kind of 'biographical decision-making' (Giddens 1999) in this excerpt, his decision-making process is contingent upon local Lebanese–Australian structures and the ways in which gender roles are ascribed. In this excerpt, the 'head flick' is a gesture that carries enormous weight for the ways that Adam reflects on his creative passion. The head flick suggests that he has made the wrong decision by enrolling in a bachelor of design. His sexuality is called into question and different degrees become gendered and sexualised. Older members of his migrant community associate creative degrees as feminine and business degrees as masculine; the latter is preferred by the family. These assessments leave Adam wondering whether the investment in a creative passion is worthwhile, not only in a financial sense but also at a cultural level.

Between passion and profession: 'Holding it all together'

Childhood leisure interests, as we have seen so far, are typically described by informants using the language of passion. A consequence of having a creative passion is that it leaves informants fearful about how they will develop adult identities. Work is supposedly central to the youth-to-adulthood transition in Western societies (Willis 1977; Morgan and Cohen 2006; Price *et al.* 2011) and a key marker of masculine identities (Willis 1977; Donaldson and Howsen 2009), but these informants feel there is little guidance within their communities about how to turn a creative interest into a creative career. Creative careers are also emergent (Taylor and Littleton 2012) and as such, informants cannot replicate the actions of other successful creative workers. They are required therefore to be self-reliant in constructing their creative biographies but are fearful about how to do this without falling out with their communities. The kinds of attitudes that these informants have towards creative interests represents a departure from the existing literature on creative vocational aspirants (Morgan 2006). The young men in this study appear not to celebrate their creative passion but treat it as problematic, as something to work through. Creative identities are a site of struggle within the family because these informants are breaking new ground by pursuing a creative passion. Creativity is foreign to parents and they are unsure about how to respond.

One way of making sense of these attitudes towards creative passion is to draw on the research that examines the higher education and vocational aspirations of young people from disadvantaged backgrounds (Modood 1993; Ball *et al.* 2002; Shiner and Modood 2002). As Bourdieu (1973) has proposed, higher education is often the primary means of achieving social mobility and as empirical research has revealed, migrant youth are highly likely to pursue further study on this basis (Modood 1993). It has been suggested that "in the twenty-first century growing numbers of the working classes are caught up in education either as escape, as a project for maximizing and fulfilling the self or a complicated mixture of the two" (Reay *et al.* 2001:336).

However, the transitional phase from school to higher education is not always smooth. Research on disadvantaged university students reveals their inner struggle to retain a sense of 'authenticity' that is often derived from attachments to their local communities and simultaneously take advantage of the opportunities that higher education presents to them, namely to transcend the limited working options in those local communities (Reay 2001; Archer 2012; Matthys 2013). In this book, I argue that the ways these young men invest in creative identities, in which passion is central, are also carefully articulated as a bid for social mobility. Thus far, I have shown that these kinds of social mobility projects are problematic as they create tensions within the local communities in which they were raised – first, because some creative vocations are perceived as immoral and second, because they contradict the gendered expectations that parents have for their children. Hence, we may be able to draw connections between these seemingly disparate sets of literature. In what follows, I look how informants try to make links between their creative passion and major life decisions, generally about higher education, that reflect their attempts to hold together what they see as competing interests.

Talal, a Lebanese–Australian Muslim young man, relayed to me some of the conversations he had with his relatives about his higher education choices. They clearly capture the ways that informants feel torn between their creative passions and the familial and communal pressure to develop professional identities.

Talal graduated from high school with very good grades and while this was a source of pride for the family it also created some problems for him in terms of balancing his personal aspirations with the pragmatic approach by parents and relatives about enrolling in more 'traditional' prestigious degrees such as medicine. He said,

Talal: Remember when I told you about the generational clash? Well, I faced a bit of that with my parents. Like, I got 90 point something in my HSC[3] year, anyway I was content. But all my family got involved then. You'd know from Lebanese families, all my aunties and uncles and grandparents and cousins were like "oh wow you can become a doctor! You can become a dentist and earn 80 bucks a patient" but I was like, I said to my grandfather, "I don't want to look at people's teeth for the rest of my life". Like, no.

Sherene: (laughs).

Talal: Like, I have a passion! They're looking at me like "what's this concept of passion?" They're like "go earn money, feed your family!" It's like, "hello it's not your lives". Like, I respect them and everything and I do know that they're looking out for me but it's very hard for them to understand when you do have a passion for something, like, money means nothing. Like, I'm not drawn to money at all.

In this exchange with his grandfather, we see two competing ideas of the value and purpose of higher education. On the one hand, parents and other family members are concerned about the economic situation that Talal could end up in if he does not choose a practical, clear-cut career path such as dentistry or medicine. On the other hand, Talal sees university as valuable for its capacity to fulfil his lifelong passion for journalism and media production. Of course, the obvious contradiction in this piece is that Talal claims to not be "drawn to money at all" and yet he chooses to enrol in a double degree of communications and law. Most commonly, law graduates enjoy better-paid careers than freelance journalists, and Talal, being aware of this, has clearly taken this into consideration when choosing his degree.

Ball *et al.* (2002) have said that families play a critical role in the higher education choices among young people in the United Kingdom. They say parents who have weak English language skills and may have studied overseas are less likely to be able to offer real guidance to their children apart from emotional support (Ball *et al.* 2002). In these instances, young people have to become 'experts' in dealing with the plethora of choices and pathways available to them (Reay and Ball 1998; Forsyth and Furlong 2003). We can see this occurring in Talal's exchange with his grandfather. His choice around higher education and specifically his articulation of how higher education enables him to fulfil a 'passion' is part of his "personalised educational project for self-improvement" (Reay *et al.* 2005:84).

I would suggest that Talal's decision to do a law degree reflects his uncertainty about the likelihood of his aspiration transpiring into reality, which is a commonly held fear among young people across all ethnic and class backgrounds (Roberts 2007). The choice to pursue this double degree can be seen as both a response towards modern working conditions in which jobs in media sectors are highly sought after (Gill 2002; Ross 2007) and as a response to the meddling of his family members. When asked what drew him to studying law, Talal said,

> I did my research about two months before I selected journalism and law and everyone I spoke to, like I told you, kept saying it's very competitive, hard to get a job, so everyone said do law as a backup. And a lot of 'em were telling me these days the stock standard is a double degree, especially when you want to apply for a job. So I'm like, ok I'll do it. But then I realised law is a hard enough degree in itself. Um it's really, really challenging.

In Talal's case it appears that his original interest in media occupies a less central role than earlier on in his life. Journalism is classified as a segment of the creative industries, but it falls outside the core creative fields such as fine arts, film and television, and literature (Hartley 2005). Nonetheless, Talal frames journalism as a lifelong passion. Here, the commitment to this passion wanes and education for the sake of employability becomes prioritised. Talal's renegotiation of creative passion fits with Forsyth and Furlong's (2003) research on higher education amongst disadvantaged youth in Scotland whereby they find "many disadvantaged young people were attracted to specific courses because these were seen as having a job at the end" (Forsyth and Furlong 2003: 222). Of primary concern for my research is trying to understand what this leap, from a creative passion into an unrelated tertiary education course, does to the formation of a creative biography.

Returning to Ibrahim's life-history narrative, I noted that he also felt torn between his creative passion and the social mobility projects of his mother, who demanded he apply to university. He said,

Ibrahim: I didn't even study for my HSC. I didn't because in my mind it was like, nah, I don't need uni because I wanna do film. And back then there wasn't any film school, so the only person that took a strong stand was my mum. She said, you still gotta go to uni, find something similar and get an education. If it wasn't for her I probably wouldn't have done it.

Sherene: And with her telling you "you have to go", how did that feel?

Ibrahim: We had fights over it, probably for about three or four months until I got in. And I only got my last preference in nursing.

Ibrahim's post-schooling choices are mediated by family expectations, though he notes that the particular details of the higher education course are less important than the respect to be gained from university qualifications. In contemporary society, whereby young people are positioned as 'students', there are few clear alternative routes available to young people who cannot or do not want to pursue further study (Dwyer and Wyn 2001; Riele and Wyn 2005). Thus, although

Ibrahim resisted going to university, he says that in hindsight he was relieved to have done so as it opened up future working opportunities for him.

So the broader social expectations placed on young people to pursue higher education, as well as familial aspirations for social mobility through education, become the few available narrative models that these young men can draw on to imagine their lives. According to Bruner (1987), our life narratives – the ways we tell stories about who we are – are interpretive projects about 'possible lives' and possible selves in which we navigate through these available narrative models for future lives. In what follows, I look at Adam's descriptions of the kinds of narrative models for future vocations available through the community, none of which appear satisfactory for the kind of creative person he aspired to become. He said,

> My uncle, my dad's brother, umm, he's always been asking me "when are you gonna get into the business?" "Why aren't you working with your dad?" It's never really been on my mind to get into that and, um, this started at about the end of year nine. Going into year ten and from that it caused a lot of I don't know, not mental issues but it played on my mind a lot. And I went into a state of depression a little bit. And that continued into year eleven and twelve. I had two voices in my mind. One that was set on a career in design or art ... but the other half of my mind was like 'what's going to happen to dad's business?' Like noone is going to take over. My older brother is already in his career and my uncle would always come over and pull me aside and be like "when are you taking – like are you going to take over your dad's business?" "When are you going to drop out of school or are you going to keep going?" Umm "if you go to uni would you study a business degree or, you know you have to study maths and know finance and that" ... and that played on my mind a lot. I don't want to let my dad down. If he were to die there's – he's got people to take over the business but like, it's sort of like I feel with me it's hereditary if that makes sense but uh yeah it was hard.

Adam is wrestling here with divergent logics – the communal pull towards business, self-employment, and familial obligation, and the push towards 'a career in design or art' and, by extension, the chance for social mobility in ways that deviate from what is culturally expected. He uses the interview process to map out the various options ahead of him, rather than presenting his creative aspirations and identification as fully formed and fully rehearsed. Unlike the youthful confidence displayed by Hamid in putting his hand up to have his story published, we can see here that Adam is conflicted and conceives of creative passions as something that might have to be abandoned in order to meet the obligations of the family.

This particular excerpt emerged within the first few minutes of our interview, after I asked him what his father did for work. One interpretation of this excerpt might suggest that he speaks of the 'hereditary' nature of the family business as related to, or perhaps code for, inherited scripts about Lebanese–Australian masculine identities. Donaldson and Howsen (2009) explain that for migrant men, the markers of masculinity in Australia are often not drastically different from those in their home country. These migrant men "strongly adhere to the ethos of the breadwinner, a belief in 'natural' gender differences and a gendered division of labour" (Donaldson and Howsen, 2009: 215). These ideas about masculinity are reinforced by the newly formed community within Australia. It becomes evident then that Adam's father and the older migrant members of his family are confronted by this idea of creative passion and by his reluctance to 'inherit' the family business because of the ways they understand gender and masculinity.

Ibrahim and Adam's discussion of how creativity complicates the process of social mobility through higher education closely align with the findings of Ball *et al.* (2002) in their research on higher education choices of ethnic minority youth. They categorise some youth as 'contingent' choosers, saying,

> The contingent chooser is typically a first generation applicant to higher education whose parents were educated outside of the UK. The student can expect little financial support from them in choice making or in funding higher education itself, although there may well be emotional support and high levels of encouragement and expectation within the family for the achievement of credentials.
>
> (Ball *et al.* 2002: 337)

Considering Adam's narrative about university course selections, we can see that he has to actively work against family members' attitudes towards education whereby its value is measured by its ability to improve one's chances in the labour market. Among ethnic minority and working-class youth in different parts of the world (Shiner and Modood 2002; Forsyth and Furlong 2003), it has been found that "not only are ethnic minority students enrolled in different types of higher education institutions" but they also follow different subject choices than youth who come from more privileged socio-economic backgrounds (Pasztor 2012). The choices of Ibrahim and Adam differ from these findings whereby they remain committed to their creative vocational aspirations but struggle to justify this to parents and members of the extended family. To return to postmodern theories of choice and individualisation we see that templates for life are not strictly adhered to by these young men, but nor are they entirely abandoned in favour of individual preference.

In another study, Smith (2007) explained that students of disadvantaged backgrounds and ethnic minority backgrounds are less likely to choose subjects or courses out of personal interest but rather, use higher education as a means to an end. Adam spoke about this, saying,

> The reason I picked design is because I thought "hey I'm not going to get a career out of drawing my whole life", so I told my teacher that and she actually suggested design. But I was just thinking, "how am I gonna make a career out of drawing stuff" so I was just like, alright I'll try design and if I don't like it I can always change. I have thoughts in my head about graphic design in general, making flyers, posters, business cards, starting a company

> ... There's a lot of stuff I can do that I haven't thought of. I can do advertising or illustrations for children's books...fashion photography ... there's a lot of excitement. And, you know, I can always do teaching and become an art teacher.

As an extension of the risk society thesis, Cote and Brynner (2008) have argued that,

> under circumstances where well-structured socialization processes have diminished, young people find that they must exercise their own agency in ways that have both risks and benefits. This process involves choosing which values and roles will constitute the basis of adulthood, but doing so can require additional time in making the transition to adulthood, often on a trial-and-error basis.
>
> (Cote and Brynner 2008: 262)

The way Adam weighs up his vocational options shows that he hesitates to take up this 'trial-and-error' approach to work because he does not have the support of his family and cannot rely on their contacts or networks to open doors for him in his chosen creative field. He reins in his idealistic, youthful creative aspirations to avoid potentially facing poverty, as he recognises that there is no obvious career outcome that follows from his interest in drawing.

Adam makes the leap from speaking about drawing as a passion, to drawing as the basis for his interest in a design course, and finally to the ways that drawing can inform a career in a range of industries – from advertising to children's books. The way he articulates his aspirations for the future appears to be an attempt to create some linearity between youthful creative hobbies and a stable sense of career. In this way, he tries to establish some control over his vocational destination rather than adopting the trial and error approach to creative biographies. In other research (Banks 2007), the trialanderror approach to working lives in the creative industries appears to be the one that can reap the greatest rewards. As such, Adam's reluctance to do so could become problematic for him in the future.

Although he frames his future as one filled with 'excitement' because of all the possibilities that may become available, this moment from my interview with Adam is full of contradictions. On the one hand he suggests that if he does not enjoy design, he "can always change". On the other hand, he displays a lack of confidence in the investment he has made in a creative passion and in his post-schooling educational choice by saying, "I can always become an art teacher". As such, it appears that Adam is willing to take the risk of pursuing a creative passion but does so with hesitation and caution. His caution might be seen as an inherited disposition (Lahire 2003); an approach towards future life planning that can be traced back to broader migrant aspirations for educational and career success. Creativity and passion are therefore not neutral concepts but floating signifiers that are interpreted and renegotiated by informants according to familial and communal definitions. In effect, their entire creative biographies are ones that are framed in relation to familial definitions and are moderated by informants' attachments to their local communities. As such, across the remaining chapters I explore how creative identities develop in different social contexts, such as school and formal employment, but continually return to the ways that familial dynamics become shaped over time because of these young men's creative aspirations.

'Passion' as a discursive tool

The language of passion is central to the creative biographies of these informants, as I have already noted in some interview exchanges in this chapter. Interestingly, informants do not reflect on childhood memories of being creative with reference to any natural *talents* as we would expect creative aspirants to do (Taylor and Littleton 2012). Claims to being talented are entirely absent from the life-history interviews and replaced instead with the language of passion. This might be related to the fact that within their familial dynamics, they are never told they have a talent. The lack of dialogue between parents and children about their creative interests can be understood, in part, by the language barriers that exist between them. As Guerra and White (1995) explain,

> A situation common to many NESB (Non English Speaking Background) young people born in Australia and fluent in English is that their parents, who were born overseas, are fluent only in their first language so that the child and the parent cannot communicate fluently in a common language; any detailed or complex discussions about school or work are almost impossible. These young people miss out on the role modelling and support provided in families from an articulate middle class background.
>
> (Guerra and White 1995: 4)

To highlight these points, Ibrahim said,

> My mother never understood the arts, never understood that world at all. I had paintings and drawings in the garage and she chucked them out for garbage collection. People walking past actually took them...there's only, I mean there was only a few I actually cared about, but I did care about the paintings I had done ... I mean, painting is a passion of mine.

This distinction between referring to yourself as having a creative passion as opposed to saying you have artistic talents is a critical one. Passion represents the investment informants make in their own aspirations. Passions have to be defended whereas talents are self-evident and need little further justification. Talent is generally established through dialogical processes; other people evaluate whether or not we have talent. According to the data presented in this chapter, there is little scope for parents and other members of the local community to confirm whether these young men actually have artistic talent. This is because, as in the case of Bashir, creative interests are not shared with the family; they are actually hidden from parents or seen, as Ibrahim calls it, to be part of a separate 'world'. An excerpt from Hamid's interview also helps make sense of the difference between passion and talent and the ways that passion can be risky in the local community. He said,

> My dad, my family, or the kind of family I live in anyway, they can't actually appreciate you as an artist. All they can comment on is you doing well. He can't read a story and say "this is a good story Hamid, you're a good writer". Or "this is a great show, you performed well". They can only say, "well everyone liked it". So all they are really analysing is whether your son or your child is succeeding. He doesn't care too much about what I'm doing; all he cares is that everyone else thinks I'm succeeding.

Again, we can draw parallels between creativity and the ways that higher education choices are negotiated within family contexts based on Hamid's statement. That is, the value of creative activities or creative labour (like higher education) is measured in terms of the kinds of success it can produce for these young men and their families. As Hamid explains, parents of these informants are unfamiliar with and, as Ibrahim illustrates, disinterested in creativity and art in itself. Ball *et al.* (2002) have explained that in the case of 'contingent higher education choosers', families of ethnic minority or disadvantaged youth are limited in that they can usually only offer emotional support and not informed evaluation. The same appears to be true in Hamid's discussion of creative aspirations. A key difference is that these informants find it much more difficult to explain how creativity can be mobilised as part of a larger project for social mobility – which all of these young men believe creativity to be. It is much more obvious to parents how educational credentials can improve one's life chances especially because there may not be any monetary gains to be made from drawing, acting, or writing.

The kind of validation these informants receive – that they have creative talents and that these talents are worth being pursued – often comes from outside of their local networks. Thus, when explaining their creative vocational aspirations to their family members and their broader ethnic communities, they resort to the language of passion. As we can see in Hamid's case, pursuing a creative passion can be risky because there is little certainty that his passion for writing or acting can result in a successful career path. Of course, this is the perspective of many creative aspirants in contemporary society because the creative industries are extremely competitive. However, in Hamid's case, as is the case with many of my informants, the uncertainty involved in creative vocational pathways is problematic not because he might fail to meet his own aspirations, but because he comes from a family in which the most important thing for his parents is that "everyone else thinks [he is] succeeding". The language of creative passion thereby says something broader about the ways that creative biographies are contested processes and involve continual justification and rationalising to the families of these Arab–Australian youth, whereas in other research, the creative identity is a taken-for-granted identity position (Hesmondhalgh and Baker 2010; 2011).

I argue that this theme can also contribute to the ways we understand risk in contemporary society. Giddens (1999) explains that the conditions of risk that individuals face in contemporary Western societies should not be characterised purely in negative terms. He says, "risk is also the condition of excitement and adventure … Risk is the mobilising dynamic of a society bent on change, that wants to determine its own future rather than leaving it to religion, tradition or the vagaries of nature" (Giddens 1999: 8). He adds that risks need to be exercised with caution but, ultimately, "active risk-taking is a core element of a dynamic economy and an innovative society" (Giddens 1999: 11). This argument can also be applied to individual identities; that is, active risk-taking is a core element of individual lives.

Giddens' emphasis on the positive dimensions of risk-taking does not address the question of what degree of risk is appropriate? For the purposes of this research we have to also ask, what does 'active risk-taking' look like in the case of the Arab–Australian young men from Bankstown? In one sense, we might see their incorporation of the language of passion in their life planning projects as a discursive strategy to meet their 'ideal' self. This is perhaps one way of 'active risk-taking'. However, one of the criticisms levelled against Giddens and other writers on reflexive modernity and individualisation processes is that they seem to claim that "neither self-identity nor social actions are tethered to class position" (Atkinson 2010: 28). Here we have seen how the lives of Arab–Australian young men, and the ways they articulate their life experiences, continue to be directed by socio-economic factors and connected in a myriad of ways to their local communities (Reay *et al.* 2005; Thompson 2011).

Of course, the aim is not to present informants as simply structured by fixed categories of class, ethnicity, gender, sexuality, and so on. In the telling of one's biography it is certainly true that the young men in this study reconstruct past events to plan for their futures; this is an important feature of the reflexive individual in contemporary risk societies. However, there are clear differences in how we speak about our lives and how they are actually lived. We see this disjuncture operating quite clearly in the narratives discussed in this chapter where some young men have an earlier creative passion or calling that is then mediated by communal expectations. Ultimately, these informants' interactions in their families and local communities leave them with the impression that they will confront difficulties in parlaying their passions into lifelong careers that make sense to the members of their social networks. Because membership of these networks is important to these young men, the challenge of communicating to the ethnic community the value of a creative career is a particularly poignant one and does impact how they develop their creative biographies as they move into young adulthood.

Conclusion

This chapter has been concerned with the ways that creativity, creative passion, and risk appear in the biographical interviews within the context of family and community dynamics with several overlapping aims. In the first instance, it has presented the perspectives of Hamid and Ibrahim, who make similar claims that their local Arab, Muslim communities reject creative leisure interests and some creative vocational pathways on moral or religious grounds. In their aspirations to become creative people, this is the first challenge they have to overcome. By analysing the strategies they deploy to overcome these negative views of creativity, I have aimed to show how the dialectical processes in this local ethnic community reveal an alternative way to understand the risks involved in developing creative identities. Creative vocational pathways are not only risky because of the working conditions or the kinds of self-exploitation that creative workers are expected to endure, but can be risky even in the case of creative aspirants who have yet to work under these conditions.

This chapter also challenges contemporary ways that risk has been conceptualised whereby it is argued that traditional communities offer stability and security, whereas individualistic lifestyles that are heavily shaped by the employment market leave people in a perpetual state of riskmanagement. If we take as a starting point that the families of these Arab–Australian young men generally perceive creativity as something of little value or benefit to these informants, then creative passion becomes something that must be continually justified, rationalised, and defended by these young men. One of the ways that these young men persevere with their creative interests in the face of criticism from their families is by receiving validation from individuals external to their ethnic-based social networks. This is a critical moment for some young men in this study because it means that the individual investments they have made in themselves, by remaining true to their 'passion', becomes legitimated by an authoritative figure; a kind of validation they have yet to receive in their childhood and early adolescence.

Through exploring these themes, this chapter has shown how investing in a creative identity is risky because it can result in the struggle to imagine futures whereby informants can be both creative and simultaneously develop respectable, adult identities that adhere to parental and communal definitions of success. However, I have not only shown how ethnicity, gender, and social class shape one's creative vocational aspirations, but also how the firm commitment these young men have to their creative passions can result in social change within local Arab–Australian communities. We saw this in Ibrahim's case where he sought to bring awareness to the community about the value of the arts and show how Islam and creativity do not have to contradict one another. We also saw this in Adam's case where, although he was tentative and afraid, he could show his family that being a creative person is not necessarily indicative of one's sexual preferences and thus, future generations of Arab–Australian young men might come under less scrutiny about their gendered identities if they choose to follow creative vocational pathways. Of course, these are not large-scale revolutionary processes of change, but I would argue that they still go some way to showing how the discourses of individualisation and personal choice are felt by these creative aspirants so that they challenge, rather than passively accept, familial expectations of vocation and social mobility.

Notes

1 Small business enterprise would not generally be considered 'stable' because of the enormous amount of personal responsibility involved. However, small business ownership is common among Arabic-speaking migrants and as such, self-employment is seen as secure and stable (Collins *et al.* 1995). This does not mean that these young men are naturally disposed towards business ownership; we know there is nothing intrinsic to one's ethnicity that makes this possible (Anthias and Cederberg 2009). It simply means that the ethnic community perceives self-employment or business ownership as realistic, even ideal, career options. The discourse of self-employment within the biographies of these informants is analysed in Chapter 4 of this book.

2 http://www.huffingtonpost.com.au/entry/charlie-hebdo-cartoons-paris-french-newspaper-shooting_n_6429552

3 The HSC refers to Higher School Certificate and is completed by all final-year secondary school students in New South Wales. The score determines what course they can enrol in at university.

References

Anthias, F. (2006) 'Belongings in a globalising and unequal world: Rethinking translocations', in *Situating Contemporary Politics of Belonging*, Ed. N. Yuval-Davis, London, Sage Publications, pp.17–31.

Anthias, F. and M. Cederberg (2009) 'Using ethnic bonds in self-employment and the issue of social capital', *Journal of Ethnic and Migration Studies*, 35(6): 901–917.

Appadurai, A., Ed. (2001) *Globalization*, Durham, Duke University Press.

Archer, L. (2012) 'Between authenticity and pretension: Parents', pupils' and young professionals' negotiations of minority ethnic middle-class identity', *The Sociological Review*, 60(1): 129–148.

Atkinson, W. (2010) 'The myth of the reflexive worker: Class and work histories in neoliberal times', *Work, Employment Society*, 24(3): 413–429.

Ball, S., D. Reay and M. David (2002) '"Ethnic choosing": Minority ethnic students, social class and higher education choice', *Race Ethnicity and Education*, 5(4): 333–357.

Banks, M. (2007) *The Politics of Cultural Work*, Basingstoke, Palgrave Macmillan.

Bauman, Z. (1993) *Postmodern Ethics*, Oxford, Blackwell.

Bauman, Z. (1998) *Work, Consumerism and the New Poor*, New York, Open University Press.

Bauman, Z. (2000) *Liquid Modernity*, Cambridge, Polity Press.

Bauman, Z. (2001) *Community: Seeking Safety in an Insecure World*, Oxford, Polity Press.

Bauman, Z. (2002) 'Foreword by Zygmunt Bauman: Individually, together', *Individualization: Institutionalized Individualism and its Social and Political Consequences*, Eds. U. Beck and E. Beck-Gernsheim, London, Sage Publications, pp. xiv–xx.

Bauman, Z. (2007) *Liquid Times: Living in an Age of Uncertainty*, Cambridge, Polity.

Beck, U. (2000) *Risk Society: Towards a New Modernity*, London, Sage Publications.

Beck, U. (2007) 'Beyond class and nation: Reframing social inequalities in a globalizing world', *The British Journal of Sociology*, 58(4): 679–705.

Beck, U. and E. Beck-Gernsheim (2002) *Individualization: Institutionalized Individualism and its Social and Political Consequences*, London, Sage Publications.

Bourdieu, P. (1973) 'Cultural reproduction and social reproduction', *Knowledge, Education, and Cultural Change*, Ed. R. Brown, London, Tavistock.

Bourdieu, P. (2005) 'Habitus', *Habitus: A Sense of Place*, Eds. J. Hillier and E. Rooksby, Aldershot, Ashgate, pp. 43–49.

Bruner, J. (1987) 'Life as narrative', *Social Research*, 54(1): 11–32.

Christopherson, S. (2009) 'Working in the creative economy: Risk, adaptation, and the persistence of exclusionary networks', in *Creative Labour: Working in the Creative Industries*, Eds. A. McKinlay and C. Smith, Basingstoke, Palgrave Macmillan, pp.72–91.

Collins, J., K. Gibson, C. Alcorso, S. Castles, and D. Tait (1995) *A Shop Full of Dreams: Ethnic Small Business in Australia*, Leichardt, Pluto Press.

Connell, R. W. (2005) *Masculinities*, Sydney, Allen and Unwin.

Cote, J. and J. M. Brynner (2008) 'Changes in the transition to adulthood in the UK and Canada: The role of structure and agency in emerging adulthood', *Journal of Youth Studies*, 11(3): 251–268.

Devadason, R. (2007) 'Constructing coherence? Young adults' pursuit of meaning through multiple transitions between work, education and unemployment', *Journal of Youth Studies*, 10(2): 203–221.

Donaldson, M. and R. Howsen (2009) 'Men, migration and hegemonic masculinity', *Migrant Men: Critical Studies of Masculinities and the Migration Experience*, Eds. M. Donaldson, R. Hibbins, R. Howsen and B. Pease, New York, Taylor and Francis, pp. 210–218.

Du Gay, P. (1996) *Consumption and Identity at Work*, London, Sage.

Dwyer, P. and J. Wyn (2001) *Youth, Education and Risk: Facing the Future*, London, RoutledgeFalmer.

Forsyth, A. and A. Furlong (2003) 'Access to higher education and disadvantaged young people', *British Educational Research Journal*, 29(2): 205–225.

Furlong, A, Woodman, D. and J. Wyn (2011) 'Changing times, changing perspectices: Reconciling 'transition' and 'cultural' perspectives on youth and young adulthood', *Journal of Sociology*, 47(4): 355–370.

Giddens, A. (1990) *The Consequences of Modernity*, Cambridge, Polity.

Giddens, A. (1991) *Modernity and Self-Identity*, Cambridge, Polity.

Giddens, A. (1999) *BBC Reith Lecture Series: Runaway World*, Delivered April 1999 in London, Retrieved from http://www.looooker.com/wp-content/uploads/2013/05/Giddens-lectures-in-london.pdf

Giddens, A. (2003) *Runaway World: How Globalisation is Reshaping ourLives*, New York, Routledge.

Gill, R. (2002) 'Cool, creative and egalitarian? Exploring gender in project-based new media work in euro', *Information, Communication & Society*, 5(1): 70–89.

Guerra, C. and R. White (1995) *Ethnic Minority Youth in Australia: Challenges and Myths*, Hobart, National Clearinghouse for Youth Studies.

Hartley, J. (2005) *Creative industries*, Malden, Mass, Blackwell Publishers.

Heinz, W. (2009) 'Youth transitions in an age of uncertainty', *Handbook of Youth and Young adulthood: New Perspectives and Agendas*, Ed. A. Furlong, New York, Routledge.

Hesmondhalgh, D. and S. Baker (2010) '"A very complicated of version of freedom": Conditions and experiences of creative labour in three cultural industries', *Poetics*, 38: 4–20.

Hesmondhalgh, D. and S. Baker (2011) *Creative Labour: Media Work in Three Cultural Industries*, Abingdon, Routledge.

Hibbins, R. and B. Pease (2009) 'Men and masculinities on the move', *Migrant Men: Critical Studies of Masculinities and the Migration Experience*, Eds. M. Donaldson, R. Hibbins, R. Howsen and B. Pease, New York, Taylor and Francis, pp. 1–20.

Lahire, B. (2003) 'From the habitus to an individual heritage of dispositions. Towards a sociology at the level of the individual', *Poetics*, 31: 329–355.

Lash, S. (1996) 'Tradition and the limits of difference', in *Detraditionalization: Critical Reflections on Authority and Identity*, Eds. P. Heelas, S. Lash and P. Morris Oxford, Blackwell Publishers, pp. 250–275.

Matthys, M. (2013) *Cultural Capital, Identity, and Social Mobility: The Life Course of Working-class University Graduates*, New York, Routledge.

McRobbie, A. (2002) 'Clubs to companies: Notes on the decline of political culture in speeded up creative worlds', *Cultural Studies*, 16(4): 516–531.

Modood, T. (1993) 'The number of ethnic minority students in British higher education: Some grounds for optimism', *Oxford Review of Education*, 19(2): 167–182.

Morgan, G. (2006) 'Work in progress: Narratives of aspiration from the new economy', *Journal of Education and Work*, 19(2): 141–151.

Morgan, G. and P. Cohen (2006) 'Introduction to the special issue: Narratives of education and work', *Journal of Education and Work*, 19(2): 105–107.

Noble, G. (2007) 'Respect and respectability amongst second-generation Arab and Muslim Australian men', *Journal of Intercultural Studies*, 28(3): 331–344.

Pasztor, A. (2012) 'Imagined futures: Why business studies dominate the higher education choices of second-generation Turks in the Netherlands', *Ethnic and Racial Studies*, 35(4): 704–717.

Price, R., P. McDonald, J. Bailey, and B. Pini, Eds. (2011) *Young People and Work*, Surrey, Ashgate.

Raffo, C. and M. Reeves (2000) 'Youth transitions and social exclusion: Developments in social capital theory', *Journal of Youth Studies*, 3(2): 147–166.

Ramadan, T. (2006) 'The Danish cartoons, free speech and civic responsibility', *New Perspectives Quarterly*, (Spring): 17–18.

Reay, D. (2001) 'Finding or losing yourself? Working-class relationships to education', *Journal of Education Policy*, 16(4): 333–346.

Reay, D. and S. Ball (1998) '"Making their minds up": Family dynamics of school choice', *British Educational Research Journal*, 24(4): 431–448.

Reay, D., M. David, and S.Ball (2005) 'Working class students', in *Degrees of Choice: Social Class, Race and Gender in Higher Education*, Eds. D. Reay, M. David and S. Ball, Staffordshire, Trentham Books, pp. 83–107.

Rentschler, R., Le, H. and Osborne, A. (2008) *Western Australia Intercultural Arts Research Project: An Investigation into Issues Faced by Culturally and Linguistically Diverse Artists in Western Australia Prepared by the Centre for Leisure Management Research*. Accessed at [http://www.omi.wa.gov.au/resources/clearinghouse/WA_Intercultural_Arts.pdf]

Riele, K. t. and J. Wyn (2005) 'Australia: Transformations in youth transitions', *Youth Transition in a Globalised Marketplace*, Ed. N. Bagnall, New York, Nova Science Publishers Inc, pp. 119–141.

Roberts, K. (2007) 'Youth transitions and generations: A response to Wyn and Woodman', *Journal of Youth Studies*, 10(2): 263–269.

Ross, A. (2007) 'Nice work if you can get it: The mercurial career of creative industries policy', in *My Creativity Reader: A Critique of Creative Industries*, Eds. G. Lovink and N. Rossiter, Amsterdam, Institute of Network cultures, pp. 17–39.

Shiner, M. and T. Modood (2002) 'Help or hindrance? Higher education and the route to ethnic equality', *British Journal of Sociology of Education*, 23(2): 209–232.

Smith, H. (2007) 'Playing a different game: The contextualised decision-making processes of minority ethnic students in choosing a higher education institution', *Race Ethnicity and Education*, 10(4): 415–437.

Soganci, I. O. (2004) Islamic aniconism: Making sense of a messy literature, *Marilyn Zurmuehlin Papers in Art Education*, 2004(1): p. 4.

Taylor, S. and K. Littleton (2012) *Contemporary Identities of Creativity and Creative Work*, Surrey, Ashgate Publishing.

Thompson, J. B. (1996) 'Tradition and self in a mediated world', in *Detraditionalization: Critical Reflections on Authority and Identity*, Eds. P. Heelas, S. Lash and P. Morris, Oxford, Blackwell Publishers, pp. 89–109.

Thompson, R. (2011) 'Individualisation and social exclusion: The case of young people not in education, employment or training', *Oxford Review of Education*, 37(6): 785–802.

Willis, P. E. (1977) *Learning to Labour: How Working Class Kids get Working Class Jobs*, Farnborough, England, Saxon House.

2 Nike TNs and Dry Fit

The importance of style among creative aspirants

> I mean, the Leb guys were smart but when they hung out, I don't want to make generalisations at all here 'cause I did have some Lebanese friends at school, just not when they were all together. Because when they were all together it just felt like, I don't know, just this weird kind of macho thing and didn't have anything interesting to talk about. It just wasn't fun and there was an element of cruelty and an element of a gang and that just wasn't appealing to me.
>
> (Walid, twenty-six-year-old community arts worker/film editor)

School is thought to be a key site of cultural and social production (Bourdieu 1973), and countless studies have examined the ways that youthful masculine identities are actively produced by the cultures of educational institutions (Willis 1977; Mac an Ghaill 1994; Archer 2003). Within schools, gendered and classed hierarchies emerge whereby "popular masculinity involves 'hardness', sporting prowess, 'coolness', casual treatment of schoolwork and being adept at 'cussing', dominance and control" (Frosh *et al.* 2002: 77). In this chapter, I will trace the ways that Arab–Australian young men with creative interests do not fit into the locally dominant version of masculinity and who therefore experience marginalisation within school-based peer groups within Bankstown. Rather than treat this as problematic, the chapter examines how the informants in this study frame their marginalisation and exclusion in positive terms, as part of their broader strategies to distance themselves from Arab–Australian young men from Bankstown that are stigmatised and demonised in the Australian media and public discourse more generally.

As such, I will look at how creativity is used by these young men with creative vocational aspirations as a metaphor for their broader aspirations for social mobility. Creativity becomes associated with, and even substituted at times for, personal characteristics such as open-mindedness, respect for women, and intellectual capacity. These are not randomly-made associations, but rather, as I will show, are often carefully articulated as reactions against the characteristics they associate with problematic peer groups in their secondary schools. Importantly, the student population of each of the informants' schools were described to me as largely made up of other Arab–Australian youth, especially where some of these young men attended specific Islamic or Maronite Catholic schools. Across all of these schools, the most commonly cited youth culture was that of the 'Lebs', that is Lebanese or Arab–Australian young men who display exaggerated performances of masculinity and who often live up to the negative stereotypes made of young Lebanese boys, as Walid describes in the opening paragraph. Therefore, I will show how the conflict between an informant's personal sense of creativity and the school-based, male-dominated youth cultures they describe point to contemporary manifestations of intra-ethnic tensions.

The specific interest in this chapter is not only that there exist intra-ethnic tensions because of preferences of style, but that creativity is at the core of these young men's constructed boundaries of 'self' and 'other' among their co-ethnic peers. I will argue that these boundaries have two important narrative functions. First, they enable these young men to undermine the physical dominance that other 'Leb' boys in their school have over them. In order to develop this argument, I draw on the points of connection between theories of masculinity (Haywood and Mac an Ghaill 1996; Connell 2005), youth subcultures and style (Hebdige 1979; 2002), and the concept of distinction as developed by Bourdieu (and adapted by others such as Giddens (1991) and Savage (2000)). Second, these constructions of self and other reveal how school becomes a key site of struggle wherein Arab–Australian young men feel restricted in their ability to develop creative interests and creative identities more generally. By looking at the constructions of self and other among Arab–Australian young men during school, I note how creative interests and youthful creative style comes to redefine these young men's attachments to their ethnic communities.

Formations of Lebanese-ness

> Lebanese-ness is a symbolic value from which some ... who have a Lebanese background derive a sense of unity, security and strength.
>
> (Noble and Tabar 2002: 136)

The status of Arab–Australian young men as the figure of the demonised folk devil has emerged over time and through various key conflicts (Morgan and Poynting 2012). The September 11, 2001 bombing of the World Trade Centre in New York, the Cronulla Riots in 2005, the stabbing of Edward Lee in 1998 by Lebanese–Australian young men; the criminal activities of Kings Cross club owner John Ibrahim and his Lebanese–Australian friends and relatives are all moments where processes of racialisation in the media and public discourse connected criminality with images of Lebanese–Australian males, creating panic over ethnic Arab gangs in Australia (Collins 2002). The phrase 'of Middle Eastern appearance' became shorthand for ethnic crime in the early 2000s; an association that has maintained its longevity partly due to the establishment of the New South Wales (NSW) Police Middle Eastern Crime Squad. The result, as Dagistanli suggests, is that "the racialization of 'gang' crime plus the fear of terrorism drew a fundamental divide between the culture of the perpetrators of these crimes and that of mainstream society" (Dagistanli 2007: 181).

The public discourse around Arabs, Muslims and young men in Sydney's West has generated a sense of alienation among Arab–Australian communities (Collins *et al.* 2000) and resulted in structural inequalities for many youth especially in the employment market (Nilan 2012). Research has highlighted that second-generation Arab–Australian young men establish a sense of ethnic solidarity as a defence against exclusion within broader Australian society (Poynting *et al.* 2004; White 2007; Wise 2009). The available literature on these youths has tended to frame their everyday lives in terms of the ongoing divides between Arab–Australian diasporic groups and broader Australian society. The young people in these studies speak to the pain of racism and everyday experiences of discrimination. It is this common suffering as the 'Arab Other' that united young Arab–Australians after their communities were "tainted by the media brush of *ethnic crime*" (Collins 2002: 2).

Despite conjuring images of solidarity, some research has refuted traditional multicultural discourse in which ethnic groups are assumed to be homogenous and clearly demarcated. For instance, Noble and Tabar (2002) explore the strategic essentialism and strategic hybridity displayed by many young Arab–Australians in which the informants oscillate between *versions* of Lebanese-ness, Arabness, 'woginess' and Australian-ness to various degrees and in a variety of contexts. By doing so, they assert power and control, albeit a limited amount, over the positions ascribed to them by broader social perceptions. The young men may predominantly speak Arabic with their parents, learn traditional folklore dances such as the *dabkeh* or insert Arabic words into conversations with friends, but omit their ethnic and religious heritage at job interviews or in the presence of white people in positions of power, feeling that their ethnicity is a disadvantage (Noble and Tabar 2002; Nilan 2012; Mansouri and Wood 2008). The majority of the young men in Noble and Tabar's study confirm the bonds they share with other Lebanese–Australian youth, highlighted in this statement by Nadim who said "It's just that we always stick by each other. Be there when others need you. Protect others, just stick together as one group". (Noble and Tabar 2002: 139)

Displays of unity among second-generation Lebanese–Australian men are often found in schools whereby they claim to defend one another against peers who might be involved in arguments with a fellow Lebanese–Australian student. In doing so, they exhibit a type of collective identity, one founded on challenging subtle (and not so subtle) racist behaviour (Poynting *et al.* 2004). Much of the work on Arab–Australian youth holds that ethnicity involves processes of identification in which groups are produced in an ongoing way and come to symbolise community despite the heterogeneity of the migrant experience (Noble *et al.* 1999). In narrating what it means to be Lebanese in Australia, the young men in Noble *et al.*'s (1999) study classify individuals from various cultural groups, such as Anglo–Australians or 'Asians', as 'Other', creating boundaries along ethnic lines. In doing so, the young men map out a space in which they belong and define the parameters of a Lebanese–Australian identity. This is a key point of difference between my research and the findings of Noble *et al.* (1999). By looking at how creative identities develop among this group of young men, it has become evident that creativity can drive a wedge among Arab–Australian youth and those with creative vocational aspirations become ambivalent about their attachments to a local Arab–Australian community. To return to Noble and Tabar's (2002) argument that "Lebanese-ness is a symbolic value" that can be a source of security and strength, I would argue that the opposite is more likely true of creative vocational aspirants. Their sense of Arabness, as will be demonstrated in this chapter, is weak, mainly because they do not subscribe to the kinds of performances of 'protest masculinity' that was captured in the excerpt provided from my interview with Walid.

One of the limitations in existing studies of Arab–Australian youth is that narratives of peer relations (provided by both young people and the researcher) are framed as responses towards adversity or prejudice within the nation. This limitation can be accounted for by considering the time in which this literature was produced, namely in the aftermath of September 11 or the Cronulla Riots. While some have alluded to disparities within this ethnic youth group (Mansouri and Wood 2008), distinctions among Arab–Australian males beyond obvious differences of religion or class have yet to be fully explored. Instead, much of the framing that has been done revolves around myths of ethnic crime, social exclusion, and performances of protest masculinity. The research I conducted confirms the nature of identity making as operating at the interplay of self-identification and identification by others in the same way that other youth researchers (Stokes 2012; Shildrick *et al.* 2009) have demonstrated. However, the relations explored in my study are not only between Arabs and Australians but within local Arab migrant communities themselves and specifically with young people who share common creative aspirations. As such, the young men in this research, when asked about the secondary schooling experience, were more likely to refer to the ways that their creative identities were at odds with localised versions of Arabness and dominant versions of masculinity.

Lebs, *Habiibs,* and ethnic minority masculinities

At the end of my interview with Bashir, the nineteen-year-old psychology student we were introduced to in Chapter 1, I asked whether there was anything he wanted to add that I might not have asked about. He paused to think then said, "Well, your topic is about Lebanese guys and being creative, yeah? But the thing is everything creative is non-Leb". The interview was clearly not over. Young Arab–Australians, he said, don't understand creativity. They see no value in it and the elements of being a 'Leb' contrasts with creativity. By creativity he was referring not only to art in a more traditional sense but also to vocations that are not based on manual labour or hard sciences such as accountancy, a field many of his peers entered into at the end of their high school lives. He continued, "Lebs just don't *get* what it means to be creative. Like, you're weird for being into film or writing or whatever".

His strongly-held beliefs about the incompatibility between creativity and 'Leb' identities stem from interactions with other Lebanese–Australian young men in the local community and reveal a system of classification in which some Lebanese–Australian young people demonstrate an intensified version of 'Lebness' which others, such as Bashir, refuse to take part. This 'weirdness' that is attributed to Bashir and the others in this study with creative interests becomes a kind of cultural capital (Bennett *et al.* 1999) where, although intended as an insult, they imagine it can be advantageous for them later in the creative industries where the ability to cultivate a distinctive look and style is celebrated. We might understand the youthful label of 'weird' as a label that comes to stand as a link to an occupational lifestyle that "gives them opportunities to begin to shape an occupational identity" (Stokes and Wyn 2007: 507). I explore this theme further in the latter half of this chapter.

However, his assertions are contradictory. After all, Bashir is Lebanese–Australian and grew up in Bankstown, an area highly populated by Lebanese migrants. For him to argue that creativity is inherently at odds with Arab–Australian identities, especially youthful identities, but spend an hour discussing his passion for fiction writing and plans to be an author, hints at the ways that categories such as ethnicity are not robust but subjective and used by individuals, as Bashir does here, to map out one's identity in light of the perceptions others have of us as well as the boundaries we impose within our imagined communities. The sentiments behind his statement, that "everything creative is non-Leb", capture some of the intra-ethnic tensions among the young people in this sample that I had previously overlooked when designing the interview questions yet one that emerged very strongly in the course of the interviews nonetheless. It seems that the tension exists because of the creative, artistic dispositions of a small number of Arab–Australian young men in a local community where the dominant masculine roles are played by 'tough' young men.

At the level of narrative analysis, it appeared that the ways informants describe Lebs as part of a hierarchical masculine order within Bankstown is based on their 'interpretive repertoires' about the interplay between ethnicity and masculinity (Edley 2001). Interpretive repertoires, according to Potter and Wetherell (1987), are defined as "basically a lexicon or register of terms and metaphors drawn upon to characterise and evaluate actions and events" (Potter and Wetherell 1987: 138). In this chapter, I refer back to the repertoires these informants use to talk about schooling cultures, Lebs and creative and subcultural interests following Edley's argument that "masculinity is something constructed in and through discourse" (Edley 2001: 191).

Edley's (2001) argument about how masculinity is constructed through linguistic devices is one sustained in earlier studies of Lebanese–Australian youthful identities. Tabar *et al.* (2010) for example, offer a detailed description of the term *habiib.* This Arabic word, which technically translates to 'beloved' and a take on the word *habibi,* meaning my love, is appropriated by young Arab–Australians in two ways. The first is that "the term *habiib* [is used] to mean a sense of ethnic comradeship that binds them together and draws the line between them and the Anglo–Australian other" (Tabar *et al.* 2010: 89). The other meaning behind the word habiib is that it is a label, used to refer to an "aestheticized mode of living" (Tabar *et al.* 2010: 89). In their study, informants explain that "*Habiibs* from Bankstown, automatically you assume it's a Lebanese gang. But if my friend was to say to me *habiib* I'd say it's a friendship" (Tabar *et al.* 2010: 90). The respondents in that study, while noting the importance of dress, manner of speaking and driving certain types of cars as key indicators of a *habiib,* point out that trust and solidarity based on a common ethnic heritage is equally important and many represented *habiibs* in generally positive (though also in complex and contradictory) terms.

In my research, the label *habiib* was rarely used by informants. However, the term 'Leb' appeared frequently and was used to describe relatively similar performances of masculinity and youth cultures. For example, Bashir described Lebs in the following way,

> They talk in certain ways to people, they break shit, they graffiti … walk around with your gang and piss on everyone else and you sort of feed your own ego and your mates.

The image of the Leb, like that of the *habiib*, is one defined by "the performance of gang-like behaviour" (Collins *et al.* 2000: 137) without necessarily undertaking criminal activities. Thus, being feared by youth of other ethnic backgrounds is a source of comfort as it reinforces ethnic, class and local geographical bonds. Often, these ethnic minority youth are scarred by racism and discrimination so that they become uninterested in forming relations with those outside their local communities; this is a defence mechanism. By contrast, the young men in my study classify Lebs and *Habiibs* in generally negative ways, associating them with the attributes of 'thugs' and 'hoods' and instead develop friendships with other youth outside of their local, ethnic communities who perhaps share similar creative or leisure interests whenever they get the chance.

Existing research about *habiibs* and stylised experiences of Lebanese–Australian youth concludes that ethnic youthful solidarity is a response to racism. These studies have also highlighted the positions *habiibs* occupy in multiculturalist discourse, challenging what they see as an unacknowledgement of these specific ways Lebanese–Australian young men speak, dress, listen to music, or drive cars.

> When the definers of this discourse talk about the cultural manifestations of these young people's experience, they name and define them in a way that erases their symbolic value and makes them the opposite to what they consider to be the defining characteristics of a valorised ethnic capital: their linguistic invention is unrecognised and even degraded (it's bad language), their social gathering is perceived to be a grouping of "Lebanese gangs" with intention to commit various crimes, and their style of music and dressing are symptoms of a pathologised gang identity.
>
> (Tabar *et al.* 2010: 94)

Similar arguments have been made in the UK case in relation to the 'chavs' who also represent localised versions of masculinity (Shildrick *et al.* 2009). Shildrick *et al.* (2009) explain, "what makes the 'chav' or 'charver' discourse so powerful, under the guise of either harmless light entertainment or unreflective, uncritical social science, is its role in pinning the mass of young, poor, white working-class people to the social pathologies of, *inter alia*, welfare dependency, moral degeneracy, academic failure, fecklessness, and excessive and tasteless consumption as if these were (a) accurate depictions of their life situations, (b) the common problems of all and (c) rooted in individual failings" (Shildrick *et al.* 2009: 461).

In Chapters 4 and 5 I examine how these sorts of negative associations affect the opportunities available to young Arab–Australian men in creative-based employment fields but in this chapter, my interest is how Arab–Australian youth who may be excluded and who exclude themselves from this 'ethnic comradeship' can also perpetuate 'Leb' discourse, for example as Bashir calls them 'a gang' in his brief description. Hamid, a twenty-five-year-old writer and community arts worker I introduced in the previous chapter, attended an all-boys public high school and was angered by how the 'Leb' boys treated females quite poorly when they were teenagers. He said,

> Like, if I was on the phone at school with a girl I was talking to, you know that I was going out with or even just a friend, they (Leb boys) would come over and snatch the phone off me and be like "hey slut" or they'd call out derogatory things while I was on the phone to her. And it was just disgusting.

The important difference between the intentions behind the definers of 'Leb' discourse, similarly to the definers of 'Chav' discourse, and the young men in this study like Hamid and Bashir is that the latter group use the term Leb and call themselves non-Leb to signify their ambivalence about their own membership and identification with the Bankstown, ethnic community, and their own sense of masculinity as young men. To return to earlier studies of Lebanese–Australian young men, we see that there are differences though between the labels (*habiib* and 'Leb') which can be accounted for by looking at the kinds of informants in each study. The sample that has comprised previous studies is made up by those who participate in this style; it is logical that they use the term *habiib* to imply endearment and friendship. 'Leb', according to my informants, signifies none of these positive attributes because of the status of the informants in that group – as outsiders or fringe members. They are categorised as outsiders not because of their ethnic background but because they actively reject the type of dominating masculinity the 'Lebs' perform. While Tabar *et al.* (2010) raise the way some youth in their sample, mostly the young women, disapprove of the *habiibs,* they do not consider the intra-ethnic conflict or the hierarchies of power that exist among young Lebanese–Australian men themselves. Further, their discussion of the *habiib* stops short of categorising them as a subcultural group. But this is a fragmented group, wherein the creative 'types' are usually marginalised or subordinated by local versions of hegemonic masculinities (Connell 2000). In what follows, I introduce informants' own accounts of the markers of Leb style and discuss how they frame this style as one that stems from local schooling cultures.

"Do you know what TNs are?" The markers of Leb style

My interview with Fawaz, a twenty-one-year-old disk jockey and construction worker, revealed a life-history trajectory that was unlike the pattern that had generally emerged across the other interviews. He did not complete high school, he was not enrolled in university, and he was less concerned than the others about adhering to cultural and religious traditions. He had "done a lot of bad shit growing up, stuff that I try to block out … but you know it's bad when your parents find drugs under your bed … (shrugs)". He tells me that music 'saved' him from following a life of gang crime. Fawaz's coloured past meant that pursuing his creative passion, music, was less risky than the young men discussed in Chapter 1. This is because while his parents and the broader Lebanese/Syrian Muslim community found his chosen career choice to be both unconventional and 'shameful', they were relieved that he had given up on dealing drugs and 'hanging out in gangs'. Being a deejay was not something to be justified because his father had already come to terms with the fact that Fawaz had rejected their familial aspirations for him to pursue higher education; to fulfil what has been called 'the migrant success story' (Ho and Alcorso 2004). In Arabic, he told me that his fathers' reaction when he brought home his first DJ set and began mixing music in his bedroom was "*rah e sabe*" which translates to "the boy has gone"; signifying that they had lost their sense of authority over Fawaz's life decisions.

What his father may not have noticed however, is that Fawaz's entry to music and club cultures was actually a turning point in his transition to adulthood. This is reflected, for example, through the ways he suddenly adapted his personal style and the reasons he gives for his makeover, as highlighted in the following exchange:

Sherene: How did becoming a deejay change you?

Fawaz: Umm … I used to be the biggest hard c*nt. I used to have a mullet down to my back … always wearing the Dry Fit (Nike clothes), never in jeans, always in the TNs. You know what TNs are?

Sherene: Sneakers?

Fawaz: Yeah, what every other Leb wears. That was my image back then before I was a deejay, that's how I wanted to be seen back then. And now I changed my whole wardrobe, become the biggest pretty boy. Now I can actually stop someone in the middle of the road, have a conversation with them without them thinking "oh my god this guy is actually trying to rob me". You know what I mean? Like back in the day I *wanted* people to think that I was gonna bash the shit out of you.

Subculture, although a widely disputed and critiqued concept (Bennett 1999; Hesmondhalgh 2005), is defined as "the expressive forms and rituals of subordinate groups" (Hebdige 1979: 2). Without spending too much time discussing whether or not 'Lebs' constitute a distinct subcultural group, what we can say is that the stylistic markers that Fawaz refers to "take on a symbolic dimension" (Hebdige 1979: 2). Here, the figure of the 'Leb' is premised on markers of dress – TNs, mullet hairstyles, and Nike clothing. As Hebdige has argued, the styles of those who participate in subcultures act as codes, as gestures and as forms of "resistance to the order which guarantees their continued subordination" (Hebdige 1979: 18). Following Cohen, Hebdige suggests that style is a useful way to see class in practice rather than as in abstract terms, "as a material force, dressed up, as it were, in experience and exhibited in style" (Hebdige 1979: 78). The markers Fawaz describes achieve particular aims; they create fear and, as such, provide Fawaz with a sense of power in a society where Arab–Australian young men from Western Sydney are generally perceived to be powerless, thus reversing the imbalance of class power if only temporarily and in a limited sense. His descriptions of being a Leb ring true with the descriptions of *habiibs* noted earlier, where one young man said, "*Habiibs* from Bankstown, automatically you assume it's a Lebanese gang" (Tabar *et al.* 2010: 90).

Creative vocational aspirations are seemingly inseparable from the cultivation of personal style. In these highly competitive industries that many young people want to work in, qualifications are generally insufficient to landing a position (Haukka 2011). As such, young people incorporate their sense of dress as well as their leisure interests as part of their creative identities, thereby increasing their chances of success in gaining entry into creative, media and other cultural sectors; thus subcultural style becomes a form of cultural capital (McRobbie 2002). The other theme to be drawn from this excerpt is that being creative, in this case being a disk jockey, impacts on other aspects of one's identity. This is illuminated by Fawaz when he says "I became the biggest pretty boy" adding that this has shifted the public perceptions of him. Being 'hard' is constructed by Fawaz as oppositional to a creative identity.

Willis (1977), in his ethnographic study of working class young men in a UK school, found that performances of 'hard' masculine identities are central to working-class youth culture. The young men he studied often referred to the other boys in their school who were academic and aspired to continue with further education as feminine and weak. We might see parallel patterns emerging in this excerpt, although my research is more concerned with the interplay between gender, class, and ethnicity. Thus, Fawaz's description of how creative labour has changed him might be understood as one part of a larger narrative about social mobility whereby 'hard' Leb youth are located within working class, migrant communities. When he stopped dressing like a Leb, he may have felt that he symbolically became dislocated from these communities.

Giddens, in his theorisation of the postmodern self, argues that markers such as "dress remains a signalling device of gender, class position and occupational status" (Giddens 1991: 99). Further, in the United Kingdom, as elsewhere, studies show how "the police construct populations of 'permanent suspects' based on socio-economic status as much as on serious offending" (Ralphs *et al.* 2009:

485). Included in the gang labelling done by authorities are factors such as area of residence and ethnic background, thus revealing "the enduring significance of class and place in youth experiences" (Ralphs *et al.* 2009: 486) for the Arab–Australian young men in this study. It is these kinds of labelling processes that inform the changes Fawaz made to his sense of style. Fawaz interprets his new dress sense as a deejay as representing adherence to what he understands as the aesthetics of the middle class male bodies, where they are less likely to be seen as threatening. The tacit understanding of the ways that personal style is related to broader class and ethnic backgrounds offer a much clearer account of how being creative is essentially about being non-Leb, to return to Bashir's assertion.

To return to the interview with Bashir, he emphasised the collective dimension to this ethnicised subcultural style through his repeated use of the word 'they'. He said,

Bashir: They talk in certain ways to people, they break shit, they graffiti ... They, they, you know! Hoods man ... geez I don't know how to describe it, how do you describe it? It's always just sort of been acting like *habiibs* ... walk around with your gang and piss on everyone else and you sort of feed your own ego and your mates.

Sherene: Can anyone be a *habiib* or Leb? Or only if they act that way?

Bashir: Err I'm not sure. I think you need a group of mates to be one but I'm sure you could be mistaken for one by acting that way. Especially if you look like one.

Sherene: Could *you* look like one?

Bashir: (Shakes head) I could never put myself through, you know, the mullet and the tats and the working out at the gym.

Connell has argued that the body is "inescapable in the construction of masculinity" (Connell 2000). The 'mullets', the 'tats', and 'working out' represent a particular version of masculinity expressed through the body; namely a working-class masculinity. Masculinity, a relational identity position, is also about the negotiation of power. Haywood and Mac an Ghaill (1996) have suggested that "power is differentiated so that particular styles of masculinity become ascendant or dominant in certain situations" (Mac an Ghaill 1996: 52). In my exchange with Bashir, we see that the body – the ways that Arab–Australian young men walk, talk, and look–is central to the distribution of power among these youth. Lebs have a specific kind of power among youth in Bankstown, one based on intimidation and physical domination. But this is not an aspirational masculine identity for all young men in Bankstown, as we see through Bashir's rejection of the processes required for him to become a Leb. His rejection of Leb style not only reveals the intra-ethnic differences among Arab–Australian young men but his essentialist categorisations of the Lebs also reproduce the existing power relations between Anglo–Australian culture and ethnic minority groups (Marotta 2008; Pryke and Dang 2003).

This rejection can also be interpreted as Bashir's strategy to deal with potentially being mistaken for a problematic Leb youth by the broader public outside of Bankstown who may not recognise the nuances in youth style that differentiate Arab–Australian young men from one another. Ralphs *et al.* (2009) studied the experiences of young people living in areas that are associated with criminality, particularly youth-based gang crime, in the United Kingdom. They found that for many youth who were non-gang members, a common strategy was to "behave in a superficially friendly manner to potential gang members they knew … to avoid being victimised by them" (Ralphs *et al.* 2009: 490). We do not know whether this was something Bashir did, but in the course of the interview, he has a chance to assert his difference as he knows too well that there are serious consequences for being associated with the pathologised image of a Leb later in life, in the world of work, for example. In Chapter 5, I return to the implications such labels can have on the creative biographies of these young men in spite of all their assertions, here in the life-history interviews, that they are decidedly non-Leb.

The ways in which Leb masculinities are described in this excerpt from Bashir resonate with the literature on youthful subcultures. Blackman (2005), in his summary of Cohen's theorisation of subculture, says

> Youth subcultures are interpreted as a language: the meaning of their style is imaginary – that is to say, it is 'real' in that it derives from their contradictory class position but young people are not fully aware of this repression; it is only fully 'realized' in their semiotic displays of subcultural style. Working-class youth through their subcultures attempt to resolve ideological contradictions that remain hidden or unresolved in the parent culture.
>
> (Blackman 2005: 5)

Bashir shows how the cultivation of Leb style is empowering for some Arab–Australian young men; it helps them develop their 'egos' as he says. Following Blackman's conceptualisation of subculture, we might say that this grab for power is a response to their exclusion within the nation, as the contemporary figure of the Other, which is a similar argument made by Tabar *et al.* (2010) and others (Mac An Ghaill 1994). However, Bashir's claim that "I could never put myself through that" should be seen as a broader statement than his personal preference for particular hairstyles, for example. In fact, it reveals that he does not see Leb style as a strategy to overcome 'repression', as Blackman calls it. His association between Leb style and 'hoods' is significant in that it supports Gidden's argument that personal style and dress are 'signalling devices'. Further, as writers on youth transitions argue, the ability of young people to articulate high level aspirations shapes their chances of success as they move into adulthood (Stokes 2012; Abada and Tenkorang 2009). Following this exchange with Bashir, it appears that the stylistic markers of Leb style are ones that lock them in to positions of disadvantage. By contrast, Bashir cultivates a creative identity, which is constructed as synonymous with being non-Leb, to avoid being locked in to this position of disadvantage and thereby reveals the investment he makes in his future.

Missing from these brief interview moments with Bashir and Fawaz are the ways that Leb identities are situated within school settings. In the narratives of schooling experiences, it is evident that school heavily influenced the ways in which Leb subcultural practices and styles were produced. This finding supports the argument that schools produce particular masculine identities, ones that are interconnected with the class backgrounds of its' student population (Willis 1977). In what follows, I analyse what informants do with their constructions of 'Lebs' in the interview process, following Taylor's argument that "to understand what it is being done with language, it is necessary to consider its situated use, within the process of ongoing interaction" (Taylor 2001: 7).

Bashir attended a Lebanese–Catholic school in Bankstown that ran from kindergarten to year twelve. Naturally, all of the students came from a Lebanese background. The boundary between his identity, what he calls a creative, "open-minded" one, with that of his peers, was sharply demarcated during secondary school. He said,

> There's, umm, there's something about putting a whole bunch of people from the same culture in one school. They don't learn about any other culture and they sort of develop this pack habit. They become really tight knit, especially the guys, and they become the *habiibs* and wogs and Lebs you see on the street. A few people actually escaped that but most of the guys, most of them ended up like that and the girls ended up in a similar way as well. I was completely different. I tried to fit into that culture in year five and six and realised I absolutely couldn't do it. And so I sort of became … I was different. Most of my friends in year five and six were outside school. Umm I had a few inside but then by year eleven and twelve I was, I had the most of the cohort I was friends with them. I was the guy in the middle, I was everywhere … but I could never fit into what the school was breeding as a mentality, it was, if you try and shoehorn one culture then they're not going to learn anything else and they have to end up that way. That's why I didn't like it, no one was different. Every day was the same thing.

A valuable aspect of Connell's conceptualisation of masculinities is the argument that gender roles are "defined collectively in culture and are sustained in institutions" (Connell 2003: 15). Here, Bashir shows that schools are central to the construction of one's ethnicity and masculinity, where these categories are performed in shifting ways at different moments in the life course. Bashir is keen to emphasise a clear distinction between two opposing youth styles or cultures, the Lebs and the non-Lebs. Enough empirical work has demonstrated the confrontational and hierarchical nature of young men's relationships (Frosh *et al.* 2002), but what Bashir additionally reveals is that these confrontations and hierarchies become intensified when the majority of the students at school come from the same ethnic background. Their shared ethnic background results in other, newer kinds of hierarchies based on youthful leisure interests and vocational aspirations.

A key point to note from this excerpt is Bashir's claim to 'difference'. It ran through his entire life-history interview, as we also saw in Chapter 1, and underscores the way he narrates his creative biography – that within Bankstown, but specifically among Lebanese young men in a Lebanese/Catholic school that encourages solidarity along ethnic lines, he is different. This recurring narrative of difference, made in relation to creative leisure interests and unorthodox subcultural practices, may be understood as claims about taste and distinction and can be seen as a strategy for personal projects of social mobility. That is, Bashir associates the sense of comfort other Arab–Australian youth gain from being surrounded by young people of the same ethnic backgrounds with 'the street'. The street is symbolic, as it conjures up images of crime and violence particularly as it relates to Arab–Australian young men, whose presence in public spaces is often a source of discomfort for some members of general Australian public (White 2007).

It has been argued that the consumption of art or music is not the only arena in which we can make connections between a person's tastes and preferences and their class backgrounds (Bennett *et al.* 2009; Bourdieu 1984). In fact, Bourdieu (1984) argues "nothing is more distinctive, more distinguished, than the capacity to confer aesthetic status on objects that are banal or even 'common', or the ability to apply the principles of a 'pure' aesthetic to the most everyday choices of life" (Bourdieu 1984:5). We can draw in these arguments of taste and consumption to analyse how Bashir harshly judges the choices of other youth in his school to remain 'tight knit'. Essentially, by doing so they reaffirm their ties to an imagined working class, migrant community and in Bashir's view, this choice reduces their ability to achieve social mobility and escape Bankstown entirely. By contrast, his claim of being 'totally different', through his creative interests and his rejection of Leb style, is a distinction that enables him to break with his migrant background and what he sees as a confining and restrictive future.

The school-based hierarchies around subcultural style were also raised during my interview with Usama. Usama was a nineteen-year-old fine arts university student. He had attended a Muslim-based high school where the vast majority of students came from Middle Eastern backgrounds. High school was a difficult time for Usama; he says he was bullied by other students because of his 'unusual' interests. When I asked him to describe what he meant by the term Leb and *habiib*, a reference he made quite often in our interview, he likened them to the cliques in American films, saying,

Usama: The whole like mullet thing. (Laughs) I think that's the best way to describe them [Lebs]. Yeah and like sports clothing, Nike shoes and that sort of thing.

Sherene: Yeah. Were a lot of the people that didn't like you, were they like that?

Usama: Yeah (laughs) yeah they were. It's like in American movies you have the jocks and the geeks.

One of the advantages of employing interpretive repertoires as an analytical tool is that it offers speakers "a whole range of different rhetorical opportunities" (Edley 2001: 202) and so Usama, for example, can speak about masculinity in a range of ways that ties in to subculture and youth practices. However, the excerpt also shows that there are also limitations to how informants construct versions of self and other in the schooling context – they are either 'jocks' or 'geeks'. Therefore, Usama has a choice to make about where he fits in these opposing descriptions of youthful masculine identities, both of which are reductive. His descriptions support the argument that performance is central to gender politics (Butler 1988). Boys who 'do' masculinity in ways that adhere to the codes associated with Leb style occupy positions of power within the school, whereas those who do not, like Usama, are classified as 'the geeks'. Further, schools can be thought of as 'discursive spaces' (Yon 2000) in which students feel they have to name themselves as part of a youthful category to indicate to others where they feel they belong in school-based hierarchies. However, as Usama intimates in our exchange, these labels are not always productive as they fail to capture the ways that young men imagine themselves as complex subjects. This idea was reiterated again in the interview when he said,

Usama: High school in general was a bad experience, I didn't like high school. Maybe it was because I went to that certain school but basically like I felt out of place a lot of the time because of my interests and then, um, like me as a person I didn't fit in that whole thing so like yeah, I don't know. I had a few friends, but it was also the case of like bullying as well in high school. And that's why I wanted to go to university real bad 'cause when you're there no one cares and you basically be yourself and study what you want.

Sherene: What was the bullying about?

Usama: Umm, just the way I dress. It was also like what I was interested in um music. They were interested in the traditional things, like engineering um architecture, medical science.

Sherene: And what about their interests outside of their studies?

Usama: Sports … I wasn't sporty. Um, like I was sort of sporty but maybe, I don't know, I did different sports, like I don't know if you know Parkour? I used to do that back in high school with a few friends, they were like "why are you jumping all over the place"? So like during the sports session everyone would be playing footy and me and two other friends would be – we'd go off and do our own thing. 'Cause I was always into extreme sports, I used to ride BMX with my brother and then I started skateboarding, I still do that now, and then I got into Parkour. Umm yeah and also the skateboarding thing. At times we'd have Saturday school and I would come on my skateboard and that was a big issue.

In this exchange Usama constructs certain leisure interests, such as skateboarding, as unusual among Arab–Australian young men in Bankstown. He does this to help explain why he was 'out of place' within his school and why he generally did not find school to be a positive experience. It is not only leisure interests that create youthful hierarchies but also vocational aspirations according to Usama, where 'traditional' vocational pathways such as engineering and medical science are aspirations shared by his peers to which he cannot relate. Usama had planned to pursue his passion for 'drawing and painting' but his school did not offer visual arts subjects to senior students, encouraging them instead to study math and science. As such, he left the school at the end of year eleven and completed his final year at the local TAFE.[1] This broader schooling culture, one that emphasises 'traditional' routes to educational success and social mobility, sets the scene for how and why Usama may have felt excluded on the basis of his leisure and vocational interests. Following the arguments made in Chapter 1, we can see that tradition and creativity are framed by these Arab–Australian young men as competing ideas. For these young men to retain their sense of membership in a broader Arab–Australian community, they feel they may have to abandon their creative vocational aspirations at some point especially since their schools, their peer groups and their families (as I explored in the previous chapter) simply do not support these vocational aspirations.

This excerpt also points to the connections between ethnicity, masculinity and subcultural distinctions. Frosh *et al.* (2002) have suggested that the construction of masculinity is centrally related to power and dominance. Within schools, boys who do not engage in physical dominance through sport, fighting or performing 'hardness' are subordinated by those who do (Frosh *et al.* 2002: 75). Usama's reflections of school support their statement about the relationship between sport and gender hierarchies – that he was excluded and bullied by the Arab–Australian boys who played 'footy'. However, Usama actually does engage in sporting cultures; he is not academic or a 'reader', for example, like Bashir. His exclusion then is the result of ethnicised subcultural distinctions whereby BMX riding and Parkour are perceived as foreign and interpreted as inferior and feminised as compared to 'footy' and other leisure interests that are presumably integral to Leb identities.

Usama says, "I wanted to go to university real bad 'cause when you're there no one cares and you basically be yourself". This statement is significant as it reveals how intra-ethnic otherness, based on subcultural style, is articulated as a main reason to pursue further education. Usama's project for social mobility – in which higher education plays a major role – is not about financial gain, nor is it about necessarily improving his job prospects. University becomes a way to explore his creative identity further and to celebrate what he calls his 'eccentricities'. He is not looking for acceptance at university, but he imagines that in university, he can participate in subcultural practices, like BMX riding or Parkour, without those interests acting as a basis for exclusion. In Chapter 3, I look at how this aspiration, to 'be yourself', to express one's authentic sense of self, is not realised once Usama and others in this study arrive at university, particularly those enrolled in creative arts degrees. As such, the subcultural capital (Thornton 1995) they gain from being called 'weird' by the Lebs in their school is limited as it may not necessarily be transferrable into other social institutions and contexts outside of Bankstown.

Finally, Nabil, who had also attended a Catholic high school in Bankstown, echoed the sentiment of other informants that Bankstown-based schools produce 'Lebs', emphasising that this was a problematic process. Nabil was twenty years old and studying Law at university. He once had aspirations to become a writer, and as such he took on extra English subjects in his senior years of school and participated in after-school writing workshops at the local youth community centre. He had some of his short stories published in a Western Sydney literary magazine while in school. However, he was deterred by teachers and family members to pursue this aspiration because "there's no money for authors, even published authors like my Extension English teacher said this". He quickly changed his mind about becoming an author and instead decided to pursue Law because he "would like to do something that would make me comfortable, like financially" rather than "chasing an unrealistic dream". I inferred from his discussion about pursuing Law as tied into his broader aspirations to move out of Bankstown, away from the students who made his time at school unpleasant. When I asked about why he did not enjoy his time at school, he said

> In our school people would go and pee in the soap dispensers in the bathroom and they wouldn't get in trouble for it or they would do untowardly [sic] things to unwanting [sic] people and nothing would happen to them because they're in a school and they're Lebanese and it just wouldn't end well. They would have their friends to back them up, and they would get in a fight outside of school and they would just call their friends down 'cause they know so many from school who know so many other people 'cause we're Lebanese we're related to half this side of Sydney. They just act like because they're Lebs nothing could touch them. I mean, I hated going to an all-Lebanese school, 'cause it creates an idea within our minds that we're always going to be surrounded by Lebanese people. You put any one of those *habiibs* or whatever you want to call them in Cronulla or somewhere and I'm happy to bet you that they – if they don't come down to Bankstown every day just to get away from it.

This particular excerpt reaffirms the statements made by Bashir and Usama in their respective high schools. He notes the impact that school, as a site of cultural and social production, has on the mentality of the students (Archer 2003, Yon 2000) and how it reinforces the dominant position Lebs occupy within the school and outside of it, where he says 'they just act like because they're Lebs nothing could touch them'. In this way, he seems to be saying something more broadly about the problem with 'ethnic ghettos'; that Arab–Australian (or specifically Lebanese–Australian as he has mentioned) communities remain unassimilated in society because they are surrounded by too many Arab migrants and their children. The challenge for these young men with creative aspirations and unorthodox leisure interests is how to pursue their 'passions' in what they describe to be a hostile environment.

Returning to the earlier discussion in this chapter about the ways that Arabs have been constructed as Other within public discourse, we can see that it is not only 'the definers' of society who have negative perceptions of Lebs and *Habiibs*, but that some young people of the same ethnic background, like Nabil for example, also make similar judgements. We can take from Nabil's statements that ethnic boundaries are fragile and that ethnic minority youth are ambivalent about their cultural heritage as well as their locality; similar arguments are made with reference to working-class youth in the United Kingdom living in impoverished cities, although not specifically in relation to ethnicity (Reay and Lucey 2000). We can also read Nabil's statements as examples of how interpretive repertoires operate in life-history interviews. That is, Nabil does not construct the image of an 'ethnic ghetto', isolated from Australian society and heavily dependent on migrant structures, of his own accord. Rather, his judgements reflect the ways he has internalised the broader discourse of the politics of Australian multiculturalism and the kinds of fears held by policymakers about community relations. It is by relying on this broader narrative model that Nabil can assert his rejection of Arab–Australian Bankstown communities and the kinds of youthful, masculine identities they seem to produce.

Where do these complicated narratives of ethnicity, gender and school-based identities fit within existing studies of ethnic minority youth, particularly against the background of secondary schooling experiences? In Mansouri and Wood's (2008) study of the educational experiences and outcomes of Arab and Muslim youth, the authors recognise the politics of framing whereby "engaging with the identity constructions of Arab and Muslim Australian youth … has focused on issues of social tension and marginalisation" adding that we could enhance our understanding of these youth by looking at "the experiences of these particular groups in their critical formative years of secondary schooling" (Mansouri and Wood 2008: 45). They make valid points on both accounts. Looking at educational experiences and the hierarchical nature of peer relations, which Bashir, Usama and many other informants were heavily affected by, has the potential of rectifying this framing. However, there is another gap overlooked by Mansouri and Wood. That is, when educational experiences are explored, they continue to be framed by assumptions of marginalisation and disadvantage by virtue of ethnicity or informants' non-English-speaking migrant backgrounds (Nilan 2012).

Despite Mansouri and Wood advocating for a shift away from sociological frameworks of minority cultures up against social structures, they too fall into this trap, saying

> being at the margins means a lowering of expectations around educational outcomes and possibly even participation. One way of dismantling the hegemony of whiteness is through the construction of discursive counter narratives. Through stories, young people are encouraged to build mutual understanding and recognition.
>
> (Mansouri and Wood 2008: 37)

Thus, while the authors originally allude to the diversity and complexity within ethnic communities, they revert to the minority positions *all* Arab–Australian students occupy in relation to middle-class Anglo–Australians. This is problematic because it reduces the ways that subjectivities transcend issues of nationhood. Boundary work, as seen in the interviews with Fawaz, Bashir, Usama, and Nabil, are conducted on multiple levels for varying reasons.

What remain common between them are their aspirations to construct an identity in ways that are not limited by the negative elements of their socio-economic positions. This is where creativity and subcultural interests fit. Claims to creative identities dramatically alter the kinds of peer relationships these young men develop with other Arab–Australian youth in their local neighbourhoods. As a result, the creative biography is one that pulls Arab–Australian young men away from the kinds of solidarity that might be available within Leb youth cultures but, on the other hand, offers them a symbolic space in which they can construct a sense of self free from their cultural baggage.

Taste classifies: On being non-Leb

Hamid was a community arts worker who frequently dealt with school-aged Arab–Australian youth in the writing workshops he ran at various schools in Sydney's West. I had attended these workshops over the course of my fieldwork, and had many conversations with him about my project over a two year period. In some ways, Hamid acted as a quasi-gatekeeper to the creative arts scene in Bankstown and helped secure some of the interviews for this study. When I interviewed Hamid, I was interested both in the ways he had developed a creative identity in relation to his Lebanese/Syrian migrant background and also in the kinds of insights he had gleaned from being a community arts worker helping other young people, especially those of Arab–Australian backgrounds, develop their creative vocational aspirations.

I told him about some of my findings pertaining to the intra-ethnic tensions among Arab–Australian boys and explained that I took an empathetic approach to their sense of exclusion, saying that it must have been difficult for them during school when they felt so isolated on the basis of their unorthodox interests. Surprisingly, he was suspicious about some of the responses I had collected throughout the interview process. This is shown in the following exchange

Hamid: I think that a lot of them actively ostracise themselves.

Sherene: Ok, I would agree with that to an extent …

Hamid: Like it's not that they don't have friends it's that … (long pause) a lot of them are lying to you, that's what I'm saying. Like, a lot of them. Because we come from a community (Bankstown, Western Sydney) that is so extremely underprivileged and disadvantaged. The kids that are in those communities that are doing really well are in competition with other kids that are doing well. I'm saying be wary of talented, creative Lebanese kids that are actively trying to be different and better than the kids around them. You know, they get called out by the other kids as being elitist and like (puts on a deep voice) "you think you're fucking better than me". You know, like, when I was at school a lot of kids would be like, "you think you're better than me?" And I was like, no I don't, but there was something that I was doing that was offending them. Do you know what I mean? Like, I know a guy, he works with me. He'll tell you "I got ostracised and I didn't fit in" but it's like no, no. It's not that *they* pushed *you* away, you actively distanced yourself … you get off on the fact that you were 'the best Leb'.

Before this interview with Hamid, I had read the data that spoke to creative aspirants' exclusion within schools as a straightforward case of intra-ethnic differences and of the ways that masculinity and gender organises social relations within school environments. On one level, this argument is sustained by the interview material presented thus far in the chapter. But we can also analyse this data on the basis of Hamid's claim, that these young men who experienced exclusion display more agency and have more say in the fact that they were ostracised than they give themselves credit in the course of their life-history interviews. He links his observations of the youth he has worked with to his own experiences of school. While he does not use the term creativity, he implies that his creative identity was the basis for other students' perceptions of him as an 'elitist'. This is evident where he says, "there was something that I was doing that was offending them".

Hamid attended a public high school that was largely populated by Arab-Australian boys, simply by virtue of its location within Bankstown. It was ranked, at a time, one of the most disadvantaged schools in the state. Despite the limited resources available in the school to assist his learning, Hamid excelled in many subjects, especially English and Drama – subjects that most of the other students in his all-boys school struggled. In his senior years, he actively petitioned to the principal to ensure that the school ran an extension English course even though only two students in his year group had elected the subject (the school required at least four students to nominate the subject). It was these kinds of actions Hamid referred to that left him ostracised by other Arab–Australian boys who conformed, more or less, to the Leb masculine identity.

There are potentially strong links to be made here between creativity and the 'elitist' attitude that Hamid spoke about. Unlike most of the available literature which suggests that 'vulnerable' or disadvantaged young people are drawn to, or encouraged to engage in, creative self-expression for therapeutic purposes (Podkalicka and Campbell 2010), Hamid's excerpt shows that there are stronger correlations to be made between creativity and personal projects of social mobility. As Bourdieu has argued, tastes classify the classifier (Bourdieu 1984: 6) and if Arab–Australian boys reject 'Leb' masculine style, they do so to classify themselves as 'the best Leb' according to Hamid. In what follows, I look at moments where informants treat their creative interests and subcultural differences as markers of distinction, where they confirm Hamid's suggestion that talented Lebanese kids *actively* try to be different and better than the kids around them.

Walid attended a public, all-boys high school. There was a mix of ethnic and religious groups in his student cohort, although he says that it was largely populated by Lebanese–Australian young men. He was twenty-seven years old when we spoke and worked as a film editor and community arts worker. In his adolescent years, he says he was 'obsessed' with watching films and inventing alternative endings or alternative scenes for the films he had seen. This was not something he discussed with his peers at school, but despite concealing his interest in film, he found other ways that he differed from the Leb boys. Apart from the 'element of cruelty' that he saw displayed by Leb young men, as highlighted in the opening of this chapter, he also explains that different leisure interests were a main reason behind his disassociation with those Arab–Australian young men. He said,

Walid: I mean here's the other thing I (pause) in high school most of my friends weren't Lebanese umm because I wasn't interested in what the other Leb kids were interested in.
Sherene: Okay so like what for example?
Walid: So music wise I wasn't interested in the same music.
Sherene: Okay ... You weren't interested in Tupac?
Walid: (Laughs) I wasn't interested in Tupac .... I had an older white cousin named Brad who was half Aussie half Lebanese. He influenced me a lot, like in what I grew up listening to music wise, we used to hang out in his car and listen to heavy metal and stuff ... so it was a bit different.

Both Hall (1999) and Gilroy (1993) have celebrated the cross-cultural appropriation of music scenes whereby Black and Asian youth cultures have entered the mainstream in the United Kingdom and become part of mass culture. Their celebration of the wider absorption of diasporic youth culture has been criticised by some, who argue that Hall and Gilroy contribute to furthering essentialist images of Asian youth (Ahmad 2001). Irrespective of whether cultural appropriation of Black and Asian youth culture is problematic, at the very least it suggests that some ethnic minority youth in the United Kingdom are confident and comfortable with being associated with the styles and subcultural interests of their diasporic communities. By contrast, this excerpt from Walid suggests that some creative aspirants of Arab–Australian backgrounds feel the need to disassociate entirely with the youth cultures in their schools and local communities in order to develop a creative biography. Walid's interest in heavy metal, a music genre constructed as the opposite of hip hop, is the influence of his 'white' cousin. The reference to his cousins' whiteness is crucial as it reveals how Walid maps different musical genres according to different ethnic groups; as though the association between heavy metal and 'whiteness' are naturally linked or, more importantly, *better* than the association between hip hop and Lebs.

Bourdieu has suggested that our cultural, educational, and other kinds of capital shape our consumption patterns and cultural practices. His central argument is that our tastes and distastes, sympathies, and aversions are more than personal opinions; they actually reflect the unconscious unity of class (Bourdieu 1984: 77). Of course, Bourdieu's arguments are particularly aimed at theorising how and why different groups of people enjoy highbrow art whereas others are more likely to be drawn towards popular art forms. He says that the ease with which some groups of people enjoy 'high art' is dependent on their educational, social, cultural and economic backgrounds. In Walid's case, the differences between hip hop and heavy metal are not distinctions between high and popular culture. In fact, as contemporary class researchers have argued (Peterson and Kern 1996), the distinctions between high and popular culture are less relevant today in terms of allocating class positions. Rather, the distinction drawn here by Walid is more broadly between Leb youth cultures and non-Leb youth cultures.

We can refer back to Bourdieu's conceptualisation of distinction, in a limited sense, to read Walid's ability to enjoy heavy metal as a display of social mobility, whereby he attempts to use his cultural practices and music consumption as an account for why he is non-Leb. Bourdieu does not discuss the interplay between ethnicity, class and gender, but I would argue that Walid's interest in heavy metal and rejection of hip hop is certainly a statement that results from these intersecting identity positions. The distinctions and hierarchies Walid has constructed are subtle, but they nonetheless enable him to identify as 'different'. If creative identities are premised on the rejection of youthful, Leb masculinity, this means that being different to the Lebs, even if only in terms of music interests, is essentially a good thing for the development of a creative biography.

Being 'non-Leb' has far-reaching implications for identity-making processes beyond the differences between musical interests. For example, Adam had this to say about the kinds of attributes that distinguished him from the Lebs in his school.

> I'm not a typical Lebanese person, I don't walk around like in my TNs and say like 'fully sick' and stuff like that ... because I was brought up, me and my brother were brought up, to respect others. They don't do that.

Being 'non-Leb' is a contingent identity position. As Du Gay has suggested, a contingent identity is one that "can never manage to constitute itself fully because it relies upon something 'outside' of itself for its very existence" (Du Gay 1996: 2). In this case, informants rely on a carefully crafted description of what it means to be Leb, and the kinds of negative attributes that are associated with this youth culture and use their positions as outsiders and as creatives to this group to make their claims of being non-Leb. Thus, their contingent identities are obviously constituted in relation to what they are not (Du Gay 1996: 2). In this short piece we can see that identity claims about being non-Leb do not only offer informants a way to show their difference, as Walid did, but also to show how this difference makes them *better* than the Lebs. These particular 'tastes' (preferences for TNs) and manner of speech (saying 'fully sick') classifies these young men as Lebs according to Adam, which is a problematic place to be because it represents their attachments to Bankstown and their 'disrespect' for others. This takes us back to Hamid's argument that it is 'talented' Lebanese–Australian youth that are more likely to engage in these processes of intra-ethnic Othering.

Relatedly, Nabil equated his creative identity with a broader sense of 'eclecticism'. He suggests that he was more intelligent that his 'Leb' cousins and that this hindered the relationship he had with them. He said,

> I just find they can't keep up with me. I'm very eclectic for the most part, I go off on random tangents really quickly and follow that through and jump around again and most of them have trouble keeping up with me ... most of them dropped out in year ten.

Here, Nabil makes no references to creativity or style or subcultural practices to build his case that creativity is at odds with Leb identities. In spite of the absence of these discursive signals, I would argue that this excerpt can be read as indicative of the ways that Arab–Australian youth construct creative identities during the moment of secondary schooling. The correlation between creativity, intellectual capacity and being 'very eclectic' represents the ways that creative identities are only vaguely defined among informants at this stage in their lives. This is because there is no 'creative' subcultural group to which they belong in their local neighbourhood. They can only construct their identities as creative in limited ways and on the basis of their exclusion from the Lebs. As a result, they define creativity very loosely but with reference to very specific examples.

For instance, their creative identities are ones that involve 'respect' for others as Adam explains; it reflects their ability to assimilate as Nabil and Bashir argued earlier; and includes their capacities to take up unorthodox leisure interests as Walid and Usama have shown in their respective consumption of heavy metal music and Parkour and skateboarding. Informants rely on an implicit and generally agreed upon understanding of youthful Leb identities as problematic in order to establish that creativity is a kind of cultural capital they can use in their projects of social mobility and not simply a 'different' youthful identity position. In Chapter 3 I explore how far their subjectively constructed notions of creativity as a type of cultural capital take them in their creative arts degrees.

Do the excerpts discussed in this chapter reveal informants desires to be 'the best Leb' as Hamid suggested in our interview? My conclusion is that this is not quite the case, but that there are processes of distinction operating within the narratives about Lebs that cannot be ignored. First, we might say that the interview process enables informants to symbolically and discursively reverse the imbalance of power they saw as unfair while they were students as they all claim to have been bullied and excluded. Johnson and Clare (1986) have suggested that the ways in which we reorder our life histories are often done to imbue our identities as agency-driven; to make the struggles and contradictions of our past dissolve in to a seamless story of who we are. Second, the techniques for telling the self (Skeggs 2002) involve the mobilisation of cultural resources. The interview moments analysed in this chapter have shown that informants rely on their educational capital to narrate a version of selfhood that is flexible and able to achieve the escape from local, ethnic networks that stifle their sense of creativity. This is a common strategy, and, as Skeggs has argued, narrating the self as mobile requires informants to introduce characters to the interview they compare and contrast themselves to who remain stuck in place. The Lebs function in this way in the interviews; as figures that informants draw on to display their own ascendancy.

Conclusion

This chapter has aimed to show how the interplay between ethnicity, masculinity, and schooling cultures affect the ways that Arab–Australian young men become creative people. It has shown how subcultural interests are subsumed within the broader narrative about the development of creative biographies. That is, participating in 'Leb style' represents a rejection of creativity. In exploring this theme, I have aimed to show how creativity is interpreted and used by informants as symbolic of social mobility. Creativity thereby offers informants ways to deviate from the templates of masculinity on offer during school.

The chapter first addressed the ways that Lebanese–Australians and Arab–Australian communities more generally occupy subordinate positions within the nation. We can see, based on the data presented in this chapter, that the young men in this study seem to be aware, almost hyper-aware, of these hierarchies and where their communities are positioned. Arabness, specifically the conjunction between Arabness and youthful performances of masculinity is a source of moral panic in Australia. This chapter has examined the strategies informants employ to overcome these broader public perceptions. During school, they do this by convincingly articulating the ways that their subcultural interests – which feed in to their creative identities and vocational aspirations – position them as unlike or different from the negatively stereotyped Leb, masculine youthful identities.

There are particular performances of masculinity produced in these local spaces to which these informants refuse to engage and this is organised in the life-history interview as one of the bases for their claims to a creative identity. As such, creative identities are not natural but are strategically developed by these young men with specific objectives in mind. These objectives are not simply about particular vocations or career possibilities, but also include the possibilities to escape the disadvantaged status ascribed to them on the basis of their gendered, youthful, cultural, and migrant affiliations and specifically the connections between those points of identification and their local neighbourhoods, as inhabitants of the often negatively stereotyped Bankstown.

There are obvious differences in how interpersonal relationships are represented in this chapter as compared to the familial relationships described in Chapter 1. In the previous chapter, where creativity was seen at odds with parents' expectations and as something that should not be broadcast to the ethnic public, informants work to justify and defend their aspirations to resolve the tensions brought about by their creative passions. Here, we see that the more distance informants can create between themselves and the Lebs, the better positioned they are to achieve social mobility and to realise their creative vocational aspirations as their leisure interests and style do not conform to the hegemonic masculine order in these local youth cultures.

I would argue that we can see a particular model of social mobility established by the informants in this chapter; one that involves the ability to move among people from other ethnic backgrounds and to be perceived as a legitimate member of broader Australian society. This is not always explicitly stated by the young men in this chapter, but there are references that hint to this, such as the 'respect' for authority and towards women that these creative aspirants show but Lebs supposedly lack; their ability to be 'open-minded' in their consumption patterns for instance listening to heavy metal instead of hip hop; and finally, how well they apply themselves to their studies. Creativity is perceived to be a powerful commodity in the ways that it can be used to distance oneself from an ethnic community. Whether others acknowledge or notice this distance is the focus of the next chapter.

This chapter has also shown that these young men's identification as 'creatives' emerges out of these peer relations within their high schools, and rests on their unorthodox leisure interests. Informants are not actually named as 'creatives' by the young men around them, but as 'weird', unusual, or different. When we situate this data in relation to other moments of the interviews, one conclusion to be drawn is that these identity labels give the informants the confidence to pursue their creative passions through formal higher education courses that form the basis of their careers. But, as I explore in the next chapter, they are shocked to learn that being called 'weird' or creative among Arab–Australian boys in Bankstown is not enough to propel these young men in to the 'art world' and the creative industries.

Note

1 TAFE refers to the Technical and Further Education body of New South Wales, which provides vocational education and training at 130 campuses across the state where students can receive Diploma or Certificate level qualifications (https://www.tafensw.edu.au/).

References

Abada, T. and E. Y. Tenkorang (2009) 'Pursuit of university education among the children of immigrants in Canada: The roles of parental human capital and social capital', *Journal of Youth Studies*, 12(2): 185–207.

Ahmad, A. N. (2001) 'Whose Underground?' *Third Text* 15(54): 71–84.

Archer, L. (2003) *Race, Masculinity and Schooling: Muslim Boys and Education*, Buckingham, Open University.

Bennett, A. (1999) 'Subcultures or neo-tribes? Rethinking the relationship between youth, style and musical taste', *Sociology*, 33(3): 599–617.

Bennett, T., M. Savage, E. Bortolaia Silva, A. Warde, M. Gayo-Cal, and D. Wright (2009) Culture, Class, Distinction, New York, Routledge.

Blackman, S. (2005) 'Youth subcultural theory: A critical engagement with the concept, its origins and politics, from the Chicago School to postmodernism', *Journal of Youth Studies*, 8(1): 1–20.

Bourdieu, P. (1973) 'Cultural reproduction and social reproduction', in *Knowledge, Education, and Cultural Change*, Ed. R. Brown. London, Tavistock.

Bourdieu, P. (1984) *Distinction: A Social Critique of the Judgement of Taste*, London, Routledge and Kegan Paul.

Butler, J. (1988) 'Performative acts and gender constitution: An essay in phenomenology and feminist theory', *Theatre Journal*, 40(4): 519–531.

Collins, J. (2002) 'Youth, ethnicity and crime in Australia', Paper to the Les Recontres du CEDEM, Centre for Studies on Ethnicity and Migrations, Université de Liege, 25 April 2002, pp. 1–29.

Collins, J., G. Noble, S. Poynting, and P. Tabar (2000) *Kebabs, Kids, Cops and Crime: Youth, Ethnicity and Crime*, Sydney, Pluto Press.

Connell, R. W. (2000) *The Men and the Boys*, Berkley, University of California Press.

Connell, R. W. (2003) 'Chapter 1: Australian Masculinities', in *Male Trouble: Looking at Masculinities*, Eds. S. Tomsen and M. Donaldson, Melbourne, Pluto Press.

Connell, R. W. (2005) *Masculinities*, Sydney, Allen and Unwin.

Dagistanli, S. (2007) '"Like a pack of wild animals": Moral panics around 'ethnic' gang rape in Sydney', in *Outrageous! Moral Panics in Australia*, Eds. S. Poynting and G. Morgan, Hobart, ACYS Publishing, pp. 181–197.

Du Gay, P. (1996) *Consumption and Identity at Work*, London, Sage.

Edley, N. (2001) 'Analysing masculinity: Interpretive repertoires, ideological dilemmas', in *Discourse as Data: A Guide for Analysis*, Eds. M. Wetherall, S. Taylor and S. J. Yates, London, Sage Publications, pp. 189–228.

Frosh, S. A. Phoenix, and Pattman, R. (2002) *Young Masculinities: Understanding Boys in Contemporary Society*, Hampshire, Palgrave Macmillan.

Giddens, A. (1991) *Modernity and Self-Identity*, Cambridge, Polity.

Gilroy, P. (1993) *Small Acts: Thoughts on the Politics of Black Cultures*, London, Serpents Tail.

Hall, S. (1999) 'Whose heritage? Un-settling the 'heritage', re-imagining the post-nation (keynote speech)', *Third Text*13(49): 3–13.

Haukka, S. (2011) 'Education-to-work transitions of aspiring creatives', *Cultural Trends*, 20(1): 41–64.

Haywood, C. and M. Mac an Ghaill (1996) 'Schooling masculinities', in *Understanding Masculinitities: Social Relations and Cultural Arenas*, Eds. M. Mac an Ghaill, Buckingham, Open University Press, pp. 50–60.

Hebdige, D. (1979; 2002) *Subculture The Meaning of Style*, Hoboken, Taylor and Francis.

Hesmondhalgh, D. (2005) 'Subcultures, scenes or tribes? None of the above', *Journal of Youth Studies* 8(1): 21–40.

Ho, C. and C. Alcorso (2004) 'Migrants and employment: Challenging the success story', *Journal of Sociology* 40(3): 237–259.

Johnson, R. and M. Clare (1986) Nationalism, narrative and identity, Conference of the Association for cultural studies, pp. 1–15.

Mac an Ghaill, M. (1994) *The Making of Men: Masculinities, Sexualities and Schooling*, Buckingham, Open University Press.

Mansouri, F. and S. P. Wood (2008) *Identity, Education and Belonging: Arab and Muslim Youth in Contemporary Australia*, Melbourne, Melbourne University Press.

Marotta, V. P. (2008) 'The hybrid self and the ambivalence of boundaries', *Social Identities: Journal for the Study of Race, Nation and Culture*, 14(3): 295–312.

McRobbie, A. (2002) 'Clubs to companies: Notes on the decline of political culture in speeded up creative worlds', *Cultural Studies*, 16(4): 516–531.

Morgan, G. and S. Poynting (2012) 'Introduction: The transnational folk devil', in *Global Islamophobia: Muslims and moral panic in the West*, Eds. G. Morgan and S. Poynting, Burlington, VT, Ashgate, pp. 1–14.

Nilan, P. (2012) 'Young, Muslim and looking for a job in Australia', *Youth Studies Australia*, (31): 48–60.

Noble, G. and P. Tabar (2002) 'On being Lebanese–Australian: hybridity, essentialism and strategy among Arabic-speaking youth', in *Arab–Australians Today: Citizenship and Belonging*, Ed. G. Hage, Carlton, Melbourne University Press, pp. 128–144.

Noble, G., S. Poynting, and P. Tabar (1999) 'Youth, ethnicity and the mapping of identities: Strategic essentialism and strategic hybridity among male Arabic Speaking Youth in South-Western Sydney', *Communal/Plural*, 7(1): 29–44.

Peterson, R. A. and R. M. Kern (1996) 'Changing highbrow taste: From snob to omnivore', *American Sociological Review*, 61(October): 900–907.

Podkalicka, A. and C. Campbell (2010) 'Understanding digital storytelling: Individual voice and community-building in youth media programs', *seminar.net*, 6(2): 208.

Potter, J. and M. Wetherall (1987) *Discourse and Social Psychology: Beyond Attitudes and Behaviours*, London, Sage.

Poynting, S., G.Noble, P. Tabar, and J. Collins (2004) *Bin Laden in the Suburbs: Criminalising the Arab Other*, Sydney, Institute of Criminology.

Pryke, K. and T. Dang (2003) '"FOB" and "whitewashed": Identity and internalized racism among second generation Asian Americans', *Qualitative Sociology*, 26(2): 83–106.

Ralphs, R., J. Medina, and J. Alridge (2009) 'Who needs enemies with friends like these? The importance of place for young people living in known gang areas', *Journal of Youth Studies*, 12(5): 483–500.

Reay, D. and H. Lucey (2000) '"I don't really like it here but I don't want to be anywhere else": Children and inner city council estates', *Antipode,* 32(4): 410–428.

Savage, M. (2000) *Class Analysis and Social Transformation,* Phildelphia, Open University Press.

Shildrick, T., S. Blackman, and R. MacDonald (2009) 'Young people, class and place', *Journal of Youth Studies,* 12(5): 457–465.

Skeggs, B. (2002) 'Techniques for telling the reflexive self', in *Qualitative Research in Action*, Ed. T. May, London, Sage, pp. 353–378.

Stokes, H. and J. Wyn (2007) 'Constructing identities and making careers: Young people's perspectives on work and learning', *International Journal of Lifelong Education*, 26(5): 495–511.

Stokes, H. (2012) *Imagining Futures: Identity Narratives and the Role of Work, Education, Community and Family*, Melbourne, Melbourne University Press.

Tabar, P., G. Noble, and S. Poynting (2010) *On Being Lebanese in Australia: Identity, Racism and the Ethnic Field*, Institute for Migration Studies, Beirut, LAU press.

Taylor, S. (2001) 'Locating and conducting discourse analytic research', in *Discourse as Data: A Guide for Analysis,* Eds. M. Wetherall, S. Taylor and S. J. Yates, London, The Open University, pp. 5–48.

Thornton, S. (1995) *Club Cultures: Music, Media and Subcultural Capital,* Cambridge, Polity Press.

White, R. (2007) 'Lebanese young people in a climate of conflict', in *Social Cohesion in Australia*, Eds. J. Jupp, P. Nieuwenhuysen and E. Dawson. Melbourne, Cambridge University Press, pp. 70–79.

Willis, P. E. (1977) *Learning to Labour: How Working Class Kids Get Working Class Jobs*, Farnborough, England, Saxon House.

Wise, A. (2009) '"Its just an attitude that you feel": Inter-ethnic habitus before the Cronulla Riots', in *Lines in the Sand: The Cronulla Riots and the Limits of Australian Multiculturalism*, Ed. G. Noble, Sydney, Institute of Criminology Press.

Yon, D. (2000) *Elusive Culture: Schooling, Race and Identity in Global Times*, New York, University of New York Press.

3 Being 'weird' is how you get ahead

Consumption patterns, personal style, and leisure interests have become increasingly important for theorising how youthful identities are made and remade in contemporary society (Bennett 1999; Du Gay 1996). Among aspiring artists, self-stylisation is critical as it functions as the outward expression of an authentic, creative self and leisure interests signal to the world exactly what kind of artist the individual is (McRobbie 2002). As Bourdieu (1984; 2005) and others would argue, developing a unique identity is not simply a natural, authentic process of self-expression but a skill that is perfected over time and that implicated in this process of continuous reinvention among many artists is the acquisition of specific cultural, social, and financial capitals. In this chapter I take as a starting point that young, creative aspirants need to have an awareness of, and ability to play with, the symbolic codes around style and taste within youth-based, subcultural creative scenes to increase their chances of success in the creative industries. In light of this, I examine what happens when Arab–Australian young men from Bankstown do not reinvent themselves or cultivate a distinctive, creative style in the same way that other youth from more privileged backgrounds are able, or eager, to do while they are enrolled in university courses.

In this chapter, I take a case study approach with two Arab–Australian young men enrolled in creative arts degrees, Usama and Ibrahim, to reveal how they become marked as outcasts during their time in university. Their sense of alienation is mainly because, as I will suggest, they are unaware of, or they refuse to adhere to, unwritten rules around style in youth-based, subcultural creative scenes. The sense of alienation that results from youthful, subcultural distinctions during university sharply contrasts with the narratives presented in Chapter 2 where isolation and being an outsider among 'Leb' youth in Bankstown was a source of pride and drawn on by informants to indicate their capacity to achieve social mobility. Here, I look at how isolation in a university context, which informants treat as a testing ground for their vocational futures, causes doubt about their creative vocational aspirations. This is especially problematic since the decision to pursue creative vocations is often done in the face of all the advice they receive from parents and members of their ethnic communities. As such, I make the case that the experience of cultural remoteness, due in part because of their inability to adapt to subcultural rules of style, essentially operates as a primary way that aspirants of socio-economic disadvantage get filtered out of mainstream creative industries before they even complete post-compulsory education or training.

The chapter will also look at how informants' sense of isolation during university is symptomatic of the discomfort they feel in social spaces outside Bankstown and with young people from non-Arab backgrounds. This is largely because they know the negative representations surrounding Arab young men in the public discourse but also because there is an intimate connection between local spaces and identity-making that results in some individuals feeling comfortable in some places and entirely uncomfortable in others. The kind of discomfort they experience in university spaces and in the subcultural scenes of the inner city, where other university students spend their leisure time, will be addressed with reference to the literature on disadvantaged students entering higher education (Ball *et al.* 2002; Modood 1993). The arguments made by those writers that structural inequalities persist in university contexts, but materialise in new ways since the 'massification' of higher education whereby students from lower class backgrounds are now almost as likely to complete post-compulsory education as students of wealthier backgrounds. Further, drawing on Massey's argument that 'space is political' (1995), I suggest that Arab–Australian young men become caught between attachments to an authentic ethnic and working-class identity, and the 'pretension' associated with university settings whereby they are expected to speak, act, and think like the more privileged students in their courses (Reay *et al.* 2010).

The irony, of course, is that the creative arts students they describe do not display pretension in the ways we commonly associate with upper classes. This further complicates the ability of these young men to participate in creative lifestyles as they become confused about why privileged youth adopt mannerisms and interests *they* would more likely associate with disadvantage. To make sense of this kind of code-switching, I draw on the work of cultural class theorists (Crompton and Scott 2005) who suggest that it is precisely this ability to adopt the practices of the working classes without jeopardising one's own class status that signifies privilege in contemporary society. Emmison (2003) calls this being a 'cultural omnivore' and it seems a particularly useful concept to apply to creative aspirants who are still working out their exact vocational pathways. The discussion to follow the two case studies will thus establish that bohemianism and youthful, creative lifestyles within higher education spaces are stratified along class and ethnic lines, thereby inhibiting the ability of Arab–Australian young men to freely express themselves among their university peers out of a fear of being 'found out' (Reay *et al.* 2005) as an outsider.

In what follows, I adopt a case study approach to explore how Arab–Australian young men in this study experience inner city youth cultures including downtown university and college campuses. The two case studies, with Usama and Ibrahim, reveal relatively similar university experiences even though there is a ten year age difference between the two young men. By analysing both of them in depth, I aim to show how narratives of higher education, specifically in creative arts degrees, incorporate strong links between localised spaces, self-stylisation, youthful identities, and class privilege.

Usama: How 'eccentric' is eccentric enough in the arts?

In Chapter 2, we were introduced to Usama, a fine arts student at a prestigious Sydney university hoping to become a successful artist but content to work as a secondary school arts teacher should his original plans fall through. From a traditional Muslim Sunni background, Usama had spent many years frustrated in his high school for a few reasons. Within the scope of his community, he was seen as having unorthodox leisure interests that his Arab–Australian and Muslim peers used as a source of mockery against him. His sexuality was often questioned because he was "pretty eccentric"– he gave an example for this by saying he wears tight purple jeans and saying this runs counter to the typical Leb style of wearing sports branded clothes. Finally, his interest in the arts was not encouraged by the Islamic school he attended which did not offer any art subjects to senior students. As a result, he left the school in year eleven, a year before graduation, and completed his senior year at a technical college. It was a risky move but one that paid off when he achieved high enough grades and developed a decent enough portfolio to be admitted into his visual arts degree. His self-identification as 'pretty eccentric' was one I found interesting and I asked whether this was a good thing for him in terms of his chosen degree and institution. He said,

Usama: Yeah it is, oh I mean there's a lot of at my campus strange people there … I'm not anyone to judge but there's a lot of 'out there' types. So like … there's this guy I don't know his name, no one knows his name but he's a very manly guy but he likes to wear skirts over his pants. I think it's just to stand out, and it's like in the arts industry the more weird you are the more people will get interested in your art. But I don't want to set out like that. I'd rather just be me and sell my art as it is.

Sherene: So do you think there's an unspoken sort of pressure to stand out, to dress a bit weird?

Usama: Yeah there is a lot of that if like, I wouldn't say it's a rule it's just like I don't know how to describe it um but it's there. It's like you know if you basically make yourself more weird, more people are gonna be interested. Especially in terms of gallery like shows, art shows. Everyone wants to meet the artist and when they meet you and you're this really strange person um like with strange mannerisms they're gonna get into you, they're gonna be interested. That's why some people do it. Most people actually. Something people put on, it's like an act.

Most striking in Usama's description of his peers in the creative arts degree is how what he calls "weirdness" is articulated as indicative of the broader culture within creative-based employment fields. Artists generally push boundaries and conventions, through their style, their lifestyles, and of course their work (Becker 1982), so the 'strange mannerisms' Usama describes is not particularly new. Of key interest for this chapter is how young Arab–Australian men like Usama respond to the call to be 'weird' for the sake of generating interest in the work he produces. It is the way weirdness operates as a kind of subcultural capital that Usama rejects. He sees the 'strange mannerisms' of his peers as an act, and by contrast he opts to 'just be me'. His negotiation of 'weirdness' points more broadly to his discomfort with reinventing himself, an expectation of creative aspirants but particularly those of working-class or ethnic minority backgrounds who are not already in the scene and cannot necessarily leverage their socio-economic status to help them achieve success.

Relatedly, in another interview with a College of Fine Arts (COFA)[1] student, Riad, he too spoke of the remoteness he experienced among the rest of his cohort, mostly due to the differences in their socio-economic backgrounds. Riad was twenty years old, of Lebanese–Australian background and studying psychology and photography but contemplating walking away from the creative arts degree entirely for several reasons noted in our exchange below. Although he does not use the same language as Usama, that other students are 'weird' or 'strange', he instead points to more precise connections between the institution, the creative arts degree, and the privilege of fellow students in his course. He said,

Riad: Umm you know it was very wanky, very 'Paddington'. Umm not about taking a good photo but about concepts and stuff … I just found it really problematic and really subjective. And I think that was the attitude shared by most people in the class. I just didn't like it. I don't like COFA. It's very Paddington.

Sherene: Paddington … what does that mean?

Riad: Well it just means that like loads of private school kids who go there because they have heaps of money and they know they won't have to try. Like they can try their hand at being a photographer but if that doesn't work out they don't have to worry too much because they'll have something else to fall back on. Like one of my best friends who went to SCEGGS[2] which is like the most expensive or one of the most expensive schools, she went to COFA and when she went there she knew most of them through school. She was even overwhelmed by the amount of private schoolies. Even if they weren't private schoolie, they seemed like they were … I don't know if that influenced me.

Sherene: And is that what Paddington means?

Riad: Yeah … I can't stand Paddington.

Riad's experience at COFA reveals that there are strong connections to be drawn between the socio-economic background of a student and the confidence they exude about their vocational aspirations. As he says, those of wealthier backgrounds have the option to rely on their families or even existing networks and contacts within the industry. In my exchanges with both Riad and Usama, it is clear that they recognise that 'weirdness' and confidence are not natural qualities but are accumulated and simultaneously produced, to some extent, by the culture of the art school. Usama recognises that weirdness is a form of cultural capital in that it has an exchange value in the creative industries, particularly for more competitive and risky avenues such as gallery artists. He does not go so far as to make a connection between the capacity to perform 'weirdness' and one's socio-economic backgrounds, but the case can be made that there is a relationship between those two things, particularly in light of Riad's statements.

In fact, I would argue that the capacity to perform weirdness is a middle class capacity in line with the 'cultural omnivore' thesis presented by Peterson and Kern (1996). Being omnivorous refers to the ability to "graze and range across cultural forms, incorporating elements from both high and popular culture" (Bennett *et al.* 2009: 18). In this model of selfhood, the omnivore relies on "attachments to practices and objects in which value is generated from the symbolic value of both the practice/object and by the relations by which they are attached (e.g. entitlement, exploitation, and appropriation)" (Skeggs 2004: 79). This model of selfhood conforms to a middle class self where

> cultural capital … is largely acquired and transmitted through the education system, to appreciate different cultural genres irrespective of their classification as 'high' or 'low'. Openness to diversity and a cultivated agility with respect to judgements of taste are its chief defining features.
>
> (Bennett *et al.* 2009: 31)

Tastes tend to carry symbolic baggage which means that consumption patterns and self-presentation become indications of one's socio-economic status. Further, the boundaries around cultural tastes are weak which makes it harder for people from lower class backgrounds aiming for social mobility to confidently participate in particular cultural practices. As Bennett *et al.* (1999) have argued,

> what is at stake in cultural choices is not simply differences in taste but the ability of the dominant class to impose the value attributed to those differences, in such a way that some choices count as 'legitimate' and others lack legitimacy
>
> (Bennett *et al.* 1999: 10)

The figure of the cultural omnivore makes it difficult to determine one's class location on the basis of their participation in only 'highbrow' or 'popular' cultural scenes. The distinctions between people of upper and lower class backgrounds are more likely to be founded on how broad one's cultural tastes are; middle and upper class individuals for example are more likely to be able to appropriate popular culture into their world (Emmison 2003). The distinctions are also about how well individuals can adapt to a range of social milieus, drawing on the necessary social and linguistic codes in order to be recognised as a legitimate member (Bernstein 1966). The emphasis on social context, whether it be in an institutional setting or a looser, Bourdieusian notion of *field,* has seen the notion of 'subcultural capital' enter the picture (Thornton 1995). Subcultural capital refers to "those assets that have a limited circulation among members of specific subcultures that might be defined in terms of specific age groups" (Bennett *et al.* 2009: 30). Alone, it might have less exchange-value in employment terms but when combined with economic and other forms of cultural capital, it can be powerful for young aspiring artists. There is a strong correlation then between confidently presenting oneself as weird and creative and having more social, cultural, and economic capital within the context of exclusive art courses at elite universities.

I then asked Usama about how he deals with the fact that everyone else in his course seems to belong to a creative scene that he does not have membership to. He said,

Usama: Because everyone is different, you've got to be different to belong. It's pretty strange like that. I have a friend at Uni, he actually looks like a *habiib*, he dresses very regular and he's seen as the weird one because yeah.

Sherene: So people think he's weird?

Usama: Yeah like he's judged for it.

Sherene: Do you ever pull him aside and say 'look man don't dress like this, you're getting judged'.

Usama: Nah we always bag out the other people as a joke, like "look what she's wearing" like, why does she have a hat on her face?

Sherene: Right, it's like Lady Gaga stuff.

Usama: Yeah some of the girls are like that, some of the guys are like that it's just like the longer you've been in art school, the weirder you get. Just so you can get that attention.

In Chapter 2, I looked at how Usama tried to adapt his mannerisms and personal style to suit the dominant group of 'Lebs' or '*Habiibs*' at his school. This had long lasting effects on his sense of self because in bending to the rules of the local dominant youth culture, Usama says he felt like a fraud. Thus, when at university, noticing that there is an expectation to 'stand out', Usama resists this pressure because he says he tried to change his identity once before and it was not a successful project. The refusal to conform to acting 'weird' while at university reflects a deeper sense of discomfort with the people he is surrounded by who are wholly unlike the youth he grew up with in Bankstown. Young (2004) found that working-class and ethnic minority youth often feel uncomfortable in higher education settings because they are in limbo between what has come before and their futures which are transformed by educational achievements.

Thus, if we compare his response to isolation and alienation to his narratives of secondary school that I explored in the previous chapter, we can see immediately a central contradiction in his life history – a contradiction that emerges precisely because of the disconnections between how we behave and how we reflect on our actions and decisions (Taylor and Littleton 2006). At school he disassociates with the '*habiibs*', this was part of his project of upward social mobility but this rejection was also because he was shamed because of his unorthodox leisure interests – "like skateboarding to Arabic school is the worst thing a person can do". But while at university he says he and his friend, who could be classified as a *habiib*, sit around and make fun of the weird people in the course. Even though Usama found the youth in his neighbourhood problematic, there is a sense of familiarity that comes with associating with a 'habiib' and that friendship provides some comfort in unfamiliar territory. There is a type of solidarity there which cuts across clear class and ethnicity boundaries, a friendship produced out of their shared sense of isolation in the course. This is known to be a common strategy among working-class and ethnic minority students in prestigious higher education institutions, as Furlong and Cartmel (2009) explain in their account of how minority and disadvantaged students negotiate higher education. They say,

> Patterns of social integration within an institution are also strongly affected by residential segregation and reinforced by the tendency of working class students ... to prefer the company of friends in their local communities. As a result, even when working class students enter prestigious courses, they may maintain a degree of social separation from their more advantaged peers.
>
> (Furlong and Cartmel 2009: 125)

Although Furlong and Cartmel are speaking exclusively about 'working class' students, the same can also be said of Arab–Australian youth like Usama who come from particularly disadvantaged regions of Sydney. The kind of 'residential segregation' demonstrated by Usama where he does in fact prefer the company of friends from his local community means that he is pulled back to Bankstown and to the ethnic community he is from rather than explicitly pushed away by middle and upper class students.

The solidarity formed with the 'habiib' friend in opposition to the typically middle class, somewhat bohemian creative arts students also has parallels with older studies of ethnic, masculine solidarity in the face of racism and discrimination from white youth (Poynting *et al.* 2004; Noble *et al.* 1999; Noble 2007). Entangled in this ethnic solidarity is class based solidarity where Usama and his friend are both cultural outsiders in a very middle class environment (Reay *et al.* 2010; Modood 2005). There is a sense of comfort to be gained from this friendship in a place that Usama otherwise uncomfortably inhabits.

Writers on comfort have suggested that feeling comfortable is a classed experience, "rooted not only in material realities but in culturally based expectations" (Weis 2009: 50). Despite the fact that it has no singular meaning, Noble maintains that comfort is a "relationship of power in a social setting" rather than solely based on individual feelings (Noble 2005: 114). Noble discusses comfort in terms of the sense of national belonging felt by Muslims in Australia but in framing this concept as "the fit we experience in relation to the spaces we inhabit and the practices we perform" (Noble 2005: 114) it becomes highly relevant to Usama's experiences of COFA. Despite these similarities with earlier studies of friendships among second generation Lebanese youth, Usama's experience is different because this friendship is based also on common creative-based interests and both are enrolled in fine arts degrees. Thus, the friendship is not just a way to deal with isolation, but also about trying to remain true to an authentic sense of self, which is intimately tied into locality, ethnicity, and masculinity. This is in spite of his previous displays of ambivalence towards Bankstown, towards his Arabness, and towards the habiibs he was surrounded by in his local community.

Risks and the ethnic community

To some extent, Usama recognises that his vocational options may be limited and frames this in two ways. The first is that the creative industries are risky and highly competitive and require one to self-stylise in quirky and unusual ways to generate interest in their artworks. The other part of his rationale for why his options might be limited is because Usama is uncomfortable with transforming his manners and appearance and this stems in some ways from his accountability to his family's reputation but mostly to his mother. He said,

Usama: The whole Arab community–there's a lot of, um, like when women get together they talk a lot and they gossip. My mum doesn't want to be the woman that they're talking about. Like she's very conscious about that thing where she doesn't want them to talk about her son.
Sherene: In a negative way you mean?
Usama: Yeah. 'Cause visual arts is a very 'out there' thing, it's not normal, it's not the thing everyone does. So they would have preferred me study the traditional jobs like lawyer, doctor or engineer that sort of thing.

The risks involved for young Arab–Australian, Bankstown-based men who have creative passions were spelled out in depth in Chapter 1, where I looked at how familial dynamics are renegotiated as informants develop their career aspirations. I draw attention to this theme again here because creative vocational aspirations are continuously negotiated over time and within different social contexts. In this moment of Usama's life history, while at university, multiple variables including class, gender, and ethnicity ultimately constrain his educational aspirations and his perception of the value of further education more generally. These constraints ultimately lead him to safer career options or at the very least forces him to ensure he has a safe backup plan. Similar conclusions have been found in other studies of the educational aspirations of migrant or ethnic minority youth (Shiner and Modood 2002). For Usama, this plan was teaching. He explains,

Usama: I'm going for the safe option and I'm going for teaching. After I finish my visual arts degree, I'm going to do like a year or two years of education and be like an art teacher. A few friends of mine had done the same thing, like they'd studied visual arts and they'd gotten jobs as teachers and then like most of the lecturers at my campus are actually people who went from high school teaching and then professors.
Sherene: And is that something you could see yourself doing?
Usama: Possibly yeah.
Sherene: So why did you choose the safe path exactly? Is it for the security that you'll have a job?
Usama: Yeah, um, 'cause in the art world it's very tough you know, I don't want to put all my chips on the table, just on like, I don't want to focus all my energy on trying to be a professional artist 'cause if that didn't work out, I'd have nothing.

Sherene: Okay.
Usama: Um so that's why I wanted to go with teaching. At the end of the day not everyone I graduate with is going to become a successful professional artist. That's not gonna happen.

In this excerpt we can see very clear pragmatic considerations for his future and a shift whereby definitions of his identity becomes "organised around jobs rather than peers and school" (Noble 2007: 337). Like other young men in this sample who rationalise their degree and career choices in the same way, the language of realistic outcomes contradicts the language of passion that dominates their narratives of creative vocational aspirations we saw in Chapters 1 and 2. One way to make sense of this discursive shift is to give enough attention to context and treat social spaces as politicised, so that some people are welcome while others remain on the periphery (Massey 1995; Noble 2007). The young people in this study struggle to articulate the relationship between social space and comfort in this way and instead simply note the local area, as Riad does when he says, "it was very Paddington", expecting me as the researcher to implicitly understand the connection between Paddington and exclusivity; Ibrahim in the next case study also makes the same reference.

While at school, Usama was surrounded by problematic students and in an environment he sought to escape. Thus, he described himself as 'non-Leb' and also as someone pursuing a creative-based career, although his definition of this career was rather loose because he had limited life experiences and social contacts in the industry to draw on. Then, while in a highly reputable university surrounded by 'weird' non-Arab aspiring artists, Usama retreats from pursuing the creative vocation he originally intended and at the same time feels that he is seen as inferior because his style is too constrained and conventional. Of course, there are key differences between the two dominant youth 'styles' (Leb/Habiibs and 'weirdness') that Usama actively rejects. As I argued in Chapter 2, Leb style has no real value outside of the masculine order of Bankstown and specifically amongst Arab–Australian youth. On the other hand, as Usama describes with reference to the gallery artist example, participating in 'weird' artistic stylisation can yield a return in the world of work. Refusing to adapt to this dominant style may actually affect his chances of employability in the future as he is marked as an outsider.

Finally, within the context of his family and his ethnic community Usama explains that his parents "love him" but do not necessarily love the things he does or his creative interests. He is not trying to please them by completing a teaching degree but in some ways he feels accountable to them and does not want his parents to be ridiculed by the community for his eccentricities and career choices. This interaction between one's style and one's career aspirations reveals the messiness of the project of upward social mobility for ethnic minority and working-class young men. Despite this, I argue it is important not to read Usama's identity as lacking because he refuses to participate in the self-accrual processes he sees other university students doing. As Skeggs has argued, expressing distance between a working-class self and privileged individuals can be about expressions of "an alternative value system ... one that cannot be framed in the shape of a self that is in any way interested in accruing exchange value to itself" (Skeggs 2004: 90). This alternate value system is partly built upon ethnic and religious-based codes of respect, morality and family duty. In Chapter 5, I examine these themes further, looking at how bohemia and the creative industries can compromise the codes of morality that these young Arab–Australian men attempt to adhere to in their projects of social mobility.

Stratification in higher education settings

As it relates to the social inequalities experienced by Usama during university, we can see that his narratives confirm that ethnic minority youth experience a sense of inferiority and isolation in prestigious social spaces. Forsyth and Furlong (2009) capture the kind of isolation experienced by ethnic minority and working class in higher education, calling this 'horizontal stratification'. They suggest that universities are inherently stratified along a number of socio-cultural divisions that cannot be addressed by simply looking at the barriers that prevent young people from gaining entry to university in the first place. In the first instance, they claim that working class students usually choose a university based on their perceptions of the "approachability of staff and by impressions of the backgrounds of fellow students [finding that] staff and students in older institutions can be seen by working class students are culturally remote" (Forsyth and Furlong 2009: 124). This argument is sustained by a number of other educational researchers looking at the preferences of working-class or disadvantaged youth (Hutchings 2003; Basit 2012; Reay 1998). In particular, Maguire *et al.* (1999) argue that in a market-led higher education sector, newer universities use marketing tactics precisely aimed at drawing in ethnically diverse, lower- to working-class atypical students.

I noted this to be the case in my interview with Adam, a nineteen-year-old graphic design student who took up a summer holiday life drawing course at COFA two years before our interview. He did not achieve high enough grades at the end of year twelve to gain entry to a degree at COFA and therefore had to enrol in Western Sydney University (WSU), a relatively new institution that caters largely to ethnic minority and working-class students. He said,

> At my first year of Uni, I saw the environment that was at WSU, it was so much more laid-back and I was like, this is the person I want to be. I looked back at COFA and it was so high class and pretentious and thought, I don't want to become that person. And I know a student from there; she's very cocky about herself.

Essentially, Adam's sense of comfort gained at WSU, with like-minded students and a 'laid-back' culture confirm Usama and Riad's sentiments, that there is a strong correlation between class privilege and youthful creative aspirants. Beyond this, he also reveals how the socio-cultural spread of students in different universities, and the kinds of cultures produced within particular institutions, shape the educational and vocational aspirations of the Arab–Australian young men in this study. What happens is that those creative arts courses are first very competitive, so they filter out applicants whose grades are not high enough. Second, the description of COFA as a place of 'pretention' and 'high class' culture deters Adam from trying to gain entry there, and makes Usama reassess his own creative identity and, further, reassess the negativity he once directed towards Bankstown and 'Leb' youth cultures.

Reay *et al.* (2005) have argued that working-class students aim to achieve social and cultural capital from entering university which they imagine will in turn help them escape from their local communities. In Chapter 2, I explored the theme of escape by arguing that Arab–Australian young men with creative aspirations develop creative identities in order to stand apart from the community during a period of their life, high school, when they are physically immobile and stuck within their local communities. However, the kind of isolation Usama feels in his course, in conjunction with the communal surveillance of his lifestyle choices, ultimately pulls him away from the creative subcultural scenes in which he imaged himself participating. Instead, he is drawn towards a more traditional career path in teaching. Even though teaching is vastly different from the manual labour work that Usama's father did, it still conforms to the more typical social mobility pathways available to the children of migrants in Australia.

The aspiration to escape one's ethnic and class community is thus only partially achievable and not even necessarily as desirable as it once was as he comes to realise, as Riad and Adam have also noted, that the cultivation of a unique creative identity are intimately tied to class privilege enabling some youth to act and be 'weird' without worrying about what kind of consequences face them in their tight-knit ethnic communities. Beyond this, Usama is especially vocal about how being weird is a performance that other creative aspirants display to help promote their work, rather than indicative of their authenticity. It is this tension between weirdness and authenticity that most strongly shapes the renegotiation of his creative vocational aspirations.

Ibrahim: 'They were all weird in some way…'

Ibrahim was thirty years old when we spoke, and the owner of a small media company that specialised in film editing for local Australian documentary makers. In this case study, I spend some time describing some of Ibrahim's experiences before he arrived at university. This is because his articulation of the structural constraints he faced during secondary school shed light on the kind of discomfort he experienced once at university. He says he was discouraged by his high school art teacher from pursuing animation and discouraged from pursuing a creative-based career altogether because it would be too difficult; he was rejected from COFA initially for reasons he can only describe as "because I was from Bankstown" and did not have enough social connections to help him secure a spot; he was ill prepared for the heavily theoretical requirements of his fine arts degree because the school he attended did not provide enough training in writing, instead teachers spent most of class time disciplining rowdy students. Finally, he felt he was 'forced' to go to university by his mother, to choose any degree just so that he could at least be a university graduate and enjoy the prestige associated with higher education. These things, as we shall see, all contributed to shaping his ideas about university and impacted also on the development of his career aspirations.

In Chapter 1, I looked at the tension that Ibrahim experienced within his family because his mother "never understood the arts" and wanted him to simply go to university instead of leaping straight into work after school. However, unlike the majority of other interviewees in this sample, Ibrahim says he had no ambition to pursue post-secondary education because he was more interested in film making and animation. The problem was that "back then there wasn't any film school … and in fine arts you couldn't major in film. You could do something called time based art so like film and video but artistic …". With limited options and the pressure of his mother, Ibrahim decided to aggressively pursue a fine arts course, also at the College of Fine Arts like Usama.

Importantly, unlike Usama, Ibrahim really struggled to gain a place there because both the institution and the course were very exclusive. He was in the top four students in his senior class in high school yet Ibrahim's Higher School Certificate (HSC) results were only high enough to only get him into his last preference, in nursing. He told me of how difficult it was to transfer out of nursing and into his preferred course.

Ibrahim: I quickly transferred to teaching art (after nursing). I did that for one year and tried to transfer again into fine arts but the person that interviewed me (for the fine arts degree) said, "Oh we've got no room for you here". So I did more teaching subjects, the core subjects. I tried again the following year but I thought, "How can I bypass the interview? There's gotta be a way". So I went into the head office, saw the head teacher – the head of the department – and said, "Look I just need a form to transfer" and he just gave it to me! So I went to the admin office to get it processed and the people at the desk said "who gave you this form?" I said, "The head of that department". And they were like "we don't have anything about this". I said, "Look what's the problem?" And they didn't know what to say so they were like, "no problem we'll process this for you". (Laughs)

Sherene: Well that was lucky! Did you think that if you did the interview again that you wouldn't get in?

Ibrahim: Yeah because … the chances are I wouldn't.

Sherene: Why is that?

Ibrahim: It was either you knew someone or … I mean I was from Bankstown first of all. Everybody there was they were all gothic, hippies, artistic and weird in their own style and look. I was the only one there wearing a collared shirt at one point. I stood out as weird. I mean, now it has changed. It's more um; more people are seeing the value in art so the doors are open.

There are quite a number of themes to explore from Ibrahim's recounted narrative of higher education, some of which have been mentioned already. First, we see immediately the connections between art students' socio-economic backgrounds and their abilities to cultivate their 'own style and look'. There is not enough evidence to suggest that other students actually were of more advantaged backgrounds but Ibrahim perceived them to be so because of his understanding that applicants were more likely to gain a place in the course if they 'knew someone'. He feels confronted by the ways that other students perform 'weirdness' and how they embody a particular artistic style that complements their study program. Ironically, he saw himself as 'weird' for being too conventional in his appearance and this dichotomy between his style and that of the 'gothic, hippies' ultimately positioned him as a cultural outsider. I will return to this discussion and how it impacted on his vocational aspirations and future life planning later in this case study.

Most importantly, his account about the difficulties of transferring to a fine arts degree reveals how active processes of Othering that can occur in these elite institutions leads to 'indirect discrimination' (Modood 2005) or 'institutional racism' (Miles and Brown 2003). This particular construction of the 'Other' is based on geographical, cultural, and ethnic differences, where young Arab–Australian men from the Western suburbs are often seen as the embodiment of the 'Other' in contemporary Australian society (White 2007; Dagistanli 2007; Poynting *et al.* 2004). As Lawler has argued, "identities are *conferred* onto subjects, so that they are marked as normal or abnormal, wrong or right" (Lawler 2004: 110) and Ibrahim seems to be saying that his identity was marked as 'wrong' before he was even granted entry into this particular institution.

Being marked as a misfit has ramifications for how far Ibrahim and many other young men like him can imagine and plan for their future careers in certain creative jobs. Participation in elite universities offers social and cultural capital Ibrahim might not access had he stayed in his local area working in a trade as did so many of his school peers. It also offers higher chances of job opportunities once he graduates. But the rejection he speaks about in this excerpt reinforces the ways that working-class and ethnic minority youth are likely to be excluded from elite social spaces and are thus afforded fewer chances to fulfil their vocational aspirations than those subjects whose identities are marked as 'normal' and 'right'.

Being from Bankstown

Ibrahim simply says "I was from Bankstown" to point out why his application might be rejected. By raising his place of residence in this narrative, he reveals how place operates as a metonym for class and classed notions of ethnicity. In a study of the treatment of Muslims in Australian society, Noble looks at how particular social and cultural markers trigger racial vilification and lead to social exclusion (Noble 2005: 118). Ibrahim's encounter with the head of the department can be thought of as a contemporary manifestation of the historical processes of systemic exclusion of certain kind of migrants, as Noble refers to in his study, but this is concealed by the explanation that the suburb in which he grew up was the basis for his exclusion rather than his visibility as a young Arab–Australian and Muslim man.

Studies looking at the experiential dimensions of university life have revealed that there are a multitude of divisions, including place of residence, which can result in exclusion from particular institutions and a sense of isolation for ethnic minority and working-class students like Ibrahim. Forsyth and Furlong (2009), for example, created a list of divisions they say results in horizontal stratification of the student experience

> including the division between 'old' and 'new' universities, between prestigious and less prestigious courses, between students living at home and those who have moved to study and between those who enjoy student-focused lifestyles and those who must combine study with specific engagement in employment-related activities.
>
> (Forsyth and Furlong 2009: 123)

In light of Ibrahim's claim, that being from Bankstown was a potential reason for his application being rejected, we need to add more to Forsyth and Furlong's list, namely, the explicit division between Western Sydney and the Sydney inner city. The former has been pathologised as dangerous, a place for 'bogans' and identifying with it can be a source of shame for many young people whereas the inner city carries notions of a creative, 'cool place' (Powell 1993; Skelton and Valentine 1998; Rossiter 2013). This was mentioned repeatedly in many of the life-history interviews, and later in Chapters 4 and 5, I develop the argument about how spatial dimensions of creative scenes lead to the exclusion of Arab–Australian young men. Two informants who explicitly spoke about the stigma associated with Bankstown, particularly in the context of their university experiences, were Adam and Talal. Adam, who I introduced earlier, followed on from his observations of COFA as 'high class' and 'pretentious' by saying,

> It's so shit that when I say I live in Bankstown people stop and go "oh". They think that's the bad side of town. But they don't know it, they haven't seen it. I don't think so much that those places, like Newtown, are very alternative but people have that in mind.

Talal, a Lebanese–Australian communications student at another city-based university, said that he was continuously frustrated by the stereotypes other students in his course made of Bankstown, where he was from. He said,

Talal: I meet people from the Eastern suburbs and the North Shore, all these other really high class areas, even medium class areas. But then I come back … then in the back of my mind I always remember where my communities come from, where I've come from. And it's very weird because I find them [Uni students from wealthy areas] very ignorant, very naïve, they don't know much. Like, you have no idea. They [the Uni students] think Bankstown is a ghetto and they're like, "I can't believe you live in Bankstown". And they started a rumour like; I dare you to sleep one night in Bankstown but like, hello! I live in Bankstown. Like you dodge a few bullets here and there but woop-ti-do.

Sherene: (Laughs) But you don't really [dodge bullets], you're just exaggerating aren't you?

Talal: Yeah definitely.

Talal creates a clear distinction here between the North Shore/Eastern suburbs students and Western Sydney students in terms of upper class and lower class, one that is slightly superficial but potentially reveals the ways that public discourses of the association between place, class, and crime become internalised by young people. It is also often the case in Australia that people identify themselves by the local suburb in which one was raised and local geographies thus become one way of categorising people into class and racial hierarchies within the nation. While we cannot take his perceptions as reflecting an accurate portrayal of social hierarchies, Talal's peer relations in university do shed light on how stereotypes are felt differently and can have different outcomes depending on who is doing the stereotyping (Miles and Brown 2003). In Chapter 2, it was suggested that many of the informants, including Talal, participate in denigrating other young men who appear to be 'Leb' and in doing so disassociate themselves from the demonised figure of the folk devil. When young people that Talal senses are embedded into more privileged social networks and from 'white' backgrounds make similar stereotypical judgements of Bankstown or the Western suburbs he appears much more offended. It could be that this stems from the fact that these other university students are perpetuating media-instigated myths about Arabs in Australia and about 'ethnic ghettos' because they have not actually lived or spent much time there.

Talal, like other informants, is sensitive to these stereotypes because he anticipates that these judgements might turn into exclusionary practices in the world of work, whereas the jokes made by Lebanese–Australian young people about other Lebanese–Australian young people are perceived as the articulation of a personal sense of belonging and as indicative of a type of camaraderie. Additionally, the confidence these other students exude in making judgements about Talal's background reflects their position of privilege and it is possibly this that Talal is reacting to. Bennett *et al.* (2009) summarise Bourdieu's position on social distinctions saying, "there is a fundamental difference between those who feel they have a right to pass judgement or hold views, and those who do not" (Bennett *et al.* 2009: 71).

Further, realising that 'being from Bankstown' is a disadvantage in the world of work is particularly frustrating for Ibrahim, Adam, and Talal because they have pursued higher education as a way to achieve social mobility and break ties with the working-class status associated with their local communities. Further, they articulate their creative passions and their creative identities as ones that they hope will allow others to recognise them as 'non-Leb' as I discussed in Chapter 2. Yet, what we see from Ibrahim's observations as well as Adam and Talal's encounters with students in their course is the performative and dialogical nature of identity-making. These young men cannot simply obtain educational qualifications and expect this to transform their class identities, they have to also use the linguistic codes (Bernstein 1966) and adopt the bodily dispositions of the middle classes in order to be recognised as such (Bourdieu and Waquant 1992). We know from the work of cultural class theorists that such transformations are difficult ones to make because of the fluidity of cultural tastes and social distinctions (Crompton *et al.* 2000). 'Getting it wrong' in terms of accents, style, or simply being from the wrong place thereby makes them more likely to be victims of social inequality (Bennett *et al.* 1999).

To return to Forsyth and Furlong's account of horizontal stratification, it becomes evident that the suburb one hails from is potentially more important for my informants than, say, the division between students who have to work while attending university and those that do not. Thus, one's geographic location within Sydney is not incidental to these young men's experiences of university peer relations but can, in itself, be a primary reason for their sense of 'cultural remoteness' (Furlong and Cartmel 2009). We see this most prominently in Talal's higher education experiences but it also comes across in many of the informants' life-history interviews as well. As a way of dealing with the prejudice facing them, Adam, Talal, and Ibrahim try to revert the balance of power in their life-history narratives by labelling peers that came from wealthier suburbs as 'pretentious', 'ignorant', or 'weird'.

But there are other aspects of being from Bankstown that affected Ibrahim's university experiences, namely the inadequate preparation he received during secondary school. Once enrolled in the course, Ibrahim found the assessment tasks challenging because he lacked the writing skills exhibited by other students in his course. This put him in a dangerous position of almost failing his degree. He said,

Ibrahim: The degree in fine arts, I learnt more theoretical … how to analyse things, which I didn't learn at school. I didn't learn analysis. I didn't learn how to write. It was either I fail at university or I – the first essay I only just passed! And I would ask people, I would go out of my way to ask people in class I thought could help.

Sherene: The weird people?

Ibrahim: (Laughs) Yeah. To show me their essays after they were marked so I could see how it's done. It was more the structure that I didn't understand. They (teachers) tell you to state what you wanna do, and then state your points and then you conclude. To me they all meant the same thing. Even though they would say the conclusion is a summary of the whole thing, to me the beginning and the summary are the same. What are the distinctions between them? No one at school went into that detail to explain it to us. And when you got low marks, just like everybody else in the class, umm teachers would need to explain to us what's going on, but they didn't. There was nothing done about it.

The inadequate preparation Ibrahim received for further education establishes how and why he may have felt overwhelmed while at university, which is elaborated on in another interview moment detailed below. His frustration at being unable to deal with the difficult theoretical assessments is consistent with findings in the existing literature suggesting that students from disadvantaged schools and from particular ethnic backgrounds are less prepared to deal with abstract, conceptual arguments having been immersed in cultures and schools that emphasise vocational, hands-on learning (Watkins and Noble 2008; Tranter 2012). In addition to feeling underprepared in terms of his writing capabilities, he added that his high school art teacher was unsupportive of his aspiration to study film and animation in university. He said,

Ibrahim: My art teacher at one point – we had to do a year twelve piece of work and I told the art teacher that I wanted to do an animation but I was waiting for my father to buy me the camera that would allow me to do it. Because the school didn't have the technology, the resources for me and so … at one point the teacher said to me "are you gonna work on something you *can* do?" He just didn't believe I could do it. But then I got into Art Express.[3] Yeah I was the first one in that school ever to get in.

Sherene: And why, why would the teacher think you couldn't do it?

Ibrahim: Umm … he thought I couldn't do it because umm he said "people are always struggling very hard in the art field no matter what". All this negativity all the time.

The fact that his father had to purchase the camera for his course, that the school did not have the available resources, confirms the position of disadvantage that Ibrahim was coming from in comparison to some of his peers at COFA. Despite the lack of support offered by the art teacher, Ibrahim's achievement of being the first in his school to be recognised in a national art competition for senior high school students allowed him to feel confident enough to pursue art as a vocational pathway. The 'negativity' from the art teacher towards Ibrahim seems to be less aimed at his creative and technical abilities, and more about preparing Ibrahim for the struggle that would await him if he was to pursue animation as a career choice. Studies have shown that the kinds of encouragement and support offered to ambitious students from disadvantaged backgrounds are limited to pushing them into degrees in 'new' universities that are more likely to offer financial security in the long run (Basit 2012; Modood 1993). They are often discouraged by teachers to pursue more unusual studies in competitive fields such as the creative arts industry. This was confirmed by Ibrahim's recollections of the lack of support offered by his art teacher.

The disadvantages of being 'normal' in a 'weird' place

It is safe to say then that Ibrahim found university life challenging and rather overwhelming and a large part of that can be accounted for, similarly to Usama, by looking at how puzzled he was by the youthful subcultural styles and practices of the other creative arts students in his course. He spoke for example about the "culture shock" he felt in his first two years.

Ibrahim: For me it was a culture shock. It was a culture shock. You know I thought maybe there is something wrong with me. Maybe I'm not normal. I actually saw the counsellor at one point. She said, "oh do you have friends in your area?" I said "yeah", she said, "well, you know, you've gotta think about that, they don't see you as weird".

Sherene: Did that culture shock affect you to the point where you ever thought, I don't want to do this anymore?

Ibrahim: Oh yeah … you know … it became, I became self-conscious wondering I wonder what they think …

Sherene: Of you?

Ibrahim: Yeah of you and all that stuff … And after a semester I didn't care anymore. It came to a point and that was it. It was really weird. I found out later, like two years later, that most of the people in the course were women. 90 per cent of them were probably gay or weird in some way and there was only a handful of people … The only ones that I thought that were normal and they were doing teaching, like a combined degree. I mean I was at the College of Fine Arts. In the heart of Paddington. Just off Oxford Street. So it gives you an idea of the sort of place that it was. Other issues were, why I didn't get along were, a lot of them would go to the pub for a drink. I didn't drink so I couldn't join them. And they had parties all the time and I would attend them. Everybody would be drunk or intoxicated to a high, a high level. And umm it was a weird bunch so it wasn't my cup of tea.

For Ibrahim, 'weird' identities are constructed around one's unusual artistic style, homosexuality, heavy partying, and consumption of alcohol. Presumably, there are many other characteristics that shape his view of these students but he seems to struggle to adequately describe them and offers instead an explanation of the location of the university, indicating that there is a local subculture in and around Oxford Street that celebrates non-conformity and underground scenes to which he does not belong. So the separation between weird and normal is not strictly a matter of class difference in terms of highbrow and lowbrow culture but about consumption, leisure interests, and youth-based subcultural practices within a creative arts scene.

Savage and Bennett (2005), amongst other cultural class researchers, point out that the emphasis on patterns of consumption does not dissolve the existence of class or persisting forms of social inequality but is a more contemporary way of understanding the ways that cultural capital organises social hierarchies. Therefore, it is possible to make the case that the aspirations for social mobility are awkwardly experienced by Ibrahim and indeed many young men in this sample because they seem to have distinct ideas about what it means to be middle class and usually this is bound up in a locally defined ideas about 'respect' and 'respectability' (Noble 2007). Respect is perceived to be awarded to young men by society through their achievements within legitimate, formal educational institutions, by their displays of good citizenship, and by their adherence to moral and sometimes religious codes. It seems that upon arriving at university they are bewildered by the consumption patterns and leisure interests of their middle class art school peers leaving them confused about how to actually achieve the upward mobility they were originally seeking.

The labels of 'weird' seem to reflect this bewilderment. If we compare Ibrahim's perceptions of his peers to Usama we see that Ibrahim does not see that the 'weird' students are 'acting' or putting on a performance for an intended outcome like Usama does. Ibrahim does say they had cultivated a particular style but does not make a connection between that style and their aspirations to make a name for themselves in the art world. One could argue that it is because he cannot see through them that he starts to question whether or not he is actually normal. He accepts that they are normal rather than the products of their social, cultural and economic positions of advantage. If we look at the traits required of creative workers in a knowledge society, namely traits such as risk-taking and individualism, his exhibition of self-doubt can only really be a disadvantage for him as he moves on from university and into the world of work (Christopherson 2009).

But beyond this, we might also see how the construction of an authentic self is articulated in relation to place, for instance when the counsellor suggests that he find comfort in the friendship circles with other Lebanese–Australian youth already established within Bankstown. By retaining membership in the friendship circles in Bankstown, who have no access to creative scenes and will not progress his career in any way, Ibrahim has chosen to go against the "ethos of omnivorousness" (Bennett *et al.* 2009: 55) which, according to the accounts of the Arab–Australian young people presented in this chapter, seem to be imperative for future success in the creative industries. Going to the counsellor to assess whether he is in fact 'normal' might also be understood in relation to the argument of Reay *et al.* (2001) that an underlying tension for working-class students in universities is a fear of being 'found out'. I would argue that this is a fear underscoring Ibrahim's narrative but is not simply a class-based tension. Rather, Ibrahim's tension is about the confrontation of being in a creative arts degree, where notions of gender, masculinity and ethnicity are challenged by his interactions with what he calls 'weird' students. The fear is about being 'found out' as neither 'cool' nor 'creative' enough and therefore ill-suited to the chosen vocational pathway.

As we see from both Ibrahim and Usama's case studies, the discussion of 'weird' students dominated a great deal of the narratives about higher education. I outlined earlier in the chapter that the capacity to perform 'weirdness' in the right way, so as to be accepted within the subcultural groups in and around Oxford Street, is an example of how some young people have accumulated particular social, cultural and financial capitals so as to be 'omnivorous' in their tastes and style. Here lies the problem for Usama, Riad, Adam, and Ibrahim. They struggle to participate in cultural scenes unfamiliar to their own and they can be, as in Ibrahim's case, entirely unaware of the social codes required for membership in the peer networks in their universities. This results in awkwardness and a sense of discomfort within their higher education institutions. I would argue that such narratives have broader implications for understanding how ethnic minority youth, particularly those of poorer backgrounds, still feel uncomfortable around people outside of their own class and ethnic groups. This discomfort is about the fact that they are still learning how to act, speak, and think appropriately in those kinds of interactions.

Because university is seen as something of a testing ground for the creative industries they seek to work in, young Arab–Australian men's lack of mastery over the codes in these particular subcultural scenes represents potential future limitations for their full participation in certain creative sectors. This is not an individual fault but the outcome of a life in disadvantaged communities with limited economic and cultural capital. Thus, the cases presented in this chapter show how the development of self-making is a form of class-making (Skeggs 2004: 91). The prejudices directed towards the young men in this chapter, as well as their own internalised sense of cultural remoteness, are part of a "class struggle made from the relationship between people and objects" (Skeggs 2004: 91). As a result, their articulations of frustration or anxiety at not fitting in are understood in this chapter as statements which come "from a social position of a future-blocked as opposed to a future that can be invested in" (Skeggs 2004: 90). The capacity for higher education to offer social mobility or escape is thus complicated by the lived experiences of these young men as ethnicised and socio-economically disadvantaged subjects. Further, it is complicated by the fact that they are seeking out creative-based careers in which they feel pressured to succumb to unwritten rules regarding self-stylisation.

Conclusion

In both of these case studies, the primary aim has been to show how university is experienced as a filtering site, where confrontations with weirdness and class privilege results in a retreat to the familiarity of Bankstown and an Arab–Australian local community. Of course, there was diversity in the narratives of higher education from other interviewees that were not explored here where isolation or tensions among peers were never flagged. But the cases I explored here all have in common that they were students from COFA, completing one of the most reputable fine arts programs in the state. The similarities between them are so obvious and the degree to which they experience isolation and cultural remoteness is so powerful in both Usama and Ibrahim's narratives.

In both narratives we saw how the capacity to perform 'weirdness' is central to developing a creative identity. Of course, what I argued is that this capacity is not one that all young people can easily do because of their limited cultural, social, and financial capitals. Even though university was originally sought out by these young men as a way to escape the surveillance of their local communities, a way to develop their sense of creativity further and play with their identities, they feel inhibited because of how much more confident other, more privileged students, seem to be able to present themselves as creatives; while they still see themselves as students and creative aspirants.

Further, the performance of weirdness does not match with the expectations they had of university life as adolescents stuck in Bankstown planning their escape. Instead, their social encounters with other students at university are confrontations too far outside the comforts of working-class Western Sydney culture. It is this that forces them to think twice about their original vocational aspirations, to consider what it means to be socially mobile and to begin planning for a safer, less risky career path that is validated from within their ethnic communities. Their reluctance to change their 'authentic self' too much accords with the cultural omnivore thesis –that cultural capital structures cultural participation and taste, and those with more cultural capital are more likely to value eclecticism and embody a range of different subcultural styles, temporarily and for a particular purpose (Bennett *et al.* 2009). Within this schema, these informants are therefore at a disadvantage in many ways. In spite of the prestige and honour they confer onto their family through their educational achievements, they still feel they are positioned by others as coming from backgrounds that are poorly ranked in social hierarchies. This positioning and these perceptions result, as we saw in this chapter, in a feeling of discomfort. Whether or not this sense of discomfort, both within the confines of the university and amongst privileged 'white' people, disappears over time is difficult to answer but some of the 'safer' career plans that these informants make, such as Usama's plan to become a teacher, suggest that it possibly does not.

Skeggs, in her theorisation of the self, argues that

> a refusal to play the game or the lack of knowledge to participate in middle-class taste culture is read back onto the working class as an individualised moral fault, pathology, a problem of bad choice, bad culture, and a failure to be enterprising or to be reflexive.
>
> (Skeggs 2004: 91)

This, she claims, is dangerous. In the context of working class, Lebanese–Australian young men in creative arts degrees or in elite universities more generally, it is dangerous to read their hesitance to participate in the local youth culture as a problem they have to overcome. Instead, one of the main conclusions to be drawn from all of these case studies is that it is *because* they value what they see as their 'authentic self' (Lawler 1999) – one embedded in a version of Lebanese-ness, and a part of Western Sydney, where they are not 'snobby' or 'pretentious', that they keep their distance from 'weird' or 'upper class' peers at university.

Essentially then, university is experienced as a filtering site for these Arab–Australian young men, most evident through the different styles, tastes, and leisure interests between the Arab–Australian young men and other students enrolled in their courses. This has serious implications for how they develop their creative identities. At the most basic level, their experiences of higher education make them aware of how creative scenes and the creative industries are stratified along class and ethnic lines, favouring creative aspirants who are the antithesis of people like them. Beyond this, it means that to continue with their creative aspirations they have to put in place alternative plans about how to pursue a creative career away from mainstream sectors in which they realise, during their time at university, that they simply do not and will never fully belong.

Notes

1 After these interviews were completed, COFA had a name change and is now University of New South Wales Art & Design. Their website states that they are located in Sydney's 'creative precinct', in closer proximity to the Sydney Opera House, the Art Gallery of New South Wales (NSW) and the Sydney Biennale. It is one of "Australia's largest community of art and design practitioners, researchers, educators and students". (https://www.artdesign.unsw.edu.au/about-us)

2 The tuition fees for Sydney Church of England Girls Grammar School (SCEGGS) Darlinghurst currently stand at $30,501 per year. http://www.smh.com.au/data-point/private-school-fees-boom-20130125-2dc27.html

3 ArtExpress is "an annual exhibition featuring a selection of outstanding student artworks developed for the artmaking component of the HSC examination in Visual Arts in NSW. It includes a broad range of approaches and expressive forms, including ceramics, collection of works, documented forms, drawing, graphic design, painting, photomedia, printmaking, sculpture, textiles and fibre, and time-based forms" (http://www.artgallery.nsw.gov.au/insideartexpress/).

References

Ball, S., D. Reay and M. David (2002) '"Ethnic Choosing": Minority ethnic students, social class and higher education choice', *Race Ethnicity and Education*, 5(4): 333–357.

Basit, T. (2012) '"I've never known someone like me to go to university": Class, ethnicity and access to higher education', in *Social Inclusion and Higher Education*, Eds. T. Basit and S. Tomlinson, London, The Polity Press University, pp. 172–192.

Becker, H. (1982) *Art Worlds*, Berkeley, University of California Press.

Bennett, A. (1999) 'Subcultures or neo-tribes? Rethinking the relationship between youth, style and musical taste', *Sociology*, 33(3): 599–617.

Bennett, T., M. Savage, E. Bortolaia Silva, A. Warde, M. Gayo-Cal and D. Wright (2009) *Culture, Class, Distinction*, New York, Routledge.

Bennett, T., M. Emmison, and J. Frow (1999) *Accounting for Tastes: Australian Everyday Cultures*, Melbourne, Cambridge University Press.

Bernstein, B. (1966) 'Elaborated and Restricted Codes: An outline', *Sociological Inquiry* 36(2): 254–261.

Bourdieu, P. (1984) *Distinction: A social critique of the judgement of taste*, London, Routledge and Kegan Paul.

Bourdieu, P. (2005) 'Habitus', in *Habitus: A sense of Place*, Eds. J. Hillier and E. Rooksby, Aldershot, Ashgate, pp. 43–49.

Bourdieu, P. and L. Wacquant (1992) *An Invitation to Reflexive Sociology*, Chicago, The University of Chicago Press.

Christopherson, S. (2009) 'Working in the creative economy: Risk, adaptation, and the persistence of exclusionary networks', in *Creative Labour: Working in the Creative Industries*, Eds. A. McKinlay and C. Smith, Basingstoke, Palgrave Macmillan, pp. 72–91.

Crompton, R. and J. Scott (2005) 'Class analysis: Beyond the cultural turn', in *Rethinking Class: Culture, Identities and Lifestyles*, Eds. F. Devine, M. Savage, J. Scott and R. Crompton, New York, Palgrave Macmillan, pp. 186–202.

Crompton, R., F. Devine, M. Savage, and J. Scott (2000) *Renewing Class Analysis*, Oxford, Blackwell Publishers/The Sociological Review.

Dagistanli, S. (2007) '"Like a pack of wild animals": Moral panics around 'ethnic' gang rape in Sydney', in *Outrageous! Moral Panics in Australia*, Eds. S. Poynting and G. Morgan, Hobart, ACYS Publishing, pp. 181–197.

Du Gay, P. (1996) *Consumption and Identity at Work*, London, Sage.

Emmison, M. (2003) 'Social class and cultural mobility: Reconfiguring the cultural omnivore thesis', *Journal of Sociology*, 39(3): 211–230.

Forsyth, A. and A. Furlong (2009) 'Access to higher education and disadvantaged young people', *British Educational Research Journal*, 29(2): 205–225.

Furlong, A. and F. Cartmel (2009) 'Mass higher education', in *Handbook of Youth and Young Adulthood: New Perspectives and Agendas*, Eds. A. Furlong, New York, Routledge, pp. 121–126.

Hutchings, M. (2003) 'Information, advice and cultural discourses of higher education', in *Higher Education and Social Class: Issues of Exclusion and Inclusion*, Eds. L. Archer, and A. Ross, London, Routledge Falmer, pp. 97–118.

Lawler, S. (1999) '"Getting out and Getting Away": Women's Narratives of Class Mobility', *Feminist Review*, 63: 3–24.

Maguire, M., S. Ball, and S. Macrae (1999) 'Persuasion and class-taste: Marketing (in) the UK post-compulsory sector', *British Journal of Sociology of Education*, 20(3): 291–308.

Massey, D. (1995) 'Making spaces or, geography is political too', *Soundings* (1): 193–208.

McRobbie, A. (2002) 'Clubs to companies: Notes on the decline of political culture in speeded up creative worlds', *Cultural Studies*, 16(4): 516–531.

Miles, R. and M. Brown (2003) 'On signification', in *Racism*, London, Routledge, pp. 87–113.

Modood, T. (1993) 'The number of ethnic minority students in British higher education: Some grounds for optimism', *Oxford Review of Education*, 19(2): 167–182.

Modood, T. (2005) *Multicultural Politics: Racism, Ethnicity and Muslims in Britain*, Minneapolis, University of Minnesota Press.

Noble, G. (2005) 'The discomfort of strangers: Racism, incivility and ontological security in a relaxed and comfortable nation', *Journal of Intercultural Studies*, 26(1–2): 107–120.

Noble, G. (2007) 'Respect and respectability amongst second-generation Arab and Muslim Australian men', *Journal of Intercultural Studies*, 28(3): 331–344.

Noble, G., S. Poynting, and P. Tabar (1999) 'Youth, ethnicity and the mapping of identities: Strategic essentialism and strategic hybridity among male Arabic speaking youth in South-Western Sydney', *Communal/Plural*, 7(1): 29–44.

Peterson, R. A. and R. M. Kern (1996) 'Changing highbrow taste: From snob to omnivore', *American Sociological Review* 61(October): 900–907.

Powell, D. (1993) *Out West: perceptions of Sydney's Western Suburbs*, St Leonards, Allen and Unwin.

Poynting, S., G. Noble, P. Tabar, and J. Collins (2004) *Bin Laden in the Suburbs: Criminalising the Arab Other*, Sydney, Institute of Criminology.

Reay, D. (1998) '"Always knowing" and "never being sure": Familial and institutional habituses and higher education choice', *Journal of Education Policy*, 13(4): 519–529.

Reay, D., G. Crozier, and J. Clayton (2010) '"Fitting in" or "standing out": Working-class students in UK higher education', *British Educational Research Journal*, 36(1): 107–124.

Reay, D., M. David, and S. Ball (2001) 'Making a difference? Institutional habituses and higher education choice', *Sociology Research Online*, 5(4): http://www.socresonline.org.uk/5/4/reay.html

Reay, D., M. David, and S. Ball (2005) 'Working class students', in *Degrees of Choice: Social Class, Race and Gender in Higher Education*, Eds. D. Reay, M. David and S. Ball, Staffordshire, Trentham Books, pp. 83–107.

Rossiter, P. (2013) 'Bogans: a sticky subject', *Continuum: Journal of Media and Cultural Studies*, 27(1): 80–92.

Savage, M. and T. Bennett (2005) 'Editors introduction: Cultural capital and social inequality', *The British Journal of Sociology*, 56(1): 1–12.

Shiner, M. and T. Modood (2002) 'Help or hindrance? Higher education and the route to ethnic equality', *British journal of Sociology of Education*, 23(2): 209–232.

Skeggs, B. (2004) 'Exchange, value and affect: Bourdieu and "the self"', *The Sociological Review*, 52(s2): 75–95.

Skelton, T. and G. Valentine, Eds. (1998) *Cool Places: Geographies of Youth Cultures*, London, Routledge.

Taylor, S. and K. Littleton (2006) 'Biographies in talk: A narrative-discursive research approach', *Qualitative Sociology Review*, 2(1): 22–38.

Thornton, S. (1995) *Club Cultures: Music, Media and Subcultural Capital*, Cambridge, Polity Press.

Tranter, D. (2012) 'Unequal schooling: How the school curriculum keeps students from low socio-economic backgrounds out of university', *International Journal of Inclusive Education*, 16(9): 901–916.

Watkins, M. and G. Noble (2008) *Cultural Practices and Learning: Diversity, Discipline and Dispositions in Schooling*, Sydney Institute of Culture and Society, University of Western Sydney, pp. i–137.

Weis, L. (2009) 'Social class, youth and young adulthood in the context of a shifting, global economy', *Handbook of Youth and Young Adulthood*, Ed. A. Furlong, New York Routledge, pp. 49–57.

White, R. (2007) 'Lebanese young people in a climate of conflict', in *Social Cohesion in Australia*, Eds. J. Jupp, P. Nieuwenhuysen and E. Dawson, Melbourne, Cambridge University Press, pp. 70–79.

Young, J. (2004) '"Becoming different": Accessing university from a low socioeconomic community – barriers and motivators', *Systemic Practice and Action Research* 17(5): 425.

4 Making money out of art

Parlaying the passion into a career

Meeting Marie

When I first set out to conduct fieldwork, I consulted with a range of artists from different community organisations that came from Arab–Australian backgrounds in order to gain access to aspiring creative workers. One of those artists was Marie, a filmmaker in her late thirties who had produced several films in the United States and had recently returned to Sydney and had turned to what she called the 'second phase' of her career, as a youth worker and project manager in a community organisation developing social enterprise projects with Muslim women. Because of her age and the fact that she was female, Marie was not included in the sample. Nonetheless, our discussion prompted several ideas and questions that I drew on when I interviewed young, male Arab–Australian creative aspirants.

Marie had worked extensively in various parts of the creative industries for fifteen years. I asked her what she thought was the biggest challenge facing creative aspirants. She said, "the biggest challenge is finding a way to make your creative interest, or your art, work in modern society". I asked how she had managed to do that considering that she came from a conservative Lebanese family and that the film industry has a reputation for being closed off in its networks, as Christopherson (2009) has argued. She said that the 'edge' she had over the other graduates from her fine arts degree was that she also majored in business administration. She says, "I knew how to write invoices, how to deal with people, how to manage a project as well as, you know, having filmmaking skills". Marie therefore saw the importance of contemporary creative workers being able to 'commercialise' their creativity, to bring together creative skills with business acumen, and be up to date with new media technologies. The ways she described this 'edge' had little to do with the buzzwords of the new economy, of creative 'talent' or 'passion'; she was pointing out pragmatic, concrete skills with applicability across a range of sectors both within and entirely distinct from creative and cultural-based ones.

McRobbie (2004) in her analysis of the creative industries in the United Kingdom describes it as

> a blend of the bohemian individualism of artists and the business ethos of the commercial art director. The small scale independent company (of perhaps

> two or three people) and the non-organised casual freelancer come to represent the dominant units of cultural production.
>
> (McRobbie 2004: 3)

In the Australian case, O'Connor *et al.* (2011) find that artists are now accustomed to the interrelations between art and business rather than viewing them as two distinct spheres. Moore and Gibson (2013) explain that artists often operate under the illusion of autonomy from the market because performances of a bohemian identity help them make a living, offering consumers an 'alternative' product as part of a counterculture movement. Finally, O'Connor *et al.* (2011) suggest that studies of creative labour often focus exclusively on creative-based industries, such as fine arts, theatre and music, but that it is much more likely that creative workers are not embedded in these traditional 'art' sectors but in fact float across a number of related creative industries. Their ability to traverse 'business' worlds and art worlds, as Marie encourages young people in the community to do, means they are arguably better equipped to deal with precarious conditions (O'Connor *et al.* 2011). We can draw from this that the idea of the self-expressive artist who works freely and independently without monetary incentive perhaps needs some re-evaluation. In cities like Sydney, artists are more likely to fit the description of the "bohemian entrepreneur" (Eikhof and Haunschild 2006: 235) who engage in forms of aesthetic labour as a way to market and self-promote their creative productions, operating in some ways like a small firm.

Marie explored what a 'bohemian entrepreneur' might look like, but her representations specifically addressed aspiring Arab–Australian artists who face particular structural inequalities. She said, "these industries are brutal; cut throat really and only a few people 'make it' because there aren't enough jobs to go around". Compounded with this problem was the fact that "in Arab communities the networks are not there to support those young people trying to find creative work". These were all sentiments echoed by other informants in this study, especially Ibrahim in Chapter 2, but what I found particularly striking from my interview with Marie was the way she emphasised the importance of creative aspirants having "a backup plan" and "to get all the business skills they can in uni, because in today's world, it's all about marketability. How can you market your creative skills to a bunch of different companies? How can you market yourself? Unfortunately, that's the way it is". The relationship between business know-how and the creativity that Marie described was at odds with the ways that the informants had identified themselves – as young people brimming with 'passion', who were not 'driven by money at all' and who were thoroughly 'non-Leb' in their capacity to view their futures differently to the dominant narrative in their local migrant communities. Of course, the majority of informants in this study were aspirants or had limited working experience in creative fields and could therefore define creativity in these ways.

Marie's experiences on the other hand accords with the literature on creative workers in fields such as new media. Gill (2009), for instance, explains how many of the web workers in her study felt the pressure to be adept in a range of skills and market themselves as experts in a number of areas to retain their competitive edge.

Beyond what Marie seems to be describing as the generally precarious conditions of creative work and the relationship between art and money, what we can also glean from my interview with her was that she was describing creative labour in recently emerged sectors. The argument that one needs to be highly qualified or cultivate a 'marketable' image to be an actor, for example, is inaccurate. But certainly, to work in media or web design, one does need to be highly qualified and entrepreneurial.

This chapter, which focuses exclusively on the working experiences of my informants in the post-higher education phase of their lives, seeks to explore how art and business converge in the life-history narratives of Arab–Australian young men. It offers an atypical account of creative identities than what has been explored so far in studies of creative labour. I am interested here in the push and pull factors that lead some members of this cohort of young men into self-employment in ways that are distinct from the culture of small business enterprise within their ethnic communities and also markedly different from the stereotype of the bohemian freelancer or the 'slashie' who takes up work in multiple but unrelated industries to make ends meet.

Eikhof and Haunschild (2006) claim "most artists understand themselves as bohemians, living a lifestyle that is distinct and distinguished from the rest of society, especially the bourgeoisie and business" (2006: 234). While this might be true of their research with theatre performers in Germany, in light of my research, this statement seems a sweeping generalisation that conjures images of nineteenth century European notions of la vie de Boheme. The ways in which artists make money is undoubtedly intertwined with factors such as class, gender, and ethnicity. Notions of bohemia will be explored more thoroughly later in the chapter, but essentially, the overarching aim here is to present and analyse narratives in which ethnic minority, working-class young men actively reject 'bohemia' as an aspirational lifestyle. Based on their experiences during university, they see clear associations between life as a 'starving artist' and the enduring safety net of the middle classes. I will present case studies in this chapter where the capacity to make a decent living and therefore achieve some kind of upward mobility from art is not perceived as problematic; in other words, you're not a sellout if you can earn a living from your creative output. Unlike other studies of artists' life-history narratives (Taylor and Littleton 2006), there appears little confliction or unease among this cohort of young men when it comes to manoeuvring their career directions in ways to earn a living rather than retain some romantic association with 'art for arts sake'.

The chapter will first look at the tradition of self-employment in Arab–Australian communities to establish the sharp contrast between this model of work that has become normalised for the young men in this study and the nature of bohemianism that underscores creative labour today. I then trace the contours of creative lifestyles that many informants in this study feel disconnected from entirely for a number of reasons. For some, bohemian living compromises their sense of religiosity; others fear being rejected by gatekeepers in these creative scenes on the basis of racial or class prejudice and others, following the discussion in the previous chapter, are deterred by what they see as the pretentions that characterise mainstream creative labour and inner city bohemia. Finally, I focus on two case studies, with Haydar and Ibrahim, who appear to have capitalised on the emerging opportunities for self-employment in niche multimedia fields to become what Florida (2003) calls 'creative entrepreneurs'.

Business enterprise in Arab–Australian communities

> Dreams by first generation immigrants of a business of their own emerged from shattered dreams about life in the 'Lucky Country'. Formal and informal racial discrimination had trapped many post-war immigrants into hard, dangerous, dirty and low paying factory jobs, regardless of their capabilities, their formal skills and the quality of their work. For most, a move into small business meant a realisation of dreams of independence and, for some, a fulfilment of dreams of great wealth.
>
> (Collins *et al.* 1995: x)

Collins *et al.* (1995) observe that family-run businesses are common in ethnic minority groups in Australia; a finding echoed in my research. All of the informants in this study said that their parents arrived in Australia and worked in relatively similar jobs; as cleaners, in factories, or working in a relatives' shop who had already migrated. Over time, some informants' parents established their own businesses. Sometimes, these businesses were based on a trade, such as carpentry, and sometimes they were in what we might call the 'ethnic retail market' selling 'exotic goods' to local co-ethnic consumers.

The young men referred to a culture of self-employment in their ethnic community, mentioning that members of their extended families ran their own construction companies for example, or had become self-employed tradesmen that could easily recruit them if they ever needed work – an option most informants eschewed as they remained wedded to their creative aspirations. For example, Youssef an eighteen-year-old studying interior design, explained that between completing high school and starting his course at Technical and Further Education (TAFE) he was "offered lots of jobs, like from friends and family". He says they were jobs such as "shop fitting, cabinet making, kitchens … ah what else? Concreting … kinds of jobs that they work in or that some relative of my dad has his own business and can give me job". He refused those jobs, calling them "shit" and "totally unrelated" to his creative passion of drawing and design; similar reactions were displayed by many other informants in this study.

Only two of the informants' fathers worked in professional roles, one in the immigration department and another as a police offer. These men migrated to Australia as adolescents. They were able to go through the schooling system and gain the required educational qualifications. Mostly though, the life-history interviews revealed a strong culture of self-employment and small business in their local migrant communities. Of the twenty participants in this study, fourteen of them had parents or other close relatives who were self-employed. I asked Bashir, a once-aspiring author who was in the process of completing a psychology course, to reflect on what kinds of jobs were most common in his Lebanese–Australian community. He said,

Bashir: A lot of them are tradies. Umm a lot of them have their own self-run business, whether it's a fruit and veg shop or mixed businesses [corner store, milk bar]; a lot of family-run businesses. I reckon only the recent generation, like my generation, they're more into offices and stuff, like professionals.

Sherene: And why do you think that is?

Bashir: Umm I think that our parents' generation when they came they were settling in and they were older, they already had their studies, they already worked you know so they stayed doing what they do. But once their children are born here and they go to the schools and they get raised and taught in the schools they head off into their own path. This country [Australia] has allowed them [second generation migrants] to do what they want to do.

Although family business backgrounds were diverse, all informants based their working experiences in these family businesses. They noted memories of spending their leisure time in those shops or at their father's offices and became accustomed to the rhythms of the seven-day-a-week business. This was not always the smoothest process. Bashir, for example, explained his frustration at working for his father's cabinet-making company, saying "you have to always be available, you can't say no. I even make sure my uni timetable is like two days a week so I can be more free for him because he won't have anyone else to help".

While some informants were involved in paid work unrelated to their families' businesses, these were secondary jobs. The presence of these businesses in their lives definitely affected the development of their own vocational aspirations, their views relating to the separation between work and leisure, and their ideas about generating an income. Haydar, for instance, a twenty-six-year-old self-employed multimedia worker, explained that working for his older brother's house painting company during the school holidays was salutary. Even though he resisted the pressure to become a partner with his brother because house painting "bored me to tears", it was the autonomy gained from being self-employed that influenced his future vocational direction as he says, "I saw my brother working for himself, not having to take shit from people. I liked that element of his job you know?" This desire for autonomy follows the same logic that Collins *et al.* suggest was the norm among older generations of migrants whereby they "dreamed of freedom: to have no boss or foreman above them, to be able to set their own work rhythms, to have autonomy in choice of tasks, methods of work and products, and to hopefully achieve prosperity" (1995: 9).

The presence of small business enterprise, or family run business, in the daily lives of ethnic minority youth is not unique to my sample of Arab–Australians (Light and Gold 2000; Aytar and Rath 2012). In fact, as others have noted, there is an over-representation of family run small business in minority migrant communities in other Western societies (Barrett *et al.* 1996). Aldrich and Waldinger (1990) suggest that this often occurs when migrant plans for return change and they settle permanently in the host country. Unlike "native workers", immigrants often have less to lose and thus "will be more satisfied with low profits from small businesses because of the wage differences between their origin and destination countries" (Aldrich and Waldinger 1990: 125). It is often this wage gap that some refer to as a way to explain rapid upward mobility among some migrant groups (Ho and Alcorso 2004). Of course, these arguments are rather generalised and work with the assumption that ethnic-based small businesses will remain small and that migrants know this to be their fate. This is not always the case, in fact, in my interview with Shaheen, he spoke of his brother's construction company developing rapidly and becoming quite profitable, but this is usually the exception to the rule.

In addition to the comparatively substantial pay increases on offer for new migrants venturing into business ownership, as outlined by Aldrich and Waldinger (1990), there are also 'push' factors that contributed to this general over-representation of ethnic minorities in self-employment. This trend of over-representation in self-employed segments of the labour market is one that has steadily maintained over time but rather than simply celebrate those figures, Anthias and Cederberg (2009) argue that it is important to identify "the wider context of immigrant disadvantage as an important factor determining routes into self-employment". This immigrant disadvantage is characterised as "the lack of opportunities and processes of discrimination in the dependent labour market" (Anthias and Cederberg 2009: 902). Although Anthias and Cederberg (2009) researched overseas-born migrants, their insights are applicable to Australia. Discrimination unfortunately remains a central factor for the ways that Arab–Australian young men with creative aspirations weigh up their vocational options. Examples of racialised prejudice have been explored in a number of case studies across this thesis. We saw how, in Chapter 3, Ibrahim felt his application from art school was rejected because of his ethnicity and visible identifiers of being from Western Sydney and in the next chapter I will discuss how Saad encountered racial prejudice during his internship at a state-wide newspaper.

Collins (2003) explains that in Australia, by comparison to other advanced societies, there is little regulation around self-employment and as such virtually anyone can establish a private business (Collins 2003: 143). Alternatively, there is little in the way of training schemes or support for newcomers looking to establish or improve their businesses (Collins 2003). What Collins calls "underdeveloped" national policy responses to immigrant entrepreneurship has implications for patterns of business ownership amongst second generation migrant youth in that they are more likely to rely on existing, local, informal knowledge about business practice rather than seek out formal institutional advice. This in turn means that second generation youth are likely to be self-employed in similar industries as their co-ethnic peers. Ibrahim illuminated some of these points. He explained how his peers from high school generally followed vocational templates influenced by their youthful working experiences helping their parents in the family business.

> They had either gone on to start their own businesses or working very basic jobs like security or … jobs that don't require you to go to university and

> judging by how everybody went, not many of them have ended up using their degrees other than, for example, if you have a pharmacy degree you open up a couple of pharmacies … There was me and probably four or five others that were top of the class, and we all went on, or most of us went on, to start our own businesses.

This accords with Collins' (2003) finding that second generation migrants who are involved in business ownership usually do so by establishing practices around a profession. Some of the more common professions include dentists, doctors, accountants, and lawyers. These are all titles that are easy to explain to the ethnic community and are also fairly predictable in terms of various job pathways. In the context of this study, parental aspirations for their children to become professionals are tied into notions of masculinity whereby the cultural figure of the entrepreneur or business owner is a venerated one, especially for these young men who happen to be the first generation of their family to be born in Australia and reap the rewards of a generous education system.

Shaheen, an actor/entertainer who was also joint owner of a construction company, revealed a sense of pride at the increasing number of successful business owners of Lebanese descent. He said,

> There's a lot of classy Lebs in the [Bankstown] area, a lot of Mercedes, BMW driving Lebs, a lot of them are rich builders and businessmen and uhh … Lebs built this or that company … I'm proud! There's a lot of successful Lebanese business people.

Shaheen's statement illustrates that status and prestige is attached to young Arab–Australian men who become business owners and, further, that there are in fact roadmaps in place for young Arab–Australian men who aim to achieve economic mobility. Of course, these roadmaps are less useful for the young men in this study who are more concerned to develop the right cultural capitals needed for creative careers. In fact, the tradition of business enterprise in their local communities is at odds entirely with the (generally) anti-commercialism with which artists prefer to be associated (Moore and Gibson 2013). Some informants in this study, like Nabil in Chapter 2, mentioned the discord between the trend of self-employment or the attraction to certain employment fields and youthful creative identities more generally. Nabil distinguished himself from the 'Lebs' because they tended to be more interested in math and science subjects or pursuing engineering degrees once they completed school.

Young men of other ethnic minority backgrounds and their families also hold similar views about the relationship between masculinity, vocation, and social mobility. In the Netherlands, for instance, migrant Turkish youth prefer choosing business degrees with the eventual aim of working in the banking and finance industry, attracted by the image of "working in suits in a nine to five job" (Pasztor 2012); a clear contrast to the hard physical labour and low waged jobs characteristic of their parents working experiences. Modood explains that in the United

Kingdom, Pakistani–Muslim young people are drawn to stable professional careers in medicine, law, and information technology while shying away from humanities or creative arts courses that can lead to ambiguous vocational outcomes (Modood 1993). In turn, we can interpret Ibrahim and Shaheen's suggestions that second-generation Arab–Australian young men tend to turn to entrepreneurship in order to achieve social mobility as examples of broader patterns of entrepreneurship among second-generation migrant males.

As Anthias and Cederberg (2009) have argued, self-employment is often a communal strategy to redress social inequalities. This is one way to interpret these short statements from Ibrahim, Shaheen, and Bashir. This interpretation follows Anthias' (2008) arguments that second-generation migrant youth "may be sponsored to social places" according to the intersections between ethnicity, gender, and social class whereby entrepreneurship, or specifically 'ethnic entrepreneurship', is promoted within their local communities as the obvious vocational outcome.

Arab–Australian young men with creative aspirations complicate the communal strategy of social mobility via 'ethnic entrepreneurship' (Anthias and Cederberg 2009) for several reasons. First, in the case of creative labour, it is much more challenging to explain to the family their vocational titles as they might work on a project to project basis, in the case of freelance graphic designers, or experience bouts of unemployment as they wait for their next gig, in the case of musicians and actors. Second, for film-editing specialists for example, difficulties arise not only because of the language barrier between the generations but also because, as Gill (2009) reports, "many of their job titles and work practices simply did not exist before the mid-1990s but are the outcome of the World Wide Web, and the rapid technological transformations since then" (Gill 2009, 161). These jobs are often highly sought after, they are 'cool' and the industries are 'hot' (Neff *et al.* 2005). Above all else, aspiring artists seek to synchronise their lifestyles with paid roles as they treat work as a vehicle for self-fulfilment rather than for monetary gain (Becker 1982). I explored this issue more thoroughly in Chapter 1.

In these situations, there arises a disconnection between parents and children about what actually constitutes, and what is the purpose of, paid work. This tension is an important one to explore thoroughly in the post-higher education moment as it affects the vocational trajectories of some informants. In what follows, I look at the clash between small business enterprise, or more specifically the venerated figure of the entrepreneur in local Arab–Australian communities, and specific elements of bohemian lifestyles that are central to working life in some areas of creative industries.

You can't be a hippy in Bankstown

Moore (2012) traces the history of bohemia in Australia from the nineteenth century onwards, describing how painters, writers, journalists, actors, filmmakers, and comedians have become as renowned for their controversial, eccentric lifestyles as for the subversive work they produce. What unites creatives in one field then is their ability to perform publicly an imagined, hoped for, and sometimes achieved autonomy from the market that involves style, behaviour, art, social formations, and even politics that transgress and subvert bourgeois society (Moore and Gibson 2013: 38). The eccentric lifestyles of creatives today were captured briefly in the previous chapter where I looked at how Arab–Australian youth in this study were bewildered by the notion that 'weirdness' is a middle-class capacity; their reactions are similar to that of Rose's (2001) historical overview of British writers and intellectuals of working-class backgrounds who were confronted by the 'untidiness' of artists living in the inner city who play with poverty but are never truly affected by it in any material sense.

In Chapter 3, and as Moore and Gibson (2013) have described, the eccentric lifestyles of creative workers revolve around inner city spaces. Florida (2003) in his 'bohemian index' suggests that the "organic" and "indigenous" street cultures of bohemians are clustered in cultural districts (Moore and Gibson 2003: 182). These clusters include coffee shops, restaurants, book stores, theatres, and even hybrid spaces such as book shops with tea rooms, often in "storefronts or old buildings converted from other purposes" (Moore and Gibson 2003: 183). While Florida's bohemian index is both static and superficial, it is telling of the centrality of cultural districts in the discourse of the creative industries, or what Landry (2008) calls the 'creative milieu'.

In the earliest descriptions of bohemians, many of whom were artists, it was not only the case that they moved exclusively within gritty and dishevelled inner cities, but also that they were nomads, living in "transient or transient-looking" accommodation (Eikhof and Haunschild 2006: 236). Public space played a vital role in their lives, but were not used simply to *appear* to belong to a creative class or as spaces for consumption as Florida (2003) seems to suggest, but also because coffee houses and pubs in nineteenth century Europe legitimately enabled artists to connect with other bohemians and develop collaborative projects (Eikhof and Haunschild 2006). These particular elements of bohemia, working and living in the inner city, using public spaces for work, and integrating leisure and consumption into one's vocational identity live on today but are entirely at odds with the ethos of small business enterprise in Arab–Australian communities.

The families of these informants tend not to venture out of Sydney's Western suburbs, and personal and social life is structured around the needs of the business. As Phizacklea and Ram's (1996) findings suggest, self-employment is part of the migrant desire to remain embedded within their ethnic communities; to do business "with others whom they know and trust either through kinship ties or social networks or membership of a close knit community" (Phizacklea and Ram 1996: 320). There is little separation between work and personal life, but not in the same way as creative workers whose leisure interests and vocational roles may overlap and interchange. Rather, as Fawaz, a twenty-one-year-old deejay, told me, his family regularly moved across parts of Western Sydney as his father bought and sold various milkbars or takeaway shops. His home was always nearby or located on the premises of these businesses; this undoubtedly shaped the family's everyday rituals. He explained,

> My dad would be awake at 6am, go from about 6am to 8.30 at night. I wasn't very helpful 'cause I was always doing my own thing but now I help out more in the afternoons … so anyway, my sisters would help out my mum and then my little brother he can't walk by himself from school, he was too young. So she [mum] would go pick him up at 3.30 and then they'd all go upstairs [where they lived].

The spatial features of working life for his parents are in stark contrast to the kinds of creative industries in which Fawaz wants to work. He told me that as a deejay "the ultimate would be Kings Cross. If you've made it to The Cross, you're set. I've done two gigs there but I haven't made it there … and that was exciting, that was really, wow! It's something different, this is party central!" According to my interview with Fawaz and a number of others, the most prized creative jobs tend to be located far from Bankstown, in trendy places like Kings Cross. Not everyone in this study was as enamoured by the association between creative work and inner city party scenes as Fawaz, a discussion I will return to later.

Morgan (2012: 1) has explained that,

> The metropolis has long been a central symbol in the modernist narrative of youth. In the big city young people can break free of provincialism and communal constraint, lose and remake themselves. It is the centre of bohemian life, the place where you can find your scene or tribe, where you can seek validation for being different … In so-called 'creative clusters', artists, geeks and start-up entrepreneurs mix in a highly caffeinated 24/7 public culture.

In his research he found that for aspiring musicians from the Western Suburbs of Sydney, migrating to the inner city to participate in cutting-edge music scenes was an integral component to their narratives of vocational aspiration. The young people in his study were constantly frustrated by the limited music cultures in their local areas, what they called 'covers land'. At the same time, travelling to the inner city as a visitor was challenging because of the time they would have to spend on public transport and, more importantly, because they had not yet worked out exactly who the gatekeepers were. The problem for the young people in Morgan's study was that some were still in high school and financially dependent on their parents, they could not yet relocate to the inner city and become more familiar with creative spaces. In spite of those limitations, some of his interviewees were adamant that if they had enough financial resources when they turned eighteen, they would attempt to leave their family homes permanently to develop their craft in Sydney's inner city. Morgan suggests though that these aspirations are unlikely to be realised because his informants appear trapped by financial constraints and limited cultural capitals required for them to confidently navigate through the risky terrain of bohemia.

Similar themes about the challenges of relocating to creative clusters and feeling trapped by suburbia also feature in my research. However, rather than only being marked by financial constraints, as highlighted in Morgan's study, the narratives of vocational choice-making and attitudes towards creative clusters among Arab–Australian young men in my research are underscored by a sense of discomfort with the inherently individualistic nature of bohemian living, questions around morality and concerns about downward economic mobility. In fact, while the young men in this study were emphatic in their proclamations of creative passions, they were reluctant to engage in the kinds of personal reinvention that seems so attractive to other creative aspirants looking to escape, for example, 'covers land'. Youssef, for instance, responded to my provocation that it is perhaps important to leave Western Sydney to develop creative enthusiasms into a career in the following way,

> Here's the thing. If you leave Bankstown and become a Surry Hills person then ahh it kind of changes you I think. But all the art I ever want to make, I feel like I want it to stay true to where I'm from. Umm and I don't, I'm not interested if it doesn't appeal to a certain, like, a Surry Hills market.

According to Youssef, there are repercussions for migrating to bohemian clusters. The idea of remaining true to where he is from is a clear statement about the classed nature of identities and how they can be compromised in new social contexts. This is an interesting statement in light of the ways that creativity is framed by young men earlier in this thesis, particularly in Chapter 2 and 3 where I discussed the schooling cultures and higher education contexts of these informants' lives, as inseparable from desires to escape the constraints of the local community.

In many ways, their reasons for pursuing creative vocational aspirations resonate quite strongly with what Hage has termed 'existential mobility' (2009). Although his is a discussion of the role of affect in transnational migration, I would suggest we can apply his arguments to the kind of migration undertaken by Arab–Australian, Western Sydney young men seeking to escape their local communities both physically and imagined. Hage says, for instance, that "people migrate because they are looking for a space that constitutes a suitable launching pad for their social and existential self. They are looking for a space and a life where they feel they are going somewhere as opposed to going nowhere" (Hage 2009: 98). Indeed, in many case studies explored in this book, creative self-expression is one of the few or only ways that any kind of mobility, a feeling of going somewhere, is achievable under familial and communal surveillance.

The primary difference is that in earlier chapters I was dealing with these young men's memories while they were still in school or in university, financially dependent on their parents and uncertain about their future vocational pathways. It was, I would suggest, easier for Youssef and others to claim that creativity was woven into a lifelong project to disembed from the ethnic community because these claims did not have to be supported by their actions; they existed only as hopes and aspirations. In the post-higher education moment of these young men's lives, the language of passion and personal self-satisfaction disappears and is instead replaced with the language of entrepreneurship and a growing attraction to small business enterprise because of, on one hand, the realisation that disembedding from the local ethnic community via creativity is fraught with pitfalls. The stakes are high and questions around 'authenticity' appear, for example, making it much more challenging for many to throw themselves into the centre of the highly unfamiliar terrain of bohemian life where the prospect of exclusion and/or prejudice is likely.

In my study, only one person out of the twenty that were interviewed rebelled against the Arab–Australian tradition of living at home until marriage in favour of migrating to the city in order to pursue his creative enthusiasms. That only one informant made this move illustrates the extent to which Arab–Australian young men in this study shy away from the lifestyles associated with creative work. Walid, who worked in community arts as a digital media producer and teacher, left home in his early twenties, after completing his degree, to live in a "mouldy little apartment in Stanmore that made my father sick". Undoubtedly this was a source of contention in the family as Walid's parents became increasingly frustrated that their university-educated son had chosen this lifestyle for himself while he worked in the community arts scene. What his parents cannot see, of course, is that these living conditions, while they may be uncomfortable for many reasons, are a rite of passage for young urban Australians. In Walid's case, he said

> I was the first person on either side of my family, out of all these cousins, and these are huge *huge* families we're talking about, to move out before marriage. And not even with a girlfriend I was going to marry! Just a mate I worked with and a random stranger. It was shocking for them and to this day they still ask when I'm coming back home. I think they [my parents] both made a decision to be supportive of me, which is wonderful, but occasionally I'll notice dad get the shits with something. Like when he found out how little I was earning he just looked at me and said, 'you do all those hours and you get paid only that much?' And it really made him angry .... he doesn't get it.

Earlier, I discussed in detail the predominant ways in which Arab–Australian young men achieve social mobility, that is, through self-employment or small business enterprise. I asked Walid whether his father offered him any such career advice to which he said,

Walid: Sometimes he says to me 'why don't you take what you do and start up your own business?' He says that, my uncle says that, they say it all the time. Yep. Especially my uncle. My dad tries not to interfere anymore but I think that's my mum saying to him not to interfere anymore. But the thing is, in my role I get to help facilitate and help a bunch of young people being able to tell their story artistically right?

Sherene: Yeah

Walid: But that doesn't translate. They don't get it. 'What's the point?' And I'm like, 'here's the point, they're expressing themselves they're given a voice', all these things that art is for ... which is the highlight of my

> job, I love it and they just don't get the point. They're shocked that I get paid anything to do it.

The tension between Walid and his father is therefore not simply that he migrated out of the family home, although as he says this was quite surprising for them. Rather, there are two interrelated issues. First, creative lifestyles seriously undermine communal ideas of ethnicised masculinity and migrant aspirations for social mobility – Walid simply does not get paid enough for his father to understand his motivation for this line of work. As a migrant, the purpose of work is understood in economic terms. By contrast, Walid as a creative worker is driven by personal satisfaction of facilitating art projects among disadvantaged youth. More broadly then, this exchange reveals yet again how creativity and bohemianism as abstract concepts are simply not translatable to the ethnic public.

It is also interesting to note that Walid's exchange with his father demonstrates a level of confidence in his personal creative aspirations that none of the others in this study display. It is difficult to offer a simple conclusion about this, but his experience certainly serves as a reminder of the heterogeneous nature of ethnic communities. On the whole though, most informants who had completed their further education framed bohemia in problematic terms and referred to the local culture of self-employment in specific industries, as well as localised ideas about work and respectability, to explain this.

Being responsible, staying away from the bad stuff

Ali, an aspiring RnB singer, told me he was frustrated with the Australian music scene because it was too easy to "slip into bad stuff very very easy 'cause you start to get these things very easily. The girls, the drugs, the alcohol – I've seen it all. I've seen the dirty side of it". Rather than adhere to the unspoken rules of the music scene, he attempts instead to clearly separate his craft from creative *lifestyles* more generally, saying "I just tell myself, I am in it for the passion of singing not for anything else. Because I don't want to do something that's like ... bad you know?" His views of creative identities can be distinguished from Morgan's (2012) account of the geography of bohemian life; that is, he does not need to be physically mobile in order to be socially mobile. This is, of course, a discursive construction, a means by which he can seemingly maintain his creative sense of self and uphold particular codes of morality. Whether this is a viable solution is yet to be seen. I caught up with Ali twelve months after our interview and he was still struggling to land a record deal while some of his friends who had "slipped into the bad stuff" had actually achieved much more success in having their music produced and played on the airwaves.

Mahmoud, a twenty-one-year-old sports psychology student who had once aspired to be an actor also spoke about the irreconcilability of the rituals and social networking practices of the acting world and his Islamic values. It was not that he was coerced by his parents to following Islamic rules, although he undoubtedly experienced some pressure, but rather his religious views were a cherished element of his identity. He said of a recent theatre show he was involved in,

Mahmoud: So it was good money but after that … like it was good but it was also bad. Every night they were drinking and I do none of that. So I said after this I'm not doing no more.
Sherene: Right, you couldn't just hang out without drinking?
Mahmoud: I did but they pressure you. Girls throw themselves at you, it's a big test. It is a struggle.
Sherene: Yeah and obviously like the more you go hang out with them, the more likely you are to get the next job, is that how it works?
Mahmoud: Yeah. Or like for example from that, um, I had another job that opened up 'cause they seen me, like there's a lot of people around …. I did a few commercials as well but I guess they were my days.
Sherene: You don't want to pursue acting?
Mahmoud: No.
Sherene: Why not?
Mahmoud: I was passionate about it and I did a few courses, like two six month courses. It was like once a fortnight and you had to go home and rehearse so it was alright. But at the end of it all, it's not my scene.
Sherene: So the actual work you like but the after bits, going out, you didn't like?
Mahmoud: Yeah.
Sherene: Are you frustrated by that? Like would you like to pursue acting but you feel like "it's against my values, it's against my morals"?
Mahmoud: Yes! That's what I was gonna say. Yeah that's the way I thought about it 'cause it did, it got to me. Like, people were like, "we saw you on Home and Away" and "we saw you on Underbelly" and it gets to someone eventually! I didn't want to lose my values or my principles, in other words, lose my religion.

What I take from both of these stories about the separation between creative work and creative lifestyles is that they are driven by the unspoken rules of what constitutes culturally acceptable behaviour. They point to the intersections not simply between ethnicity and vocation but between the codes of morality developed within migrant communities and the lifestyles associated with particular vocational choices. The problem, as Bauman (1993) suggests in his discussion of postmodern ethics, is that it has become increasingly difficult for the individual to know which sets of rules or guidelines they ought to follow as they strive to create a life of their own. He says,

> There are too many rules for comfort: they speak in different voices, one praising what the other condemns. They clash and contradict each other, each claiming the authority the others deny. The choice is not between following the rules or breaking them, as there is no one set of rules to be obeyed or

> breached. The choice is, rather, between different sets of rules and different authorities preaching them … With the pluralism of rules, the moral choices appear to us intrinsically and irreparably ambivalent.
>
> (Bauman 1993: 21)

Some informants faced exactly this crisis in their narratives of creative vocational aspirations. I offered some detail about this in Chapter 2 where the tension between aspiration and obligation was explored – Anthony, for example, said he often had "two voices in my mind" about his post-schooling decisions and his concern for the future of his father's business. However, Ali appeared to have overcome the confusion experienced because of the divergent logics – between the expectations of the migrant community and the demands of creative lifestyles. The way he negotiated the clashing and contradictory rules that Bauman has noted above, was by placing a time limit on how long he was willing to pursue his ambitions to becoming a recording artist. He modelled this time limit on the experiences of his father, who also happened to be a musician in his youth.

Sherene: If you were to get married and have kids, would you be content to stop making music, to not keep going with the music career?

Ali: I probably won't be. But if I get married at least I can say to myself, I tried everything I can. Until I try everything, I can't give up. If I get married and I know that I tried everything and nothing ever came from it, that's when I can be alright. I mean, you have to remember, my dad was an amazing musician and he gave it up for religion as well. He wanted to get married and do things right. He didn't want to keep following the music.

Based on Bauman's account of choice-making in a postmodern world, we see that on the one hand the pull to creative work is strong but offers no templates for how to balance passion with family and personal life. On the other hand, Ali has a clear template from his father's experiences of what kinds of choices should be made in this case and at what stage of life they should be made. In a risk society characterised by 'fateful moments' (Giddens 1991), Ali's vocational aspirations are potentially less likely to be realised because he cannot take "leave of the past, of traditional ways of doing things" and open himself up to a "problematic future" (Giddens 1991: 111) but one that is undoubtedly more closely aligned with how the majority of creative aspirants live.

Likewise, in a discussion of existential mobility, Hage (2005) says that people want to feel that they are 'going places' not that they are stuck in a space or condition that does not allow them to realise their true self. Physical mobility, the act of migration, is in many cases undertaken so that individuals can achieve existential mobility; not the other way around. In his research, Hage found that for many, uncertainty is better than enduring their current situation because uncertainty "also means the possibility of mobility, than the perceived certainty of immobility" (2005: 474). In the case of Ali and Mahmoud, narratives of morality outweigh their interest in physical mobility to creative clusters wherein they can perhaps realise their vocational aspirations.

Of course, neither Ali nor Mahmoud's rejection of bohemian lifestyles involve explicit references to the culture of small business enterprise in their communities. However, both of their parents run, or have owned, their own small businesses. Ali's father ran a takeaway food shop in Tasmania before they relocated to Bankstown and Mahmoud's father is a retired policeman who now runs a local corner store. These particular small businesses, within the confines of Bankstown and among like-minded Arab–Australian migrants, do not compromise their sense of morality or religiosity but rather, because of their location, simply reinforces the bonds these migrants can have to their cultural traditions. As such, I would argue that both Ali and Mahmoud have been immersed in communities where vocational choices are made primarily on the basis of balancing the need to earn an income and have some financial stability with localised notions of respect and broader attachments to a religious identity; self-employment in niche ethnic markets provides the perfect opportunity for this. Ali makes this connection quite clearly, for example, when he says his father walked away from his music interests entirely in order to adhere to cultural expectations of marriage. While Ali has chosen not to replicate his father's choices by running his own shop, Mahmoud said that he would like to one day operate his own physiotherapy practice; this aspiration is one way to witness the effects of the prevalence of small business enterprise on the vocational choices of the young men in this study.

Bohemia is precarious, exclusionary, and feminised

There is widespread concern about the precarious conditions of creative labour (Hesmondhalgh and Baker 2011; Murray and Gollmitzer 2012) and especially the ways that young people are exploited, for example, by agreeing to work for little to no pay in 'cool' industries in order to increase their chances of landing paid work in the future. Numerous academics have criticised Florida's (2003) representations of the creative class, arguing that creative work does not offer a liberating lifestyle as he suggests (Peck 2005; Ross 2008). Instead, the precarity trap means that creatives generally face difficult economic circumstances in these employment fields (Throsby and Cunningham 2009; Throsby *et al.* 2003). They can often struggle to earn a living, are required to work long and irregular hours because of the highly competitive nature of their sectors and they struggle to create coherent vocational identities in the face of contract-based work that may see them in and out of paid employment as well as "episodic migration to other parts of the economy" (Murray and Gollmitzer 2012: 419). The figure of the 'starving artist' is thus a prevailing one in the literature on creative working experiences.

Very few of the informants in this study had worked for long enough in their chosen creative industries to be able to reflect on the kinds of workplace exploitation that other studies have explored. An exception to this was Haydar, who worked at a reputable film editing and multimedia company for several years after completing a course in filmmaking at a private college. He says he was paid 'peanuts' and that his wages were at the mercy of his boss who he called 'a massive tight-arse'.

Haydar: I was on wages which were good but two months later they brought everyone's wages down and you can't say much 'cause you want the experience…

Sherene: So were you like an all-rounder?

Haydar: Yeah … Like I used to work with the head editor. I used to watch him and think I can do better than him. Shit, I can do so much better! And they used to pay him so much money. I started off on 15 dollars an hour which is good and then I got taken down to 10 dollars an hour. So I used to make coffees, vacuum the place … it's just … you're young and they take advantage of you.

Haydar was lucky in that he was paid enough not to have to wait tables or resort to supplementary jobs to make ends meet. In many cases, the main source of income for aspiring artists can be totally unrelated from their creative labour (Higgs *et al.* 2007; Higgs *et al.* 2008). The structural problems of creative work are resolved internally by many artists by their affective attachments to their work as McRobbie (2004) explains

> The role of affect in creative labour and the normative expectation of the pain of insecurity, precariousness and even failure, skewers any comparison with more standard work or employment. Professed 'pleasure in work', indeed passionate attachment to something called 'my own work', where there is the possibility of maximisation of self-expressiveness, provides a compelling justification (and also a disciplinary mechanism) for tolerating not just uncertainty and self-exploitation but also for staying (unprofitably) within the creative sector and not abandoning it altogether.
>
> (McRobbie 2004: 5)

In the context of Arab–Australian communities, there are several problems with these facets of creative labour. To begin with, service and retail work are still seen as highly feminised and stigmatised in Arab–Australian communities, although this is slowly changing, especially for young men who also happen to be high academic achievers (see Wynn 2007 for in-depth discussion of the relation between service work and gender roles in Egyptian cultures for example). Retail and service work itself is not the only problem, the larger issue is that creative interests and related leisure interests are themselves treated as feminised as we witnessed in Chapter 1 when Adam described the hurt he felt when relatives questioned his sexuality for choosing to enrol in an art degree.

An additional issue is that having multiple jobs, some or all of which are unrelated, produces 'portfolio careers' or what has otherwise been called the "slashie" effect (Olding 2011). This refers to a creative worker that holds multiple titles, some of them complementary to one another but others are random jobs that simply help pay the bills. For Arab–Australian young men with aspirations for social mobility, the fractured vocational identities that result from being a "slashie" appears to parents and the extended family as a sign of failure or, to put it more gently, a sign that they are still in the transitional space between completing university and finding a 'proper job' with a stable income. Of course, creative identities can remain fragmented well into an individual's creative biography. This is now a condition of modern working life where periods of financial insecurity have become normalised, not only for creative workers, but as Beck suggests, for all people as "the specificity of the risk regime is that it firmly rules out, beyond a transition period, any eventual recovery of the old certainties of standard work [and] standard life histories" (Beck 2000: 70).

We can draw McRobbie's conclusions into a broader discussion of selfhood in late modernity. Bauman (2007), for example, has argued that the aspiration to express one's own authentic self is at the heart of individual decision-making processes across all facets of modern life. Further, Sennett (1998), who traced a small number of workers biographies, not all of whom worked in creative industries, found that contemporary life *more generally* is now highly individualistic. This is not a personal flaw, but the condition of a post-Fordist world whereby working life is "highly erratic and discontinuous rather than routine and determinate" (Sennett 2001: 183). As such, it is important to situate the conditions of creative work within the broader 'risk regime' of late modernity, as I have suggested at various points of this book. When we do, it becomes evident that this employment field exemplifies quite strongly the mandate that "the individual must be prepared to make a more or less complete break with the past, if necessary, and to contemplate novel courses of action that cannot simply be guided by established habits" (Giddens 1991: 73).

However, some informants in this study realise during the post-higher education moment that the break with the past is not necessarily aspirational because the alternative lifestyle on offer, in bohemian clusters, is either equally fraught with problems or closed to them. Hamid for instance, hesitated to embrace the ethos of bohemianism because of the exclusionary nature of creative industries. He said,

> There are a lot of people in the community sector, but the people I'm mainly talking about are artists coming from Newtown. And they're usually Anglo, middle class and privileged backgrounds and usually live in the inner city and usually live in share houses and they'll almost (pause) look down on you for having an almost normal life. Like, they'll slander you for being married at twenty-three years old.

Hamid suggests then that it is not simply the case that Arab–Australian young men perceive creative lifestyles as incompatible with migrant traditions around marriage and family, but that the gatekeepers of creative clusters themselves are unwilling to accept the lifestyles that Arab–Australian young men choose to follow as they pursue their creative ambitions. The break with the past that Giddens

(1991) suggests is integral for the reflexive self to yield a return of some sort, perhaps in the form of a new community or new space in which individuals can belong, even if fleetingly. Indeed, that is often the lure of creative clusters for many young Australians including the young men in this study as I explored in earlier chapters where I looked at their motivations for choosing particular university courses. The hope is that they will find their 'tribe' (Morgan and Ren 2012). Not so for young Arab–Australian men from Western Sydney according to Hamid.

Giddens has argued that the "security attained through sticking with established patterns is brittle, and at some point will crack" (Giddens 1991: 73). Similarly, Bauman argues that "human bonds are … frightfully unreliable, and solidarity is difficult to practice as its benefits, and even more its moral virtues, are difficult to comprehend" (Bauman 2007: 24). I would argue that the reverse is true based on the ways that Mahmoud, Ali, and Hamid have negotiated their creative vocational options. That is, the moral virtues of creative lifestyles, that can be individualistic and exclusionary, are difficult to comprehend for these young men and perhaps even more difficult to convince their families, who still have a high level of influence on their vocational choices.

Thus far, the chapter has shown how informants articulate the challenges of bohemia and the several ways in which creative lifestyles are inherently at odds with the traditions of self-employment in local Arab–Australian communities. However, it is not simply the case that these young men abandon their creative interests and passively accept the vocational templates offered to them. Rather, as I explore in the next section, some informants attempt to reconcile these divergent logics by developing their vocational identities around the figure of the creative entrepreneur.

Ibrahim

Two informants in this study, Haydar and Ibrahim, had chosen to become self-employed in niche multimedia markets. On the surface, they present these choices as ones made entirely independently of any family pressure or expectation; in fact Haydar constructs this decision as woven into a lifelong desire to "be my own boss". However, considering the earlier discussion about the presence of business enterprise as well as familial and communal rejection of bohemianism, I would suggest that these decisions demonstrate what Atkinson calls "faux reflexivity" (2010) whereby every decision is mediated by some form of social, cultural or financial pressure. Take the following example from Ibrahim about opening up his film-editing company. He said,

Ibrahim: My brother-in-law had a cleaning business just across the road from here. I told him what I wanted to do but I never had the initiative to do it. And one day he said, what do you think of the offices across the street? They're for lease … and I said, well, that would be great if I could get it! And then one day he walks in to our house and says to me, "you know what this is? It's your key to your new office". (Laughs)

There's no way I would've got the lease on my own being twenty, twenty-one. Yeah, twenty-one.

Sherene: And then what did you do with yourself, just walk in and say, what do I do with this space?

Ibrahim: Yeah I said to him … what do I do? I struggled at first but then I started, I learnt very quickly. I got to pick up my skills to make this work … I mean, I didn't even know how to write an invoice, I didn't know how to keep track of anything … so I had to learn that quickly.

Sherene: How did you learn that?

Ibrahim: I just kept asking questions to other people running their own business. I'm still learning today.

This is the same informant who, in Chapter 1, we heard speak about the riskiness of animation, whereby his community held concerns about the religious implications of his creative enthusiasm. He comes from a family where social mobility is clearly a priority, as is the maintenance of religious traditions and values. Thus, while entrepreneurship features in recent literature on creative labour as an exciting, aspirational pathway for creative aspirants (Henry 2007), I would argue that in Ibrahim's case, his turn to entrepreneurship indicates a retreat to a familiar, conventional pathway but one that is still distinct from the particular fields of self-employment that many of his Arab–Australian peers from Bankstown enter.

His family may not understand what he does for a living, but they are aware that he is a business owner and as Shaheen explained in the opening of this chapter, being a Lebanese business owner is a source of pride. More importantly, the ability to name yourself and to be named within one's social networks, to have a professional title, gives the impression to the ethnic community of stability and success. This kind of stability is not often afforded to creative workers in precarious industries. As such, I would argue that Ibrahim's experience of becoming self-employed, with the help from his brother-in-law, confirms Atkinson's arguments that those of socio-economic disadvantage make vocational decisions based on the fact that they simply do not have the time to "meander between options in the search for self-realization" (Atkinson 2010: 116). Bohemia by contrast is characterised by the ability to meander between various cultural and creative scenes as well as probing and playing with consumerism (Moore and Gibson 2013: 39) in the hopes of finding one's true calling.

Haydar

The other informant who went into self-employment, Haydar, applied his film-making skills to specialise in multimedia and advertising. Instead of admitting that his work does not predominantly involve creative-based tasks, he reworks the definition of creativity to suit his current employment situation. After a long discussion about how he remembers being authoritative towards other students in the schoolyard and how he considered those memories as indications of his creative personality, I asked,

Sherene: Is telling people what to do necessarily creative?

Haydar: Yes it is. I'll tell you why. There's a lot of people that can do stuff but … if you don't tell them what to do then they don't do it properly. So like from a creative mind if you're doing, say for example, you can design a logo. But say you don't know how to pitch it and apply it to different mediums then you're not doing your job. There's always got to be someone telling you, not pushing you to do something. There's people that get told what to do and people that do.

Sherene: So for you creativity … is not just the actual act of drawing or designing, it's the managing?

Haydar: It's the whole process. Like from the dullest thing to … everything.

Sherene: Hmmm right. So then would you consider someone who is an accountant, but the manager of that department as being creative?

Haydar: No. It's gotta be creative field. But if you're in a creative role in a company, you've got to apply yourself in every aspect of that company from writing the invoice, to creating the creative to sourcing the materials to … you just can't … that's, that's my role so that's how I see a creative person.

His views of what it means to be a creative worker are specific, for example that being a creative person requires the ability not only to create but also to pitch the product, do the required social networking and manage the invoices. But this description is also completely vague at the same time, for example lacking any clear definition of what actually constitutes according to him a 'creative field', and thereby falls in line with policy rhetoric that urges people to see the creativity across industries and in a variety of roles rather than adhere to older notions of the crafts artist (Florida 2003). Creativity thus operates as a floating signifier, but that is not to say that his views of creativity are not entirely of his own imagination (which of course life-history narratives can sometimes include as Zigon (2008) suggests). Rather, Haydar's claims that being his own boss makes him a creative person is facilitated by the increasingly close ties between business and creativity. As Banks and Hesmondhalgh (2009) explain, "the notion that artistic values and creative work are in profound tension with commercial values has been made to appear quaint or elitist. Now, it seems, the very best artists are also some of our most effective entrepreneurs" (Banks and Hesmondhalgh 2009: 419).

I would argue that we can also account for the shift in Haydar's creative biography – originally aspiring to be a filmmaker and then, post-compulsory schooling, choosing the route of self-employment – as an outcome of interrelated issues and challenges. First, we can situate his articulations that telling people what to do is creative as a way he can reconcile the fact that his creative vocational trajectory did not go the way he originally envisioned, as "being like Steven Spielberg, holding an Oscar in my hands". Apart from the obvious fact that such an aspiration is a remote possibility for anyone, Haydar experiences moments of reckoning early in his working life within his local community that sway him from pursuing this goal. Within an ethnic community where business ownership is normalised and seen as the most conventional way for young men to achieve social mobility, he feels the pressure to turn his creative passion into a legitimate and financially viable career within a very limited amount of time.

Thus, we can situate Haydar's claims that telling people what to do is necessarily creative within broader migrant traditions of self-employment and local templates for masculine identities. Through entrepreneurship in highly specialised multimedia labour markets, both Haydar and Ibrahim manage to avoid the pitfalls of precarity, keep themselves loosely connected to their original creative aspirations, and uphold culturally acceptable views of work. In this process, notions of creativity are reinterpreted and rearticulated. However, in both Haydar and Ibrahim's case, I have not aimed to suggest that they simply reproduce older familial patterns by entering self-employment. Rather, we can see that they draw on local knowledge and exploit the opportunities for entrepreneurship in recently emerged creative sectors to try and balance competing guidelines about vocational choice-making.

Research that traces the reasons many migrants are attracted to self-employment arrive at relatively similar conclusions. Self-employment offers them protection from racial prejudice; they do not have to take on menial low-paying jobs and they can remain within a local ethnic community where social life and work become integrated (Barret *et al.* 1996; Anthias and Cederberg 2009; Song 1997). Despite the fact that this book examines the biographies of creative aspirants, this chapter has shown some intergenerational consistencies where migrants enter self-employment and their children might do the same. Haydar and Ibrahim both turned to small business enterprise as a way to avoid inequality and prejudice in mainstream creative industries although this manifests in vastly different ways in youthful cultural scenes, based on markers of style and consumption for instance, than it would have featured for their parents and older relatives. They turn to self-employment as a risk aversion strategy to avoid the challenges of creative labour.

The findings of this chapter are distinctive from other research on creative labour in that the risks I have explored here are related to these young men's fears about losing the respect of their families and extended networks and straying too far from communally-defined codes of morality. Further, while the trend of creative entrepreneurship has been examined in a number of studies as a way to understand the relation between business and creativity, the case studies presented here signal a return to community for some young men after their short-lived and brutal experiences traversing the youthful creative scenes during university and the inner city bohemian clusters more generally where they feel unwelcomed and uncomfortable.

Conclusion

There are several interrelated themes that I aimed to develop across this chapter. The first was to explore the ways that creative clusters, which I argue is central to the development of a creative biography, are experienced by Arab–Australian young men. I showed how they evaluated creative lifestyles found in the inner city in moral terms – as lifestyles that are corrosive to their religious and cultural traditions. I also showed how creative lifestyles are seen as individualistic, but more so, as co-opting one's sense of authenticity. This sense of authenticity, I argued, was tied in to an original class-based identity; a working-class migrant identity that was compromised when these Arab–Australian creative aspirants tried to manoeuvre their way through the scenes of Surry Hills, Newtown, and even Paddington. Finally, I aimed to show how the traits of creative living exemplify some of the central claims of theories of late modernity according to Giddens and Bauman. The point of situating creative lifestyles within these theoretical frameworks was to show the value of examining creative industries and creative labour – that it is no longer on the fringes of our economy, but as Garnham (2005) says, at its very core.

While tracing attitudes and experiences within creative lifestyles may seem removed from a discussion of 'ethnic entrepreneurship', I have aimed in the second half of this chapter to argue that engaging in business enterprise in niche multimedia sectors is simply one response to the challenges of bohemianism. It is not the only response of course, but as there are so few informants who had moved beyond being aspirants and held vocational titles it is difficult in this book to capture all the various kinds of responses Arab–Australian young men with creative aspirations have towards the challenges of bohemianism. Nonetheless, in the latter sections of this chapter it was revealed that the creative vocational aspirations of these Arab–Australian young men, while originally represented by informants as deviant and rebellious, can actually fall in line quite easily with existing templates for social mobility in communal terms.

Overall, we can see that the predominant way in which these young men narrate their working experiences is in relation to familial concerns about social mobility and upholding culturally acceptable templates for masculinity. Moreover, it is at this point in the life-history interviews that they cease to speak of passion and individual pursuits for creative identities, or in Haydar's case, rearticulate entrepreneurship to be an integral component of their creative passions. Most commonly, informants situate their creative vocational aspirations within the migrant traditions of business enterprise. In terms of tracing the creative vocational trajectories of this group of Arab–Australian young men, this shift or break in the life-history narratives is a very important one to capture. It means that creativity and creative identities more generally undergo, in this life moment and in the context of these creative clusters, radical transformation. Following Atkinson (2010), the chapter has aimed to show that this kind of transformation of what creativity means and what it can offer these young men in their attempts to achieve social mobility, is not one that reflects individual agency, but is the outcome of the intersections of cultural and social expectations as well as material restraints.

References

Anthias, F. (2008) 'Thinking through the lens of translocational positionality: An intersectionality frame for understanding identity and belonging', *Translocations: Migration and Social Change* 4(1): 5–20.

Anthias, F. and M. Cederberg (2009) 'Using ethnic bonds in self-employment and the issue of social capital', *Journal of Ethnic and Migration Studies*, 35(6): 901–917.

Atkinson, W. (2010) 'The myth of the reflexive worker: Class and work histories in neoliberal times', *Work, Employment, Society*, 24(3): 413–429.

Aytar, V. and J. Rath (2012) *Selling Ethnic Neighborhoods: The Rise of Neighborhoods as Places of Leisure and Consumption*, New York, Routledge.

Banks, M. and D. Hesmondhalgh (2009) 'Looking for work in creative industries policy', *International Journal of Cultural Policy*, 15(4): 415–430.

Barrett, G., T. Jones, and D. McEvoy (1996) 'Ethnic minority business: Theoretical discourse in Britain and North America', *Urban Studies*, 33(4–5): 783–809.

Bauman, Z. (1993) *Postmodern Ethics*, Oxford, Blackwell.

Bauman, Z. (2007) *Liquid Times: Living in an Age of Uncertainty*, Cambridge, Polity.

Beck, U. (2000) *Risk Society: Towards a New Modernity*, London, Sage Publications.

Becker, H. (1982) *Art Worlds*, Berkeley, University of California Press.

Christopherson, S. (2009) 'Working in the creative economy: Risk, adaptation, and the persistence of exclusionary networks', in *Creative Labour: Working in the Creative Industries*, Eds. A. McKinlay and C. Smith, Basingstoke, Palgrave Macmillan, pp. 72–91.

Collins, J. (2003) 'Cultural diversity and entrepreneurship: Policy responses to immigrant entrepreneurs in Australia', *Entrepreneurship & Regional Development*, 15(2): 137–149.

Collins, J., K. Gibson, C. Alcorso, S. Castles, and D. Tait (1995) *A Shop Full of Dreams: Ethnic Small Business in Australia*, Leichardt, N.S.W, Pluto Press.

Eikhof, D. and A. Haunschild (2006) 'Lifestyle meets market: Bohemian entrepreneurs in creative industries', *Creativity and Innovation Management*, 15(3): 234–241.

Florida, R. (2003) *The Rise of the Creative Class: and How it's Transforming Work, Leisure, Community and Everyday Life*, North Melbourne, Vic Pluto Press.

Garnham, N. (2005) 'From cultural to creative industries: An analysis of the implications of the "creative industries" approach to arts and media policy making in the United Kingdom', *International Journal of Cultural Policy*, 11(1): 15–29.

Giddens, A. (1991) *Modernity and Self-Identity*, Cambridge, Polity.

Gill, R. (2009) 'Creative biographies in new media: Social innovation in web work', in *Creativity, Innovation and the Cultural Economy*, Eds. P. Jeffcutt and A. Pratt. London and New York, Routledge, pp. 161–178.

Hage, G. (2005) 'A not so multi-sited ethnography of a not so imagined community', *Anthropological Theory*, 5(4): 463–475.

Hage, G. (2009) 'Waiting out the crisis: On stuckedness and governmentality', in *Waiting*, Ed. G. Hage. Melbourne, Melbourne University Press, pp. 97–106.

Henry, C. (2007) *Entrepreneurship in the Creative Industries: An International Perspective*, Cheltenham, UK, Edward Elgar Publishing.

Hesmondhalgh, D. and S. Baker (2011) *Creative Labour: Media Work in Three Cultural Industries*, Abingdon, Oxon, Routledge.

Higgs, P., S. Cunningham, and H. Bakhshi (2008) 'Beyond creative industries: Mapping the creative economy in the United Kingdom', London, National Endowment for Science, Technology and the Arts (NESTA).

Higgs, P., S. Cunningham, and J. Pagan (2007) 'Australia's creative economy: Basic evidence on size, growth, income and employment', QUT, pp. 1–50.

Ho, C. and C. Alcorso (2004) 'Migrants and Employment: Challenging the success story', *Journal of Sociology*, 40(3): 237–259.

ldrich, H. E. and R. Waldinger (1990) 'Ethnicity and entrepreneurship', *Annual Review of Sociology*, 16(1): 111–135.

Landry, C. (2008) *The Creative City: A Toolkit for Urban Innovators*, London, Routledge.

Light, I. H. and S. J. Gold (2000) *Ethnic Economies*, San Diego, Academic Press.

McRobbie, A. (2004) 'Creative London-creative Berlin: Notes on making a living in the New Cultural Economy', in *Atelier Europe: Creative Labour in New Cultural Economies*, Munich: 1–22.

Modood, T. (1993) 'The number of ethnic minority students in British higher education: Some grounds for optimism', *Oxford Review of Education*, 19(2): 167–182.

Moore, T. (2012) *Dancing with Empty Pockets: Australia's Bohemians Since 1860*, Sydney, Pier 9/Allen and Unwin.

Moore, T. and M. Gibson (2013) 'Fringe to famous: Bohemians, entrepreneurs, audiences and the enabling state', *Asia Pacific Journal of Arts and Cultural Management*, 10(1): 35–47.

Morgan, G. (2012) 'Leaving "covers land": Creative aspiration and social class in Sydney's western suburbs', paper presented at *Cultural Studies Association of Australasia conference*, Sydney, 4–6 December.

Morgan, G. and X. Ren (2012) 'The creative underclass: Introduction to special issue,' *Journal of Urban Affairs*, 34 (2): 127–130.

Murray, C. and M. Gollmitzer (2012) 'Escaping the precarity trap: A call for creative labour policy', *International Journal of Cultural Policy*, 18(4): 419–438.

Neff, G., E. Wissinger, et al. (2005) 'Entrepreneurial labor among cultural producers: "Cool" Jobs in "hot" industries', *Social Semiotics*, 15 (3): 307–334.

O'Connor, J., S. Cunningham, and L. Jaaniste (2011) 'Arts and creative industries- An Australian conversation', [Report] Australian Council for the Arts.

Olding, R. (2011) 'Straddle, not struggle, as slashies prove ultimate multi-taskers', *Sydney Morning Herald*, retrieved from http://www.smh.com.au/national/straddle-not-struggle-as-slashies-prove-ultimate-multitaskers-20110422-1drhg.html#ixzz1XFHHJt1X

Pasztor, A. (2012) 'Imagined futures: Why business studies dominate the higher education choices of second-generation Turks in the Netherlands', *Ethnic and Racial Studies*, 35 (4): 704–717.

Peck, J. (2005) 'Struggling with the creative class', *International Journal of Urban and Regional Research*, 29(4): 740–770.

Phizacklea, A. and M. Ram (1996) 'Being your own boss: Ethnic minority entrepreneurs in comparative perspective', *Work, Employment & Society*, 10(2): 319–339.

Rose, J. (2001) *The Intellectual Life of the British Working Classes*, London, Yale University Press.

Ross, A. (2008) 'The new geography of work: Power to the precarious?', *Theory, Culture & Society*, 25(7–8): 31–49.

Sennett, R. (1998) *The Corrosion of Character: The Personal Consequences of Work in the New Capitalism*, New York, Norton.

Sennett, R. (2001) 'Street and office: Two sources of identity', in *On the Edge: Living with Global Capitalism*, Eds. W. Hutton and A. Giddens. London, Vintage.

Song, M. (1997) 'Children' labour in ethnic family businesses: The case of Chinese take-away businesses in Britain', *Ethnic and Racial Studies*, 20(4): 690.

Taylor, S. and K. Littleton (2006) 'Biographies in talk: A narrative-discursive research approach', *Qualitative Sociology Review*, 2(1): 22–38.

Throsby, C. and V. Hollister (2003) *Don't Give Up Your Day Job: An Economic Study of Professional Artists in Australia*, Surry Hills, Australia Council.

Throsby, D. and S. Cunningham (2009) *Artist Careers: Do You Really Expect to Get Paid?: An Economic Study of Professional Artists in Australia: What is Your Other Job?: A*

Census Analysis of Arts Employment in Australia, Surry Hills, Australia Council for the Arts.

Wynn, L. L. (2007) *Pyramids & Nightclubs: A Travel Ethnography of Arab and Western Imaginations of Egypt, from King Tut and a Colony of Atlantis to Rumors of Sex Orgies, Urban Legends About a Marauding Prince, and Blonde Belly Dancers*, Austin, University of Texas Press.

Zigon, J. (2008) *Morality: An Anthropological Perspective*, Oxford, Berg.

5 Politicised ethnic performativities

In this chapter, I look at how some creative aspirants of Arab–Australian backgrounds become involved in community politics; around issues of ethnicity, racism, and representations of an 'authentic' cultural group. In a multicultural framework, artists of ethnic minority backgrounds are usually offered marginal spaces in which to express themselves. They are called upon to act as cultural brokers or offer representations of their supposedly neatly bounded communities in the name of social inclusion (Werbner 1997). In light of this position of marginality, the aim of this chapter is to address the ways in which the creative biographies of some young men in this study become shaped both by processes of racialisation and multicultural discourses.

In contrast with earlier chapters, I do not examine how familial and communal dynamics constrain creativity; nor do I focus on how being uncomfortable in unfamiliar social environments, such as university, pulls these Arab–Australian youth back to familiar vocational templates, such as creative entrepreneurship. Instead, the chapter will argue that processes of racialisation produce specific vocational identities, namely that of the ethnic minority, community artist who use their creative forms of expression in order to redress social inequalities. I suggest that this particular vocational trajectory is in part indicative of the classed, exclusionary, and hierarchical nature of the creative industries and, further, that this trajectory speaks more broadly to contemporary issues of ethnic and class prejudice.

In 2011, a Western Sydney youth-based community arts organisation hosted an internationally recognised hip hop artist, Yassin the Narcicyst. Yassin, who came from a Canadian–Iraqi Muslim background mentored young people aged twelve to twenty-five years over a two-month period, helping them write and produce original songs. These workshops culminated in a showcase at the community centre where the students and Yassin performed to an audience of family, friends, local politicians, and the general public. Yassin was the emcee of the evening and began the show by explaining his professional background as a hip hop artist and activist for global Arab issues, such as racial profiling. He also told us how he worked as an academic specialising in race relations. He told the audience of his instant affection for Western Sydney because of its cultural diversity and how it reminded him of the cultural mix in his home town. He then invited the audience to "raise your hand if you're an immigrant". Few people did so. Yassin tried again, this time adding “don’t be kidding yourselves now”. Nearly all the audience members did so the second time around. Introducing the first act, he said, “Our performers are going to rap about their lives as new migrants in Australia so please keep your hands up!”

Twelve acts performed that evening, all of them regular high school students with little to no music producing experience. They came from a wide variety of ethnic and religious backgrounds and most told stories that spoke to their everyday adolescent experiences. Some of the content was political, for example, a young hijab-wearing Muslim woman rapped about exclusion and discrimination. Generally, there was a strong connection between the youth’s ethnic identities and the content of their songs, which is understandable given that an aim of the community organisation is to empower disadvantaged youth by training them in music production, performance, design, and writing. Over the course of my fieldwork, as an observer of various local community workshops, I found it is interesting how categories such as ethnicity and ‘migrant’ were often called upon in these settings as one of the major subjects to be dealt with in creative work. The fact that Yassin encouraged the audience to identify with a migrant background points to the tensions between the push to adopt forms of clearly-defined and perhaps essentialised ethnic identities and the forms of cultural hybridity that typify their lives.

The performances at this community arts centre and the major role Yassin played in developing the hip hop/music program prompted my interest in finding out how and why some creative vocational aspirants might be attracted to working in community arts. In this chapter, I will draw on interviews with three Arab–Australian young men– Hamid, Saad, and Walid – who, like Yassin, make their living as community artists training aspiring creative young people in various organisations across Western Sydney. Drawing on Spivak’s (1990) notion of strategic essentialism, I will suggest that working in community arts enables informants to use creativity strategically, as Yassin demonstrated, to deal with broader issues of race-relations and experiences of discrimination. In effect, I am interested in the ways that those who work in community arts organisations potentially become what Brubaker calls ethno-political entrepreneurs’ (Brubaker 2002: 166) who live *off,* as well as *for,* their cultural difference, in turn becoming ‘ethnic artists’.

Further, the chapter will also look at subjectively constructed notions of authenticity. It asks, how do these young men working in community arts and teaching creative skills understand authenticity, and how is it used discursively within the life-history interview? I will argue that claims to representing authentic cultural representations can be advantageous for these young men who feel there are few other ways in which they can fully realise their creative aspirations in highly competitive industries. For example, informants can, like Yassin, refer to their status as members of an Arab, Lebanese, or Muslim community to legitimise their claims about showcasing ‘authentic’ representations of the everyday experiences of Western Sydney, ethnic minority youth. Alternatively, I will suggest that being an ‘ethnic artist’ and purporting to create authentic representations of a local migrant group is constraining, as Hutnyk (2000) argues in his “critique of exotica", because it essentially means that the creative output of these young men primarily serves the purpose of feeding into the multiculturalist project of 'freezing culture'.

This interest is prompted by Dwyer and Crang's (2002) suggestion that the relationship between 'hybridity-talk and aesthetics' – the kind displayed by Yassin that night at the Information and Cultural Exchange (ICE) – needs "critical interrogation to understand why [they are] being invoked by some people, in some places and at some moments" (Dwyer and Crang 2002: 414). We might call this 'strategic hybridity' following the work of Noble *et al.* (1999), but the focus in this chapter is not about how Arab–Australian young men perform attachments to an original migrant background and also to a sense of Australian-ness to establish their belonging within specific cultural domains, as these authors have already argued. Rather, I am concerned with how informants invoke authenticity as a resource for 'political mobilisation' (Spivak 1990: 60); as representatives of their local communities. In effect, their work as community artists means that they must re-evaluate their local communal attachments and whether creativity can be mobilised for social mobility in the ways they originally hoped.

The road to community arts: Exploitation, essentialism, and racialisation

Hamid, as I noted in earlier chapters, was twenty-five years old and worked in a local community arts organisation in Bankstown. His primary role there was as the editor of a literary magazine but he was also responsible for running creative writing workshops, as well as facilitating in-school writing programs with high school students who had been identified as 'talented' by their English teachers. Before becoming a community arts worker, Hamid tried his hand at acting but tells me that this was a short-lived pursuit. When I asked why, he said,

> I have been exploited. I've done a few TV shows. But people go, "oh, you have done stuff on TV" .... And, like, I was in East West 101, which was a big show. But, you know what? I played a drug dealer and it's like, that's really crap. But the problem is that that's something that a lot of people go, "hey I saw you in that" ... but it's like, I'm actually ashamed of that. I don't want people to say "hey I saw you in that". I'll never play a drug dealer ever again.

It appears here that Hamid is pointing out two interrelated problems that occurred in his attempt to make a living as an actor. The first is the problem of typecasting, where Arab–Australian young men are more likely to be offered roles that actually perpetuate negative stereotypes because, naturally, they are more believable in those roles due to their appearance. He is uncomfortable in this role because he is aware of the damage that these negative associations – between Arab–Australian young men and crime – can cause and does not want to be responsible for perpetuating these stereotypes. The other problem he notes is how playing those stereotyped roles is a source of 'shame', namely because of the negative communal attitudes towards acting and creative careers that were noted in Chapter 1. It may not be as bad as "being on *Neighbours* and getting on to some white chick" as Hamid put it earlier, but there is little depth to the characters that he has played. They are two-dimensional and further, they are generally the villain or the 'bad guy'. Unfortunately, there is a lack of cultural diversity on Australian screens (Jakubowicz and Goodall 1994; McClean 2011) and so there is a strong chance that Hamid will mostly be offered these kinds of roles, as a drug dealer. His stance, to never play that role again, therefore means that unless the Australian television industry undergoes radical changes, Hamid will be left with very few options.

Similarly, Saad, who might be called a 'slashie',[1] had been an actor, was a hip-hop artist, and had tried to become a journalist. When we met, his main interest was teaching young people of disadvantaged backgrounds how to produce their own rap songs, as one part of his role as a youth worker. I will spend more time expanding on his working experiences in each of these fields as the chapter progresses. Although Saad does not name it 'exploitation' like Hamid, he says he was also frustrated by the limited acting work available to him. He said,

> I think when the role is a criminal Arab, a lot of the time they (other actors) don't look believable. But I find that I'm such an easy target because I actually do look like I could be one. I have the tattoos and stuff so they probably think, "ok he can act and do all this other stuff so he's perfect for it". I would like to do other things though.

Interestingly, Saad had just finished filming a critically acclaimed, but somewhat controversial, television program on a nationally broadcasted channel when we met. The program was a fictionalised series about Sydney's gang wars, the participants in which generally came from Lebanese backgrounds. He had a minor role in the show but received good reviews for his performance. The show was criticised by some for the ways it was seen to glorify convicted criminals and reinforce popularly-held beliefs that Lebanese–Australian young men were responsible for the increase in gun-related crime in Sydney. There is a large body of literature that examines how media depictions of an event or group, even fictionalised ones, influence social attitudes (Jakubowicz and Goodall 1994; Jakubowicz and Seneviratne 1996; McClean 2011; Saha 2012). Most notably, Said's (1997) work about the Western portrayals of Islam shows how the media has a hand in rewriting the historical relations between the Middle East and colonial powers. The aim here is not to revisit these debates but to consider how creative aspirants from Arab–Australian backgrounds reflect on the kinds of jobs they have taken on within, in Hamid and Saad's case, media and television industries and how those jobs and these industries compromise what they say is an 'authentic' sense of self, based on local communal attachments.

Typecasting is a problem faced by many aspiring artists of ethnic minority backgrounds, and it is a problem not easily redressed by simply having more people of ethnic minority backgrounds on the screen because, as other research has shown, media producers of ethnic minority backgrounds also tell essentialist, reductive stories about their own cultural backgrounds because this is one of the few ways to establish their place within this sector (Saha 2012). This was noted by Hamid when he spoke of the problems of contemporary films that have been made by individuals of Arab–Australian backgrounds. He said,

> So 'Cedar Boys', 'The Combination' – they represent drug dealers and rapists. I don't know any drug dealers and I don't know any rapists. I've lived here (Bankstown) since I was ten years old. Do you know what I mean? But that doesn't mean that all the kids here are angels. I'm not saying they're the best kids in the world, I'm just saying that they're not drug dealers and they're not terrorists and they're not rapists.

Shaheen takes Hamid's issue further, suggesting the problem is not only type-casting and stereotyping but the lack of support for television shows or films to be made about ethnic minority characters in the first place. Shaheen is a working actor and entertainer who had been part of a popular television series created by an Arab–Australian producer that catered to a multicultural audience. He expressed his frustration at the lack of diversity on Australian television and how difficult it is for actors of certain ethnic backgrounds to be able to find work in non-stereotypical roles, even when those shows are produced by ethnic minorities themselves and even in spite of the commercial success of many films that specifically focus on ethnic minority characters. Shaheen said,

> The networks don't get behind anything, anything that's ethnic, wog projects … I've said this before but everything ethnic has worked. From 'Acropolis Now' to the 'Wog Boy' being the biggest box office takeout for a locally Australian made movie … uhh 'Fat Pizza' broke records, um 'Looking for Alibrandi', um the list goes on, 'Underbelly' the Kings cross one had an Arabic feel to it, the first one had an Italian feel and all the other ones did crap in the ratings. And I said that. The networks don't feed a multicultural country.

Shaheen and Hamid are speaking of a widespread problem. In 2012, one of Australia's longest running soap operas, *Neighbours*, introduced an Indian family to the cast. The fact that this was the first non-white family in the show's twenty-eight year history sparked widespread debate about whether Australian television is 'too white' and, relatedly, whether mainstream television programs only incorporate non-white actors in tokenistic ways which may reproduce cultural stereotypes. What Hamid is saying then is that actors of Arab–Australian backgrounds have to first overcome the limited working opportunities available to them, and second, have to be wary of falling in to the trap of reproducing what he sees are inaccurate and 'self-essentialised' (Spivak 1990: 51) representations of Arab–Australian, Western Sydney youth.

Mainstream Western media productions are littered with never-ending negative representations of Arabs and Muslims, a problem exacerbated by the events of

9/11 (Shaheen 2001). Further, Arab–Australians and Muslims have been subjected to forms of 'new racism' across social and political arenas whereby their cultural rather than (only) physical differences cause public anxiety as I explored in Chapter 2 in relation to the ways that young Arab–Australian boys are demonised and treated as a social problem. Individuals who appear to be from that background are potentially more vulnerable to racial prejudice and exclusionary practices. We can call this 'racialisation', following Miles and Brown (2003) who explain the concept to refer to "those instances where social relations between people have been structured by the signification of human biological characteristics in such a way as to define and construct differentiated collectivities" (Miles and Brown 2003: 101). Dunn (2007) uses racialisation to help explain the relations between Muslims and non-Muslims in Australia. He says, the repetitive use of well-rehearsed stereotypes, perceptions of threat, and inferiority, as well as fantasies that the Other do not belong, or are absent have coalesced to work against Arabs and Muslims in Australian society (Dunn 2007: 564). Racialisation is an important feature of the stories I have collected about Arab–Australian young men's working experience in the creative industries because while other research tends to treat exploitative practices in general terms, as relating to the conditions of creative work (Gill and Pratt 2008; McKinlay and Smith 2009), here I show how ethnic and social hierarchies in Australia additionally create specific kinds of challenges for these informants.

Saad, for example, found that networking was challenging as people were reluctant to work with him because of his Arab and Muslim background. He tells of how, while trying to promote his music at various clubs around Sydney, he felt pressured to lie about his ethnic and religious background or else risk stalling his career. He said,

Saad: My management, when they approach promoters and labels and stuff like that, a lot of times what happens is they're very interested at first because they like the music and stuff but they assume I'm Latino. We've been approached by promoters who liked my work but they'd ask "where's he from, like Puerto Rico?" My managers would be like "No, he's Arab" and they'll be like "oh umm nah we're not interested".

Sherene: Have you ever just lied about being an Arab, pretended to be a Latino?

Saad: No. My management feels that my religion and who I am and what I represent is important and I'm not gonna hide. Hiding behind – saying I'm this or that is eventually gonna come back to bite me. I've got enough faith in my talent and in God that eventually someone will ... see I don't even want to work with someone who's that narrow minded. But I tell my managers to tell them, come meet with me, let me ease their minds. If they're scared I'm gonna be overtly political, overtly religious or I'm gonna bring a thousand Lebs to smash the place up, that's fine. I don't expect everyone to know what the fuck is going on. Ignorance is everywhere, but we can sit with them and have a chat.

Sherene: Do they go for that?

Saad: Most of them don't. It's a business, I understand that.

Saad's experiences highlight the ways that ethnic identities are simultaneously classed, gendered, and sexualised, and constructed in relation to the hegemonic racialised ethnicities within the nation (Mac an Ghaill 1999). The position of the 'Arab Other' that Saad occupies is one associated with political and religious fundamentalism and extremism, physical aggression, violence, and gang-like behaviour. Ultimately then, the racialisation of Middle-Eastern cultural and religious groups threatens Saad's ability to find long-term meaningful paid work as a singer/songwriter. An irony of his experience is that hip hop is a music genre generally based on young men cultivating their image as rebellious, 'bad boys'. Australian hip-hop differs greatly from its urban US counterpart, both in the style of contemporary hip hop artists and in their lyrical content. The raps of popular Australian hip-hop group Hilltop Hoods, for example, invoke ideas of an imagined national community, a sense of monocultural Australian-ness from a youthful perspective. But it still remains that subverting social and cultural norms are a main part of this genre. Hip-hop artists in general already struggle to find a place in the Australian mainstream scene as hip-hop is a sub-genre in which not many artists enjoy widespread commercial success in Australia. Yet, based on Saad's experience, ethnic hierarchies persist that leave Arab–Australian or, perhaps more generally, non-white artists having to justify that they won't, for example, damage the property and the reputation of club venues as Saad has mentioned. His experience confirms Hutnyk's (2000) argument that being denied opportunities as a result of one's visibility "is much more than an absent-minded and myopic blindness of the dominant cultural group" (Hutnyk 2000: 115).

However, the problems Saad describes are not only the product of race relations in Australia but can also be attributed to the nature of the music industry itself. He says, "it's a business", which might imply that certain kinds of ethnic minorities are constructed as a liability, of having an "excess of culture of the wrong kind" (Lentin 2012: 7). It has been argued that those inhabiting a 'cosmopolitan habitus' (Allen and Hollingworth 2013), a habitus with the traits of flexibility, entrepreneurialism and mobility, fare best in creative industries (Banks 2007). In Chapter 3, I explored what it means to have a flexible, mobile, creative identity in the context of higher education institutions and suggested that to be truly accepted into bohemian, creative scenes, one has to become a cultural omnivore. Shape shifting in this way, however, requires a process of capital accumulation usually only achievable for middle-class creative aspirants.

Of course, in that chapter I was dealing with aspirants who had not yet entered the labour market. Here, we can see the effects of not being able to shake off the markers of a non-white, Western Sydney, Lebanese–Australian gendered identity in the world of work. We see that Saad is treated as a 'sticky subject' (Allen and Hollingworth 2013), seemingly contained by his ethnic, class, and religious background. As I outlined in Chapters 1 and 2 of this book, creativity and creative vocations are pursued by many of these young men as a way to achieve social mobility. Saad's experience reveals the limitation of such an aspiration.

Social networking is, of course, an integral component of the creative industries and one's ability to build the right kind of industry contacts is a strategy often employed by artists to improve their chances of future employment (Blair 2009; Christopherson 2009; Grugulis and Stoyanova 2012). This means that, in addition to the challenges of finding work, Saad must also overcome the negative stereotypes that follow him but, as he explains, doing so is not always possible if one does not even have access to the sector. What this exchange with Saad shows, however, is that social networking does not have the same outcome for people of different ethnic and class backgrounds. His experiences support the findings of Grugulis and Stoyanova's (2012) study of working practices of those in the television industry, where "working-class, black minority ethnics and female informants did not network any less actively than their white, male, middle-class colleagues, but they [still] had far less access to high-quality jobs" (Grugulis and Stoyanova 2012: 1326). There is a clear issue of visibility here, one that was implicit in the narratives of higher education in Chapter 3 but concealed by informants' discussions of subcultural practices, youthful style, and class privilege. Here, the correlation between ethnicity and disadvantage in mainstream creative sectors is much more pronounced.

Other informants also spoke about racial prejudice while working in creative-based jobs. Haydar, for example, worked in multimedia at a medium-sized company in Sydney's Eastern suburbs. The suburbs he refers to are some of the wealthiest in Sydney and also have a relatively large population of residents from Jewish backgrounds, especially when compared to Bankstown. Haydar came from a Lebanese–Syrian Muslim background and found that his Arabness was a problem for him in his workplace, even though he was not always immediately perceived to be from an Arab or Muslim background. He explains,

> I was working in [Sydney's East] umm a lot of our clients were Jewish so my boss had a real problem with me telling them my real name, my religion and things like that. I had certain situations where they were taken aback when they [clients] knew … I remember once a client asking me what my real name is, 'cause everyone calls me [X]. It's a nickname that my brother gave me and it just stuck. My real name is Haydar. And I'd be like "my name is actually Haydar" and they would go, "oh" – like surprised. They'd say "'where are you from?", I would go, "I'm from Australia but my parents are Syrian". And I never worked with that client again.

Sherene: So they asked your boss not to work with you in particular anymore?
Haydar: Yeah.
Sherene: Wow what did that feel like? That's tough.
Haydar: At the beginning I had a problem with it and then to the end, I thought, stuff 'em. If they're that narrow minded, stuff 'em.
Sherene: What would your boss ask you to do to cover up your identity?
Haydar: Oh he would say don't tell them. If they ask, say you're Spanish to avoid conflict. They ask me "what's your real name", "oh just say your nickname and then try and get out of the room quickly and go back to work". But I never said I was Spanish, I would just avoid them from then on.

The first thing to note is that working in multimedia is very different from being an actor or hip hop artist. Multimedia, which Haydar tells me might include creating advertisements or online marketing for various companies, is embedded in recently emerged sectors, possible through global technological advancements and designed to respond to rapidly-changing consumption and lifestyle practices. These new media sectors are often sold to young people as 'cool' and exciting, but in fact the day to day tasks are not altogether unlike business administration. The kind of work Haydar does is indeed a standard full-time job. On the other hand, actors and musicians live from job to job and are often required to have separate full-time jobs to support their creative vocational pursuits. Irrespective of these differences, there are similarities in the ways that Haydar and Saad experience racial prejudice and how they deal with those prejudicial attitudes, by saying "stuff 'em".

The refusal to lie about one's religious and ethnic heritage and, also, the refusal to work in creative sectors that are responsible for negative portrayals of Arab–Australian young men, as in Hamid's case, reveal more generally how informants negotiate the ways that creative labour often forces individuals to compromise their 'authentic' sense of self. McRobbie (2002a) spoke about this issue in relation to the kinds of 'makeovers' that working-class women experienced in their attempts to find work in the fashion industry. In my research, authenticity was often referred to in relation to the strong affiliations informants have with their migrant histories, although, of course, such affiliations are always ambivalent according to particular moments in the life history.

Hamid, for example, told me of how he often felt "ashamed" to be a member of "this [Lebanese–Australian] group" because

> they're [Lebanese–Australian young men] always complaining about how, you know, their culture and their communities are being picked on but their behaviour is just so inappropriate and unacceptable but they use the media as an excuse to say 'no you're just picking on me'. It's just so frustrating.

This kind of ambivalence is not a problem that needs to be resolved, but is in fact a state of being for hybrid subjects because dual cultural attachments are never robust or fixed but always fluid, contextual and, importantly, constructed for varying purposes rather than naturally assumed (Bhabha 1996; Bhabha 1997; Werbner 1997). Further, this ambivalence and 'shame' of being a member of the Lebanese–Australian community does not undermine Hamid's claim that television portrayals of Arab–Australian young men are problematic, but rather, indicates his 'self-imagining of community' (Werbner 1997: 230) that he draws on later to explain how he works in community arts to produce alternative representations of Western Sydney youthful experiences.

In Chapter 3, I looked at the ways that informants struggled during university as they felt out of place, uncomfortable with the youth subcultures in various institutions, and unable to perform a version of the self that they could capitalise on in their quests to become creative workers; they could not perform 'weirdness' in the same way and to the same degree as some of their fellow peers from more socio-economically privileged backgrounds. Others refused to engage in cultivating 'weird' identities as they feared that to do so could jeopardise their sense of an authentic identity. We can see parallel processes occurring in the working experiences I have noted in this chapter.

McRobbie (2002) argues that 'selling the self' is a key way that young people find their footing in contemporary creative sectors. She explains that the networking practices that have always been central to creative work have taken on new forms, where club culture sociality and the use of online spaces to perform and play with identities are now a main part of, and not incidental to, creative labour. I suggested in the previous chapter that the young men in this study struggled to sell a 'self' based on their ethnic backgrounds and residence in Western Sydney as these things cannot necessarily be capitalised on in the creative industries. The interview data I have analysed thus far in this chapter is an extension of the kinds of challenges facing Arab–Australian young men with creative aspirations that were described in Chapter 4. Their ethnic heritage is frequently 'called out' in the sectors they work in, often in very reductive and negative ways. Arabness becomes problematic and so 'selling the self' is no easy feat for these young men.

But Saad and Hamid don't simply say "stuff 'em" to deal with the prejudice they face in these creative sectors. They actually change the direction of their creative-based careers and move instead towards community arts. Similarly, Haydar also said he made a major career move after "putting up with" those experiences of racial prejudice, as I discussed Chapter 4 where I looked at his decision to become self-employed in the multimedia sector. As I argued in that chapter, there are limited ways in which these Arab–Australian young men imagine they can translate their creative passions into viable careers – entrepreneurship is one route and in this chapter we see that community arts is another arena in which Arab–Australian young men with creative skills can thrive.

It would be an oversimplification to claim that they make the move to community arts or small business enterprise *solely* because of the kinds of challenges they describe while working in creative industries, but it was implied that their experiences of typecasting and processes of racialisation were contributing factors. Saad, for instance, explained how his original aspiration to become a journalist was "shattered". While working as an unpaid intern at a national newspaper, he wrote an opinion piece as a response to the 2005 London bombings. He wrote in this piece that "terrorism in all forms is bad and should be stopped but the Israeli government bombing Palestine is also a form of terrorism that needs to be stopped". He says that after that article was published, he was called in by a senior writer who "bullied" him and who promptly published an article the following week about how Saad's "schooling and family environment had failed him". He says that, in a nutshell, the potential to land a job at that newspaper afterwards diminished drastically. I asked him to elaborate on this and he said,

> Well they had hired, they had given an internship to this white girl even though they told me there were no jobs available. (Shrugs shoulders) That fucked me up. I was done with it. I um I did a little bit more here and there, with ABC and SBS and it was fine. But I started to realise that everyone just wanted me for the Arab stories. Everything was just like, something happened in the Arab community, go investigate it. It's like, yeah I'm Muslim and my background is Arab but it's not my be all and end all.

By describing the experience of being a budding journalist to being burned in the mainstream sector to ultimately only being hired to chase 'the Arab stories' shows that while the creative industries might be characterised as 'precarious and risky' for all (Atkinson 2010), there are different manifestations of exclusion and discrimination which can ultimately be traced back to the relationship between ethnic, class, gender, and other identity-based differences. Even though Saad has a niche market he can access by pronouncing his Arab and Muslim insider status, he expresses the frustration at being contained by these categories; the interplay between ethnicity, religion, and gender are repressive for his aspirations for a creative career. His concerns about being "wanted for the Arab stories" echoes some of the findings of Hyder (2004) who investigated the affective politics of pleasure among British–Asian musicians, suggesting that they faced what Hall (1996) calls 'the burden of representation'. Hyder explains that

> whether they liked it or not the pioneering Asian bands have been forced into a spotlight where they have been analysed and identified as the representatives of a youthful Asian constituency. This mode of representation puts extra pressure on the musicians since attention is focused not just on their musical output but also on their supposed role as representatives of a 'community'.
>
> (Hyder 2004: 114)

The choice to be (or not be) an ethnic or cultural representative is denied to Saad in the creative industries in the same way that Hyder finds of his informants and as such, Saad feels his only choice is to opt out of that sector entirely.

Alternatively, the community arts scene, which I describe shortly, is a space that is appealing to young people from disadvantaged backgrounds even though it also a sector that encourages aspiring artists to emphasise and essentialise their cultural heritage. Hamid and Saad are exactly the kinds of people who thrive in the community arts scene because there is a market for creative projects that speak to an 'authentic' sense of self. However, authenticity is arguably a social construction, one fabricated by the discourses of multiculturalism as a way to manage and celebrate ethnic and religious 'difference'. Gunew (in Spivak 1990) made similar arguments some time ago, but since then, the multicultural policies and the landscape of community arts have changed. In a postmodern world, the hybrid subject is no longer unusual, so the focus here is on the impact that 'strategic essentialism' or 'strategic hybridity' can have on these young men's creative biographies. In what follows, I detail the relationship between community arts and multicultural policy in order to contextualise the broader discourses informing the kind of work in which Saad and Hamid were engaged when we spoke.

Community arts and multicultural policy: A brief background

In Australia, as in other parts of the western world, multiculturalism was a prescriptive set of policies implemented in the second half of the twentieth century to celebrate the nation's rich cultural diversity (Jayaraman 2000; Ang 2011) and to govern and manage group differences under democratic systems of law (Hage 2002; Modood 2007). The principles underlying multiculturalism are primarily based on what Modood identifies as "the politics of identity: being true to one's nature or heritage and seeking with others of the same kind public recognition for one's collectivity" (Modood 2007: 2). Central then to multiculturalism is not only state acceptance of different cultural groups but also recognition of cultural specificities in public discourse and ongoing dialogue with citizens which enables them to 'debate the terms of recognition' (Modood 2008).

Public performances of 'authentic' migrant traditions in song, dance, and storytelling are encouraged by governments as a strategy to promote cultural diversity. Harmony Day, for example, is an initiative managed by the Department of Immigration and Citizenship (DIAC) and takes place in schools, community groups, and local festivals across Australia every year on March 21st, the same day as the United Nation's International Day for the Elimination of Racial Discrimination. The initiative aims to celebrate and educate the broader public about both the specific cultural traditions and the common bonds between all Australians capturing the desire of many migrants to have their traditional culture(s) recognised in the host country, and the universalist ideal to be recognised as an equal citizen (Taylor 1994).

However, the Harmony Day initiative assumes ethnic communities are unchanging entities (Nagle 2008; Harris 2009; Ang 2011). In effect, "state multiculturalism … can work against cultural mixing up or the fundamental hybridity that diversity may produce, by attempting instead to consolidate difference" (Harris 2009: 190). This statement is supported by the active competition and division among minority groups as they seek out public funding to deal with community affairs (Nagle 2008; Jayaraman 2000). This trend, alongside broader globalisation and the rise of the figure of the 'cosmopolitan' has prompted some academics to question whether multiculturalism has a place in twenty-first century politics (Modood 2007). In the United Kingdom, some have gone as far as announcing the death of multiculturalism (Parekh 2001; Back 2009), others characterise current times as post-multicultural (Ang 2011), while others still argue for an emphasis on interculturalism or cosmopolitanism to counter the pitfalls of multiculturalism as an ideology that has facilitated social fragmentation and entrenched social divisions (for a further discussion of these debates see Meer and Modood 2012; Wieviorka 2012; Brahm Levey 2012).

Perhaps we can understand these 'post-multicultural' sentiments as a reflection of the shift in academic discourse away from assuming that ethnic groups only hold dual attachments between the homeland and host country to recognising that the diasporic experience is one that consists of multilayered, multi-spatial attachments, and that ethnic groups are internally differentiated in terms of class and religious hierarchies (Hage 2000; Levitt 2011; Modood 2011). The rhetoric around the demise of multi-ethnic or multicultural states cannot erase the fact that Australia and other western nations like the United Kingdom continue to be comprised of a wide variety of ethnic and cultural groups that are "more or less open communities, bounded by real but relatively vague ties of affection, collective memory and common interests" (Parekh, 2001: 693).

In earlier conceptions of migration and diaspora, migrant groups were characterised as having journeyed from one place to another in a linear fashion (Clifford 1994). Now, both policy and academic discourse recognise that diasporas are not bound by nation-states but are part of a transnational order wherein migrants "pivot back and forth between sending, receiving and other orientations at different stages of their lives" (Levitt 2011: 41). An awareness of these movements has left political commentators in Australia and elsewhere criticising multiculturalism on the grounds that notions of nationhood have been jeopardised by these divisive policies that produce citizens who demonstrate a weak sense of allegiance to the host country.

Beyond celebrating diversity and allowing migrants to retain their traditions and cultural traits, multiculturalism has also been conceptualised as welfare and a structural socio-economic policy (Hage 2002). Considering many new migrants from non-English speaking backgrounds face economic difficulties on arrival and beyond, multiculturalism was thought to be a way to combat social disadvantage by implementing strategies to help migrants navigate the bureaucracies of the housing, legal, and education departments. In Western Sydney, local community organisations use government funding to assist youth, women, newly arrived refugees, and non-English speaking migrants find employment opportunities, suitable housing, interpreter services, and other basic needs. Additionally, this funding is also granted in order to assist ethnic groups retain their cultural heritage and manage multiple levels of attachment. For the second and third-generation migrant youth who participated in this study, this type of cultural preservation is not such a pressing issue. Rather, because of the negative stereotypes that surround Lebanese–Australian communities and the fact that many have been victims of discrimination in schools and elsewhere during their youth, multiculturalism operates as a way to redress this type of social exclusion. By the same token, I would suggest that particular kinds of social exclusion in areas such as the creative industries are actually produced by the discourses of multiculturalism, for instance, as actors of ethnic minority backgrounds are more likely to be offered stereotypical roles that contribute to the vilification of young men of their communities.

The arts have been identified by local and state governments as a valuable way to deal with youth issues at a grassroots community level and this includes racial vilification and social exclusion on racial grounds. In 2006, Arts New South Wales (NSW) (the peak government arts policy and funding body in NSW) published a progress report on the Western Sydney Arts Strategy. Over the last ten years, Arts NSW has aimed to develop infrastructure to support cultural developments in the region, to increase local government investment in arts and cultural activities, and to increase the numbers of Western Sydney residents employed in cultural industries. In Bankstown, $5 million dollars has been spent specifically to build a new arts centre, and a further $1.5 million dollars has been secured to implement arts programs in the local area.[2] The report makes clear that the substantial amount of funding reflects a commitment to the arts sector, as a way to build a creative city in line with the rhetoric that creative cities drive the local economy, and finally as a way to address issues around 'community'.

ICE, a local community arts centre in Parramatta – a nearby city in Western Sydney – have also adopted notions of community in their policy framework. They say their aim is to develop and deliver "a range of community-determined creative projects that target disadvantaged, disengaged and vulnerable communities across Western Sydney. The purpose of this work is to build social cohesion, community confidence, and facilitate cultural expression and opportunity".[3] In 2009, they developed a program with a local high school called 'Digi Diaries'. This program was aimed specifically at "young people from Western Sydney's Muslim communities" with the aim of enabling newly arrived refugees and migrants with an exciting and innovative way to explore their emotional journeys, some of which were quite traumatic. The outcome of this particular program was a short book which contained many of the stories in print and a DVD that captured the stories with voiceovers by the students.

The project coordinator said of 'Digi Diaries' that "aside from being a platform for individual voices, the project was an important contribution in community building and bridging the gap of misconceptions and stereotypes between Muslim groups and other groups in the community at large".[4] In this rationale, we can see these programs are designed to do more than just provide young people with creative skills, but are also committed to the broader project of multiculturalism and social inclusion. This is a common theme among the community arts programs I observed during my fieldwork.

Capturing 'authentic' voices

Communities are not natural entities simply made up of families, neighbourhoods, and ethnic groups, but are actually sites of political contestation (Collins 2010). The language of community is central to multiculturalism because "the construct of community has long been associated with women, ethnic groups, non-Western peoples, poor people, religious minorities and similarly subordinated groups" (Collins 2010: 10). As such, community arts programs can be thought of as intermediaries between state policies and local peoples. Within community arts programs in Western Sydney, artists from various ethnic groups are likely to explore issues of identity, difference, social exclusion, and cross-generational clashes in their creative works. Community arts facilitators – those responsible for designing and organising workshops and programs to provide socio-economically disadvantaged youth with creative training skills – regularly encourage young people to engage in expressions of ethnicity and narrate their diasporic experiences. These organisations have played an important function in advancing the project of multiculturalism in Australia by promoting anti-essentialist, hybrid, and creolised views of culture and ethnicity. But issues of social exclusion, Otherness, and narratives of belonging within the nation dominates much of the content produced by young people participating in community arts programs in Western Sydney, demonstrating the politicised nature of the production of creative work among artists of marginalised ethnic groups.

For instance, I attended several writing workshops run by Hamid and another community arts worker in a local public high school. Ten students from year eight participated in this program, selected by their English teachers as the best writers in their year group. The experience of working with published authors was intended to help sharpen their writing skills. Because of the school's location in the Western suburbs of Sydney, the group of students was a multicultural one, made up of students from Lebanese, Syrian, Samoan, Vietnamese, and Anglo backgrounds.

At the first writing workshop I attended, one of the community workers began the hour session by reading a poem she had published recently, which dealt with her experience of moving from a suburb in Sydney's West to the inner city suburb of Newtown. She spoke of how the move impacted on her sense of identity; she was poked fun at by her fellow inner city friends for having lived in an area stereotyped as dangerous and "too ethnic". The poem had a humorous tone but the students did not laugh, forcing the artist to explain some of the cultural references in the text and further, explain that there are differences between Newtown and parts of Western Sydney. After a lengthy silence, a young man from a Samoan background raised his hand and asked "Where is Newtown?" After the class, one of the community workers told me they had not anticipated such a limited knowledge of Sydney's geography and were genuinely surprised that the students could not identify the class structures operating in their lives.

It appeared to me that in this moment, the community arts workers used their positions of power or expertise to call forth a particular class-based identity and ethnic minority status, making these youth aware of their Otherness. From this example we can see that creativity takes on an entirely different meaning and purpose. Creative practice – such as writing – is no longer a solitary activity, as Bashir described to me in Chapter 1, hiding his passion from the family. Rather, in the case of professional community artists, creative expression is treated as a dialogic process and the value of writing is no longer measured simply according to the intrinsic benefits to be gained from self-expression. Instead, creative writing becomes the tool for exposing ethnic and classed hierarchies.

This was again demonstrated in another writing workshop whereby students were asked to spend fifteen to twenty minutes writing a short story about who they are. One of the community workers explained that this was not a simple task, but involved some complexity because, as he told them, "what's normal to you is not normal to others, so it's important to explain every detail". Brubaker and Cooper (2000) argue that the "modern state has been one of the most important agents of identification and categorization" by holding the power "to name, to identify, to categorise, to state what is what and who is who" (Brubaker and Cooper 2000: 15) or in other words to interpellate individuals into a racial, ethnic, class-based identity. In the following exchange between the community arts worker and a year eight student from a Syrian background, it is clear that 'naming' is not only carried out by governments and dominant cultural groups but also within diasporic groups themselves. Multiculturalism thus both enables and contains particular identity positions.

Hamid (to Syrian–Australian student): Where are you from?
Hassan: Syria.
Hamid: What if you went to Syria, what would you say you are?
Hassan: Australian.
Hamid: See don't you think it is weird how in Australia, you're not Australian and in Syria, you're not Syrian? So what are you?

The question was intended to be rhetorical but Hassan appeared embarrassed that he did not have an answer. In her ethnographic exploration of everyday racism experienced by middle-class Indian communities in Britain, Raj (2003) documents the way second-generation Indian professionals experience ongoing pressure especially when asked the question "where are you from?" Raj's conversations with second generation youth demonstrate the ways difference and exclusion continue to shape one's identity formation, despite individual financial success and attempts at social integration. One young woman, having arrived back to Britain after a business trip to India, is quoted saying: "I never really realized the pressure of constantly knowing that I was a different color (sic) than everyone else until then" (Raj 2003: 151).

As we saw in the exchange between Hamid and Hassan, some community arts facilitators work with this type of internalised sense of difference and empower young people to use this cultural specificity or hybrid identification as a major element of their creative works rather than adhere to dominant Western literary traditions. As ethno-political brokers, they rely on a robust sense of community, ethnicity, diaspora, and class groupings. Hamid, then, uses creativity to tackle a range of social, cultural, political and religious topics, drawing on constructions of community and diaspora for varying political purposes.

I was interested to find out what Hamid thought his purpose was as a community arts worker. He explained this by way of recalling a dispute he recently had with a colleague who came from a more 'privileged' background, according to Hamid. He said,

Hamid: She's told me that the way I teach young people writing is dangerous.
Sherene: Why would she think that? Why is it dangerous?
Hamid: Because I teach – because she's an idiot! Because I teach social realism … I teach young people to write about the suburbs, do you know what I mean? Now she thinks it's dangerous because she thinks it's wrong for young people to be deprived of the opportunity to write about vampires if that's what they want. And she uses the analogy that maybe a kid wants to write about vampires instead of *Neighbours*. And I'm like, look! I teach social realism. You've (the colleague) grown up in a middle-class white environment where every freaken story we hear is like *Neighbours*, I'm not telling kids to write about white middle-class values, I'm telling kids to write about what it's like to have never been valued. Who have never been identified and never been respected, to talk about what it's like to live in a house where you share a bedroom

> with six brothers and sisters. Where you're breaching the divide between being Lebanese and being Australian, do you know what I mean? Like I'm doing a new thing anyway.

Based on what Hamid has said, we can make the case that the community arts scene is a space in which individuals cultivate professional identities that are simultaneously activists and artists. He draws on discourses of social exclusion, what he calls 'social realism', as a justification for why he encourages young people to explore issues of community and hybrid ethnic identities in their fictional writing. Based in Western Sydney, the young people who participate in his programs have never, according to Hamid, 'been valued' because of their visibility in Australian society as non-white and as individuals living in stereotypically working-class suburbs. In this excerpt, Hamid explains that the divisions between working-class and middle-class youth are not only that the two possess markedly different group values, but that in fictional works in Australia, it is middle-class views of the world that are deemed to be valuable. Fiction, according to Weedon (2004), "is an important medium for exploring questions of identity and belonging. It is also effective in giving readers some sense of what it is like to be the subject of racism, made other in negative ways" (Weedon 2004: 61). This seems to be a major driving factor for Hamid as he sees little separation between the arts and the broader project of social justice, made clear when he shouts, "I teach social realism!"

However, Hamid provides a rather cohesive portrait of youth from different ethnic groups. He also represents an overly simplistic account of the economic hardship facing working-class youth. It is my argument that he does this for a number of reasons. The first is simple – he wants to make his colleague aware of the privileges she has enjoyed by virtue of her social status as a middle-class Anglo individual and draw her attention to the invisibility of working class and/or certain ethnic groups in the creative industries, such as Lebanese–Australians who have experienced discrimination and marginalisation in contemporary society. Another way to understand this community arts worker's exasperation with his colleague's ignorance of the structural conditions of class and ethnicity is with reference to Mirza's (1997) discussion of the Black British experience. She says,

> Being black in Britain is about a state of 'becoming' (racialised); a process of consciousness when colour becomes the defining factor about who you are. Located through your 'Otherness' a 'conscious coalition' emerges: a self-consciously constructed space where identity is not inscribed by a natural identification but a political kinship. Now living submerged in whiteness, physical difference becomes a defining issue, a signifier, a mark of whether or not you belong. Thus to be Black in Britain is to share a common structural location; a racial location.
>
> (Mirza 1997: 3)

As someone competing for public funding for multicultural arts based programs, Hamid participates enthusiastically in the politics of difference (Benhabib 2002;

Yuval-Davis 2006). He does this by presenting, both to me and his colleague, an essentialised vision of the oppressed working-class and migrant youth, unified in their experience of social exclusion by saying "I'm not telling kids to write about white middle-class values, I'm telling kids to write about what it's like to have never been valued. Who have never been identified and never been respected". Providing simplified accounts of ethnic and class groups in which all members share the same attributes or emotions is part of what Brubaker calls the 'performative character' of ethno-political brokers like Hamid who "live *off* as well as 'for' ethnicity" (Brubaker 2002: 166). We see in this short statement that by differentiating between class groups and treating these divisions as discrete and inflexible, he constructs "inclusionary/exclusionary boundaries that differentiate between self and other, determining what is 'normal' and what is not, who is entitled to certain resources and who is not" (Yuval-Davis 2006: 199). Ironically, Hamid has positioned Anglo–Australians as 'normal' and positioned himself, and those youth he works with, as the Other.

However, Hamid is quick to note that there are broader power relations at play that almost force him to play the role of the ethno-political broker. He said,

> Jackie (an Anglo–Australian co-worker) tells me that when a white artist comes into the office, they're never interested in Jackie, they never talk to her, they never acknowledge her. They're interested in the wogs; do you know what I mean? 'Cause that makes white people more open minded. It makes white people look like "oh I'm working with refugees, oh I'm working with people of Lebanese backgrounds who are disadvantaged". Like, they love going back to their communities in Newtown and telling them that. It makes them look good! It makes them look more open minded and more progressive than the other people in Newtown. So white people love working with wogs. On the same hand, wogs have no agenda and no devotion to working with other wogs because wogs don't have authority and power in Australia, so wogs are kind of always trying to appeal to white people all the time too.

Of course these are simplistic binaries, but at the core of what Hamid is saying here is his recognition that the broader framework of multiculturalism, as I outlined earlier, encourages community arts workers to incorporate their ethnicity and location in Western Sydney into their art projects. Doing so can, first, be a way to challenge how parts of Western Sydney have become pathologised as dangerous and disadvantaged. But, second, he feels he *has* to do this because there are few alternative ways in which he can establish a career as a writer, editor, and actor in a highly competitive job market where the opportunities presented to him make him feel uncomfortable, for example playing a drug dealer on television. Essentially then, he recognises that the figure of an 'authentic' migrant representative is a social construction that he plays with strategically to further his career.

In my interview with Walid, these notions were never explicitly mentioned but, rather, the relationship between creativity and the project of multiculturalism was subsumed within the official narrative of 'capturing authentic voices'. Walid, twenty-seven years old and from a Lebanese–Australian background, had once aspired to produce films and completed a double-degree in filmmaking and teaching but, after a long period in unemployment and doing odd jobs, he turned to community arts and became a facilitator who taught digital media skills to socio-economically disadvantaged youth across Western Sydney schools. I asked whether he felt pressured to encourage his students to use their creative skills to discuss themes of ethnicity or identity, which he disagreed with. Instead, he said

> I guess theoretically it [their stories] could be about anything … the yeah the arts stuff at the moment is about Sudanese refugees 'cause our arts director is Sudanese. But yeah, I mean yeah generally speaking it's not necessarily about migration but certainly unheard stories. I mean that's the key focus is unheard stories and umm often that comes from cultural diversity 'cause television is so 'white' and you know, umm, you know, you don't hear, you wouldn't hear from these kids in Liverpool, you don't hear from a Sudanese refugee so that's what our mission is both on the artistic and the community side is it's about getting unheard stories out there somehow. We don't dictate what the story is. Umm to a degree we get criticised for it in that umm people provide funding to get a certain thing, but this is a very personal thing for me. I worked in five schools in Liverpool last year and I did not dictate what they needed to be about, I said "just remember that you're kids. Don't do anything that you need to be an adult to make" … and they all made frivolous funny you know, funny films and ah I didn't want to do a heartbreaking, heart-wrenching thing … but it was unique and authentic.

Although he makes claims to the contrary, I would suggest that in this particular excerpt, Walid draws on 'diaspora consciousness' (Clifford 1994). Diaspora consciousness refers to a sense of solidarity among diaspora groups as well as "strategies of community maintenance and interaction" (Clifford, 1994: 308). When Walid says "theoretically it could be about anything … the yeah the arts stuff at the moment is about Sudanese refugees 'cause our arts director is Sudanese" he is referring to a type of identity politics at play, where he and the arts director act as political entrepreneurs using cultural difference and categories of ethnicity to

> persuade people to understand themselves, their interests, and their predicaments in a certain way, to persuade certain people that they are (for certain purposes) 'identical' with one another and at the same time different from others, and to organise and justify collective action along certain lines.
>
> (Brubaker and Cooper 2000: 5)

In this way he demonstrates that cultural difference and categories of ethnicity and community are not natural facts but resources that can be mobilised strategically by social actors for various purposes and in specific contexts (Harris 2009; Brubaker and Cooper 2000; Collins 2010).

Identifying links between being Sudanese, the refugee experience, and creative training reflects an attempt by community arts facilitators to empower young people to celebrate their cultural specificities through art. This is reaffirmed when Walid refers to the under-representation of non-white creative and cultural producers in mainstream media. Indeed, Back (1996) suggests that the cultural forms produced by artists of ethnic and working class backgrounds have often been used to "challenge dominant stereotypes, express translocal connections and find a voice that does justice to their social location" (Back 1996: 228). Thus, creative training in community programs are not solely concerned with teaching young people new skills to be used in the labour market but rather, as Walid points out, to provide a space in which stories produced by people of diverse ethnic groups are valued and celebrated. Authenticity here is constructed as the property of the disadvantaged, ethnic minority or working-class youth. Telling 'authentic' stories is a way to disrupt and resist the dominant representatives of the everyday lives of young people; as Walid notes, "television is so 'white' and you know umm you know, you don't hear … from a Sudanese refugee".

Re-articulating the purpose of creativity

How do the roles that Saad, Walid, and Hamid occupy in community arts organisations sit within their broader creative biographies? For the most part, the young men in this study framed creativity and creative vocational aspirations as incompatible with their ethnic backgrounds and attachments to their local communities in Western Sydney; that "everything creative is non-Leb". However, we can see from this discussion about capturing authentic voices that the community arts scene is one area in which ethnicity, creativity, and identity politics merge very well. The work that these young men do in the local community arts scene is interesting because, in some respects, it is at odds with the ways they originally articulate themselves as creative people. Their original creative passions are articulated as another kind of authenticity, as ones that separate them from the other Arab–Australian youth in their community who are either disinterested in academic achievements entirely or plan for their vocational futures along culturally acceptable templates of masculinity, especially in business ownership. This is demonstrated through their practical decisions and also by the ways they draw on symbolic gestures to establish their identities as non-Leb, as clashing with their parents, and 'out of place' in Bankstown more generally. In most cases, creativity is a way to 'escape' their local ethnic communities. Here, creativity is articulated from exactly the opposite perspective, that is, ethnic identification is essential to producing 'authentic' creative forms of self-expression. Thus, the attachments these young men have to their local, migrant backgrounds become reformulated once they enter the world of community arts.

Walid, who I noted in Chapter 2 was keen to emphasise his difference from the other Lebanese–Australian young men in his school, spoke, for example, about the enjoyment and satisfaction he felt by being part of producing a show called 'the migrant project' and how this connected to his and others 'personal stories of migration'. He said,

> The concept of that show, it was a multimedia show, umm the concept of that show was addressing the idea of Sydney as a place of migration for the

> last, you know, 200 years so ahh since the first migration, thinking of them as migrants and every subsequent migration thing ah and there was an indigenous aspect as well where we were kind of acknowledging the indigenous movement as well so umm, and it was huge like there were a lot of different artists from Western Sydney involved, most of us for no pay. Yeah and so it had dancers, it had theatre practitioners. I worked on it as a video artist, that was my role, so there were video projections all throughout the show and it was really cool and everybody was exploring their own personal stories of migration and why they came here and some of the challenges, and some of the challenges of identity that people have and stuff like that. It was really interesting and it yeah it was really good.

Similarly, Hamid also emphasised how his role as a community artist facilitated positive representations of Western Sydney through creative writing projects. He said,

> What I'm trying to do is create a culture for Western Sydney. Where it's like this is interesting, this is an amazing place, this is special. Don't worry about *Twilight*, that's boring! *Neighbours* has been done to death and it's like … these are untold stories. This is a new place for the world, you know? And the thing is that when you're living in Newtown you don't need to talk about how great your life is, you know it in your blood. You don't need to act like you're better than anyone, you already know it. What I have been trying to do in the last five years is create not positive representation of the community but accurate representations. But these kids are anti-social and they do have issues just like every other community so I've been trying to represent the real life stories and experiences that they face. So I still think this community is amazing, and I still think the Lebanese–Australian community is, is worthy of recognition and isn't always positive but I don't think that they're always drug and rape associated.

There are two main points to be made about these short pieces as they relate to notions of authenticity, creativity, and community, and the intersections between these concepts. The first refers to the purpose and audience of the individual and collective creative projects to which these young men have referred. Both Walid and Hamid suggest that their projects provide counter-narratives to the negative representations of migrants and Western Sydney. However, Hutnyk (2000) in his 'critique of exotica' argues that at the level of multicultural arts, individuals and groups cannot expect to achieve material redress of problems like racialisation for example, but that in fact "all that can be fought and won at this level is 'authenticity'" (Hutnyk 200: 121).

In addition, the audience for their creative work – usually community members but also policymakers – is crucial because it changes the ways that their creative identities are perceived. What I mean by this is that the funding these young men can receive by making connections between their creative projects and their ethnic and social disadvantage – to simultaneously self-essentialise and perform cultural hybridity – provides them with a platform to have their stories told. However, as Kalantzis and Cope (1994) have argued, community arts are not an equally respected platform within the creative industries. They say that community arts have been given a "multicultural label" and as such they refer to a "category of marginalisation, something other than mainstream art" (Kalantzis and Cope 1994: 25). By foregrounding their biographies as artists with reference to their membership of a Bankstown-based diasporic group, the creative output of these informants is less likely to be critiqued or scrutinised, as art is intended to be in the public realm. Instead, these informants claim to be telling or capturing 'authentic' stories as representatives or authority figures of the local community and are applauded for simply doing so instead of being rewarded or critiqued based on the quality of their work.

At the level of narrative analysis, it also appears that at this moment in their lives, informants must ultimately rearticulate what it means to be a creative person from an ethnic minority background. The creative vocational trajectories of Hamid, Walid, and Saad see them return to their communities, the ones they originally wanted to escape as we saw in Chapter 3. This is a fate that Gunew calls the 'trap' of multiculturalism, where over time "people are wheeled in as token figures speaking for these marginalised groups" (in Spivak 1990: 63). Attachments to community become redefined as a result of their roles in community arts organisations. From those two excerpts, we see that being from a migrant, Western Sydney community is suddenly 'amazing' and 'really cool'. These are perhaps the first moments in my interviews with creative aspirants of Arab–Australian backgrounds where their local communities are described positively. To return to the discussion in Chapter 1, it is evident that the project of 'disembedding' (Beck and Beck-Gernsheim 2002) from the local Arab–Australian community through the development of a creative biography has not been realised by these young men because of the prejudice they experience in 'mainstream' creative sectors.

Conclusion

Using one's ethnic background for creative self-expression is not necessarily something that these aspiring artists originally envisioned themselves doing. Rather, to return to the earlier discussion of processes of racialisation in 'mainstream' creative sectors, I have aimed to show in this chapter how working in community arts can be thought of as individual responses or strategies to deal with their experiences of racial prejudice and discrimination. Their experiences certainly confirm Araeen's (2000) argument, based on his study of visual artists in the UK, that non-white artists generally only achieve success "by showing their cultural identity cards" (Araeen 2000: 16). As Ahmad (2001) reminds us, even when artists find platforms to present their creative works, the content of their work is reduced by "the multiculturalist will to construct them as from elsewhere" (Ahmad 2001: 76).

Ultimately, the language of escape and of using creativity as a way to break free of communal restraint, language that we might attribute to a youthful fantasy of remaking the self, disappears at this moment of the interview. In its place is the celebration of 'migrant stories', of cultural hybridity, of Arabness and of Western Sydney. Their return to their local communities is constructed as a return to an 'authentic' identity position despite the inherent contradictions with this notion as the informants themselves point out. Yet, the community arts scene, for all of its flaws and multicultural agenda-setting, is perceived as one of the few arenas in which these informants can develop a stable creative biography. At the very least, they are made to feel that they have a degree of control over what kinds of 'migrant' or Western Sydney stories they tell whereas their experiences in the broader creative industries left them vulnerable and insecure in their identities.

Notes

1 http://www.smh.com.au/national/straddle-not-struggle-as-slashies-prove-ultimate-multitaskers-20110422-1drhg.html
2 http://s3-ap-southeast-2.amazonaws.com/ehq-production-australia/cccde589b2b3a-d6ae35ab077b9845c2709d94ee8/documents/attachments/000/006/105/original/LOW_RES_BCC_COMMUNITY_PLAN_2021_v9.pdf?1394447789
3 http://ice.org.au/artistic-program/
4 http://ice.org.au/project/digidiaries/ (accessed 27 March 2011)

References

Ahmad, A. N. (2001) 'Whose underground?', *Third Text*, 15(54): 71–84.
Allen, K. and S. Hollingworth (2013) '"Sticky subjects" or "cosmpolitan creatives"? Aspirations for Work in the Knowledge Economy', *Urban Studies*, 50(3): 499–517.
Ang, I. (2011) 'Ethnicities and our precarious future', *Ethnicities*, 11(1): 27–31.
Araeen, R. (2000) 'A new beginning: Beyond postcolonial cultural theory and identity politics', *Third Text*, 50(Spring): 3–20.
Atkinson, W. (2010) 'The myth of the reflexive worker: Class and work histories in neoliberal times', *Work, Employment Society*, 24(3): 413–429.
Back, L. (1996) *New ethnicities and Urban Culture: Racisms and Multiculture in Young Lives*, London, Routledge.
Back, L. (2009) 'Researching community and its moral projects', *21st Century Society*, 4(2): 201–214.
Banks, M. (2007) *The Politics of Cultural Work*, Basingstoke, Palgrave Macmillan.
Beck, U. and E. Beck-Gernsheim (2002) *Individualization: Institutionalized Individualism and its Social and Political Consequences*, London, Sage Publications.
Benhabib, S. (2002) *The Claims of Culture: Equality and Diversity in the Global Era*, Princeton, Princeton University Press.
Bhabha, H. K. (1996) 'Culture's in-between' in *Questions of Cultural Identity*, Eds. S. Hall and P. Du Gay, London, Sage Publications, pp. 53–60.
Bhabha, H. K. (1997) 'Editor's introduction: Minority manoeuvres and unsettled negotiations', *Critical Inquiry*, Spring, 431–459.

Blair, H. (2009) 'Active networking: Action, social structure and the process of networking', *Creative Labour: Working in the Creative Industries*, Eds. A. McKinlay and C. Smith, New York, Palgrave MacMillan, pp. 116–134.

Brahm Levey, G. (2012) 'Interculturalism vs. multiculturalism: A distinction without a difference?', *Journal of Intercultural Studies*, 33(2): 217–224.

Brubaker, R. (2002) 'Ethnicity without groups', *European Journal of Sociology*, 43(2): 163–189.

Brubaker, R. and F. Cooper (2000) 'Beyond identity', *Theory and Society*, 29(1): 1–47.

Christopherson, S. (2009) 'Working in the creative economy: Risk, adaptation, and the persistence of exclusionary networks', in *Creative Labour: Working in the Creative Industries*, Eds. A. McKinlay and C. Smith, Basingstoke, Palgrave Macmillan, pp. 72–91.

Clifford, J. (1994) 'Diasporas', *Cultural Anthropology*, 9(3 Further Inflections Towards Ethnographies of the Future): 302–338.

Collins, P. H. (2010) 'The new politics of community', *American Sociological Review*, 75(1): 7–30.

Dunn, K. (2007) 'Contemporary racism and islamaphobia in Australia: Racializing religion', *Ethnicities*, 7(4): 564–589.

Dwyer, C. and P. Crang (2002) 'Fashioning ethnicities: The commercial spaces of multiculture', *Ethnicities*, 2(3): 410–430.

Gill, R. and A. Pratt (2008) 'In the social factory? Immaterial labour, precariousness and cultural work', *Theory, Culture & Society*, 25(7–8): 1–30.

Grugulis, I. and D. Stoyanova (2012) 'Social capital and networks in film and TV: Jobs for the boys?', *Organization Studies*, 33(10): 1311–1331.

Hage, G. (2000) *White Nation: Fantasies of White Supremacy in a Multicultural Society*, New York, Routledge.

Hage, G. (2002) 'Multiculturalism and white paranoia in Australia', *Journal of International Migration and Integration*, 3(3): 417–437.

Hall, S (1996) 'New ethnicities' in *Stuart Hall: Critical Dialogues in Cultural Studies*, Eds. D. Marley and R. H. Cohen, London, Routledge, pp. 441–449.

Harris, A. (2009) 'Shifting the boundaries of cultural spaces: Young people and everyday multiculturalism ', *Social Identities* 15(2): 187–205.

Hutnyk, J. (2000) *Critique of Exotica: Music, Politics, and the Culture Industry*, London, Pluto Press.

Hyder, R. (2004) *Brimful of Asia: Negotiating Ethnicity on the UK Music Scene*, Aldershot, Ashgate.

Jakubowicz, A. and H. Goodall (1994) *Racism, Ethnicity and the Media*, St. Leonards, Allen and Unwin.

Jakubowicz, A. and K. Seneviratne (1996) *Ethnic Conflict and the Australian Media*, Sydney, University of Technology Sydney.

Jayaraman, R. (2000) 'Inclusion and exclusion: An analysis of the Australian Immigration History and Ethnic Relations', *Journal of Popular Culture*, 34(1): 135–155.

Kalantzis, M. and B. Cope (1994) 'Vocabularies of excellence: Rewording multicultural arts policy', in *Culture, Difference and the Arts*, Eds. S. Gunew and F. Rizvi, St Leonards, Allen and Unwin, pp. 13–34.

Lentin, A. (2012) 'Post-race, post-politics: the paradoxical rise of culture after multiculturalism', *Ethnic and Racial Studies*, iFirst Article, 1–19.

Levitt, P. (2011) 'Transnationalism', in *Diasporas: Concepts, Intersections, Identities*, Eds. K. Knott and S. McLoughlin, New York, Zed Books, pp. 39–45.

Mac an Ghaill, M. (1999) *Contemporary Racisms and Ethnicities: Social and Cultural Transformations*, Philadelphia, Open University Press.

McClean, G. (2011) 'Cultural threats, cop drama, and "community PR": Diversity and security cultures in EastWest101', *Continuum*, 25(2): 177–188.

McKinlay, A. and C. Smith (2009) *Creative Labour: Working in the Creative Industries*, New York, Palgrave Macmillan.

McRobbie, A. (2002) 'Clubs to companies: Notes on the decline of political culture in speeded up creative worlds', *Cultural Studies*, 16(4): 516–531.

McRobbie, A. (2002a) 'From Holloway to Hollywood: Happiness at work in the new cultural economy?', in *Cultural Economy: Cultural Analysis and Commercial Life*, Eds. Du Gay, P and M. Pryke, London, Sage, pp. 97–114.

Meer, N. and T. Modood (2012) 'How does interculturalism contrast with multiculturalism?', *Journal of Intercultural Studies*, 33(2): 175–196.

Mirza, H. S. (1997) *Black British Feminism: A Reader*, London, Routledge.

Modood, T. (2007) *Multiculturalism: A Civic Idea*, Cambridge, Polity.

Modood, T. (2008) 'Multiculturalism and groups', *Social & Legal Studies*, 17(4): 549–553.

Modood, T. (2011) 'Multiculturalism and citizenship', in *Diasporas: Concepts, Intersections and Identities*, Eds. K. Knott and S. McLoughlin, New York, Zed Books, pp. 50–55.

Nagle, J. (2008) 'Multiculturalism's double bind: Creating inclusivity, difference and cross-community allegiances with the London–Irish', *Ethnicities*, 8(2): 177–198.

Noble, G., S. Poynting, and P. Tabar (1999) 'Youth, ethnicity and the mapping of identities: Strategic essentialism and strategic hybridity among male Arabic speaking youth in South-Western Sydney', *Communal/Plural*, 7(1): 29–44.

Olding, R. (2011) 'Straddle, not struggle, as slashies prove ultimate multi-taskers', *Sydney Morning Herald*, retrieved from http://www.smh.com.au/national/straddle-not-struggle-as-slashies-prove-ultimate-multitaskers-20110422-1drhg.html#ixzz1XFHHJt1X

Parekh, B. (2001) 'The future of multi-ethnic Britain: Reporting on a report', *The Round Table*, 362: 691–700

Raj, D. S. (2003) *Where Are You From?: Middle Class Migrants in the Modern World*, Ewing, University of California Press.

Saha, A. (2012) '"Beards, scarves, halal meat, terrorists, forced marriage": television industries and the production of "race"', *Media, Culture and Society*, 34(4): 424–438.

Said, E. W. (1997) *Covering Islam: How the Media and the Experts Determine How We See the Rest of the World*, New York, Vintage Books.

Shaheen, J. G. (2001) *Reel Bad Arabs: How Hollywood Vilifies a People*, New York, Olive Branch Press.

Spivak, G. C. (1990) *The Post-Colonial Critic: Interviews, Strategies, Dialogues*, London, Routledge.

Taylor, C., Ed. (1994) *Multiculturalism: Examining the Politics of Recognition*, New Jersey, Princeton University Press.

Weedon, C. (2004) *Identity and Culture: Narratives of Belonging and Difference*, Berkshire, Open University Press.

Werbner, P. (1997) 'Introduction: the dialectics of cultural hybridity', in *Debating Cultural Hybridity: Multi-Cultural Identities and the Politics of Anti-Racism*, Eds. P. Werbner and T. Modood, London, Zed Books, pp. 1–28.

Wieviorka, M. (2012) 'Multiculturalism: A concept to be redefined and certainly not replaced by the extremely vague erm of interculturalism', *Journal of Intercultural Studies*, 33(2): 225–231.

Yuval-Davis, N. (2006) 'Intersectionality and feminist politics', *European Journal of Women's Studies*, 13(3): 193–209.

6 Conclusion

Retrospective and future selves

This book has explored how processes of racialisation, socio-economic disadvantage, and local, familial dynamics, and traditions shape the ways that young Arab–Australian men articulate their vocational aspirations. In youth studies, aspirations are a key way in which we can see the effects of a young person's socio-economic background because, as Archer (2003) has argued, to develop educational and vocational aspirations requires cultural and social capitals. Our 'dispositions to believe' cannot exist solely in our imagination but reflect the social and material conditions in which we live (Lahire 2003). Other studies have claimed that some young people of low socio-economic backgrounds develop low aspirations and that these aspirations can thus tell us more about how class hierarchies are reproduced in contemporary society (Cuthill and Scull 2011). In this book however, the shaping effect that local communities have on Arab–Australian young men with creative aspirations were not grouped as either 'low' or 'high'. Instead, I used narrative analysis to refrain from necessarily 'measuring' aspirations because such conclusions do not tell us enough about the nuances and contradictions involved in career decision-making processes among Arab–Australian young men.

While Beck (2000) has argued that individual life trajectories are now more likely to be disembedded from tradition and community, this book has evaluated the enduring significance of class, place, gender, and ethnicity in the youthful identification processes of these creative aspirants. In this respect, the book shares similarities with Nayaks' study of young people's situated lives in Northeast England where he observed "highly meaningful relationships between place and identity" (Nayak 2003: 175). This was also evident in the earlier chapters of the volume where informants used local spaces to signpost where they have been and where they plan to go in future. Overall, the book has offered a counterargument to the 'risk society' and 'liquid modernity' theses revealing that in spite of many young people spending their formative years actively seeking to escape the rigidity and tradition of their local communities, the escape is not neat or smooth for many who are limited by socio-economic constraints and face racial prejudice as well as uncertainty within themselves about what an escape actually entails.

This volume has shown, essentially, that there is much at stake when ethnic minority youth choose to invest their time, energy, and resources into cultivating a creative identity. Throughout each chapter, I looked at how these young men negotiated particular tensions that emerged in particular social contexts and life history moments as a direct result of their creative vocational aspirations. Wyn *et al.* (2012) have been critical of the tendency among researchers to treat the transition from youth to adulthood and school to work as natural and aligned processes with individual autonomy and mature identities being the end goal (Wyn *et al.* 2012: 6). While this book was chronologically organised according to key moments in the youthful experience, such as familial relationships, schooling experiences, higher education, and paid employment, I have taken my lead from Wyn *et al.* (2012) by placing greater emphasis on the local and global conditions and influences that "form the possibilities for the ongoing project of performing identities. From this perspective, identity is never final or achieved" (Wyn *et al.* 2012: 8).

The effects of class on the informants' creative aspirations were not only situated within local, communal dynamics but also in relation to large-scale changes to national and global economies. Kelly and Kenway (2001) suggest that contemporary global, reflexive modernity involves "processes that restructure the demand for labour-intensive manufacturing and service jobs, and result in flexibility agendas, declining core and expanding peripheral workforces and increasing casualization" (Kelly and Kenway 2001: 22). Beck and others have argued that these features of modern life affect *all* individuals. What this book has aimed to show is that young people from low socio-economic backgrounds are particularly more vulnerable to these ruptures. They have less guidance and financial support to weather the casualisation that is characteristic of creative labour, for example, and are thus more likely to seek 'safe' degrees and career options in order to "rationally manage" (Kelly and Kenway 2001: 22) structural inequalities.

Race relations

The structural inequalities that result in challenges for Arab–Australia young men to develop what I have called 'risky' aspirations are further compounded by race-relations. On a global scale, much has changed since the completion of fieldwork for this book. The fallout from the 'Arab Spring' has resulted in over half a million applications for asylum in Europe from Syria and Iraq in 2015 alone,[1] and that number continues to climb every month. Australia's border protection policies have become even more draconian than in years past with Tony Abbotts' campaign slogan 'turn back the boats' helping him win the 2013 federal election.[2] Much of 'Operation Sovereign Borders' remains unknown, hidden from public knowledge, but we do know that in a 14-month period between 2013–2015, over 630 asylum seekers were 'turned back' to neighbouring Asian countries[3] and over 2000 reports of abuse in offshore detention camps by Australian guards have been documented in 2016.[4] The rise of the Islamic State terrorist group (ISIS) took place mostly after the completion of my fieldwork with attacks against 'the West' taking place in Europe and the United States, for example at the *Charlie Hebdo* offices and a gay nightclub in Orlando. In Australia, a Muslim teenager shot dead a worker at the police department and claimed to have done so as a member of ISIS but this connection was never fully proven. Up to 150 Australians have left to fight with ISIS in the war in Syria. Hysteria about home-grown Muslim terrorism dominated mainstream news reporting in 2015 and 2016, which we can argue helped with the resurgence of the One Nation party and Pauline Hanson in federal politics. White, upper class morning news presenters feel comfortable and confident to make statements such as "I would feel safer if we froze Muslim immigration to Australia for a while" to a national audience.[5] Britain voted to leave the European Union in a bid to 'reclaim its' borders'; it was reported that 289 hate crimes against migrants occurred within 24 hours after Brexit.[6] The Islamophobia Register has reported increasing numbers of complaints especially from Australian–Muslim who have been racially harassed on public transport following negative news reporting on Muslims or Arabs in general.[7]

What does this all mean in relation to the youth transitions of aspiring artists of ethnic minority backgrounds? In one respect, it means that claims to a creative identity have become potentially more difficult to articulate for Arab–Australian young men. In this book, I have explored why this is the case, referring to the intersections between their minority status, socio-economic positions, and the gendered expectations placed on them as they move from adolescence to adulthood in multilinear ways. It also means that we must seriously re-evaluate the discourse of 'liquid modernities' in which reflexivity is argued to be one of the key defining characteristics of our times. The question about whether these young men had the capacity to disembed from their local ethnic communities because of their socio-economic backgrounds, and thus become reflexive individuals steering an individual biographical course, was addressed across this book. This particular research question was influenced by the work of Beck, Giddens, and Bauman who have each suggested that the 'freely choosing subject' is the most dominant figure of postmodernity. They say that even those who cannot be freely choosing subjects, because of material constraints, for example, either aspire to become so or at the very least attempt to articulate their life histories as ones that are firmly in their control. Several researchers of youth have examined how this emphasis on individual autonomy that features in Beck and others work plays out among young men as they weigh up multiple and sometimes conflicting choices during the youth to adulthood transition (Wyn 2005; Roberts 2007, 2009).

This book picked up on these issues. In the earlier chapters I suggested that Arab–Australian young men from Bankstown articulate creativity and creative identities as a vehicle to escape the local community, to transcend the limiting career templates and gender constructions available to them. Then, I considered whether these young men had the right capacities to move freely and comfortably in social spaces outside of Bankstown as they encounter competitive and exclusionary scenes. In Chapters 4 and 5, I argued that in some segments of the creative industries exists thinly veiled racial, class, and gender prejudice that constrains the ability, and desire, for many of these young men to fulfil their personal projects of social mobility which includes, primarily, disembedding from their local communities. The recent global events of mass migration from the Middle East to Europe and Australia as well as the rise of far-right groups in federal politics will no doubt affect both the cohort of young men in my study and subsequent generations of ethnic minority creative aspirants in the West. It will be imperative to trace how creative aspirations play out for young people under such conditions. Where in this study I found that *some* aspirants turned to 'safe' spaces of multicultural arts, we may speculate that future generations of Arab–Australian artists will simply have no choice but to become more politicised and radical in their creative expression, even if they are ill equipped or have no interest in doing so, in light of the conditions of racialisation that force them into categories of Other.

Deradicalisation

Indeed, recent data on the make-up of the creative industries workforce paints a rather bleak picture for future creative vocational aspirants of ethnic minority backgrounds. While we simply have no recent reports in Australia about the ethnic, religious, or migrant composition of creative workers in various creative sectors, estimates put the figure somewhere around 8–9 per cent, but this includes administration roles as well as content producers, so we might assume the figure is actually lower in some creative sectors. Whether the situation for non-white artists has worsened in recent years alongside, or as a result of, the global events I mention cannot be confirmed but anecdotal evidence in the form of conversations with artists from Arab–Australian backgrounds seems to suggest that this is the case. Government funding for arts programs and projects has either decreased in some sectors or has shifted in focus. Artists of Arab–Australian backgrounds have much better chances of securing funding if they feed into the current concerns over "countering violent extremism".[8] Thus, since completing my fieldwork it appears that little has changed when it comes to the racialisation of artists of non-white backgrounds, even though the contours of this racialisation may have shifted slightly to include the language of 'deradicalisation'.

In a recent conversation with the director of the community arts centre in Bankstown where much of the fieldwork for this project took place he said that in 2016, no government funding would be given to run the projects he has been producing for the past ten years. If he simply changes the language in his proposals to state that such projects will reduce potential Islamic radicalisation, the funding is much more swiftly secured. While this arts director (not of an Arab–Australian or Muslim background) has chose to adhere to these new funding guidelines, my discussions with artists who have links to, or themselves work in, community arts sectors revealed they are deeply troubled by what they see as new forms of surveillance and additional restrictions on their freedom of expression. Much more empirical data is required in this field of research because if the knowledge industries, in which creative labour is central, is at the heart of growing our national economy, then it is important we understand *who* is contributing to this knowledge, what *kind* of knowledge is being produced and what implications it has for class and ethnic hierarchies if ethnic minority groups are continually excluded or sidelined.

'The native informant'

While this book has focused on the case study of Arab–Australian young men and their creative vocational aspirations and entry points into the labour market, it is imperative to situate their biographical life histories in the broader context of ethnic minority representation within arts sectors more generally. Zing Tsjeng offers these personal insights as it relates to UK ethnic minority artists searching for spaces to express themselves in 2016:

> If you're a person of colour, remotely creative and/or working in the arts, you probably have a memory like this. You'll be looking around a room – it could be a gallery opening or a book reading or a private view – and you'll suddenly realise yours is the only face in the room. The only face that isn't white, that is.
>
> Here's my story. I was twenty; I'd sneaked into the after-party for some university theatre group, grabbed a free glass of wine and cast my eyes around for anybody that I might know. Nobody. What I did see was a sea of white faces, laughing at this or that backstage in-joke and downing house white. The gratis booze turned sour in my mouth.
>
> Why did it bug me so much? Why did it matter? I probably had a few friends in that crowd. But there was something about the whole scene that made me feel alone in a room of a hundred people: the yellow girl in the corner, turning redder by the second. I slunk off.
>
> In February, the Warwick Commission released a damning report that stated that the creative arts have become whiter and more middle class over the last two years. It's no coincidence that the same period has seen the poisonous growth of anti-immigration rhetoric and xenophobia, from both right and left-wing political parties.
>
> People of colour (POC) rarely see ourselves reflected in British media; when we do, it's usually because one of us has done something wrong and we are immediately called on to apologise for their behaviour. We've become a cipher for someone else's anxieties and insecurities, or a quota to be massaged, fact-checked and disputed into oblivion.[9]

There is one other way that POC British artists are incorporated in the creative industries, and that is as the 'guinea pig witness' as Said (2004) has poignantly articulated in relation to Arab intellectuals in the United States. "Since you're from Iraq, you tell us about Iraq. When we're not interested in Iraq, we don't want to hear from you. The native informant" (Said 2004: 365). This has generally been the experience of my informants; these experiences are incredibly useful for witnessing how multiculturalism, migration, and racialisation operate as structuring forces in the lives of ethnic minority youth in Australia today.

Zing Tsjeng follows up her critique on a positive note saying,

> a new wave of POC artists and creatives is challenging that narrative. Between them, they publish zines, curate shows, and create platforms for people to come together, not apart. They show that British artistic identity is more than 'Keep Calm and Carry On' tea towels and cocktails at Frieze.[10]

There are some areas for optimism in the findings from my own research as well with more content production taking place within Arab–Australian communities in much more complicated ways than would have been permissible in the late twentieth century Australian arts scene under multicultural discourses of 'harmony' and cultural preservation. However, the reach of these productions to mainstream audiences remains rather limited. In July 2016, a Western Sydney-based arts centre held a two-day symposium that brought together artists of ethnic minority and refugee backgrounds, community workers, policy makers, and academics. In one panel, which dealt specifically with the limitations placed on refugee artists to tell stories in their own ways rather than as objects of study in the 'war porn' industry, an audience member who worked in community development raised her hand to make the comment that "these conversations are so valuable and it is great to have this dialogue, it is a great starting point". This is a fairly typical response at many of the workshops and conferences I have attended about the ways in which ethnic minority artists face unique sets of challenges that white artists simply do not. After the panel, I held a one on one interview with one of the artists involved, Ziad, who was an Iraqi-born twenty-three-year-old university student and designer. I asked how he felt about the audience response. He said,

> I give so many of these talks and the white person in the crowd will be like, "thanks for sharing, it is a great start". Like, what are you even saying? We have been having these conversations for fifteen years already, you should know by now. Do your damn homework, you know? It's so frustrating because that ignorance is such an easy cop out and it doesn't actually change anything. In five years time I could give the same talk and someone in the audience will say the exact same thing. They just want to give themselves a pat on the back, like good job, and then go back to their normal lives. What's the point really?

While there has been a surge of new material produced by emerging Arab–Australian artists that, as is the case in the United Kingdom, challenges notions of national identity, the distribution of these creative projects still remains hidden from the mainstream.

Future selves

Based on existing studies of how working-class youth fare in knowledge economies, I began the research process with the understanding that creative careers are financially risky and that young people of socio-economic disadvantage are less likely to pursue creative vocational trajectories. This research therefore contributes to the existing body of work that dispels the myths of the creative industries by instead highlighting some of the challenges involved in becoming a member of what Florida calls the creative class. Of course, several other researchers are working on similar issues, especially in relation to young people's transitions to adulthood. Haukka (2011) for example, conducted a large scale survey with 507 creative aspirants in Australia who were completing education and training or had worked in creative fields for up to two years (or both). Her findings revealed that there are specific features of the creative industries that makes the youth to adulthood transitions complex and challenging. For instance, she says the creative industries are not always "qualification driven with many employers recruiting workers because of their creative talent and/or job skills" (Haukka 2011: 44). In this study, I showed that these recruitment processes can easily lead to institutional discrimination where physical differences, being non-white, marks Arab–Australian young men as lacking the right kinds of talents and skills required for various jobs or alternatively leads to typecasting in fields such as television and film where these young men are only chosen to play stereotyped characters.

Haukka (2011) also suggests that creative workers are expected to have high levels of flexibility and mobility. This is problematic, she says, because in these working conditions, workers "tend to operate on short term contracts with study-based work … and workers do not have regular access to learning and development opportunities" (Haukka 2011: 44). Of course, Florida (2003) has presented these conditions in positive terms; allowing individuals to easily blend their lifestyles with paid work and have greater freedom to set their own working hours. In my research, the lack of stability available in creative labour was seen as a deterrent, not as an incentive, to pursue their creative aspirations. Coming from socio-economic disadvantage, particular career paths are pursued for betterment, to improve their life conditions – not necessarily through economic means, but rather by escaping a potentially limited future in Bankstown. Because of the kind of flexibility that Haukka suggests is widespread in creative fields, the Arab–Australian young men in this study see little prospective of improving their life conditions, usually once they arrive at university, and are thus less likely to continue with their goals beyond school or further education.

Flexibility within creative labour refers not only to working conditions but the capacities of artists to reinvent themselves and be 'loose' with their identities, omnivorous in their social and cultural interests. This book has shown the challenges some Arab–Australian young men experience in trying to live up to such expectations as they are unaware of the codes and the rules of the game. This ignorance is of course a product of class stratification, as Bourdieu has theorised in his discussions of social and cultural capital. I suggested in Chapter 3 for example that the discomfort experienced in university can be traced back to the ways that young people of more privileged backgrounds are first, able to see the value of performing weirdness and second, able to convincingly play the role of a bohemian-living aspiring artist. Particular performances of flexible identities are therefore an acquired skill that a higher education qualification simply cannot teach. This is where my book departs from much of the research on migrant youth who tend to emphasise much more the increasing rates of higher education qualification as an indicator of integration and social mobility (Modood 1993). While this cannot be disputed on a general level, the bearing that class has on youthful subcultural expression and style tends to be overlooked in youth studies; Chapter 3 of this book in particular reveals that we can pay closer attention to this to expand our understanding of how class is reproduced in complex and nuanced ways.

Importantly, this book focused solely on young men and while this has been useful for unpacking the links between masculinity, creativity, and aspiration, it does leave us with some unanswered questions. For example, the flexibility involved in creative labour is perceived as problematic for the young men in this study because, as I have argued elsewhere (Idriss and Morgan 2017), the attachment to a creative identity disrupts the gendered expectations for social mobility within the local Arab–Australian community. 'Flexible' creative identities subvert the roles these informants imagine themselves performing as breadwinners for their future families. Chapter 4 of this volume contained an extended discussion about how the culture of small business enterprise in Arab–Australian communities is regarded by parents and the extended ethnic public as the most viable means of achieving rapid social mobility and, importantly, offers individuals the autonomy to manage their daily life and not fall victim to racial prejudice in mainstream, dependent employment markets. As I showed in that chapter, creative aspirants in this study do not simply choose between their individual aspirations or succumb to parental pressure. Rather, they exercise personal agency to seek out alternative career paths, for instance as creative entrepreneurs, which resonate on some level with their original creative aspirations as well as their desire to remain embedded within the local ethnic community and fulfil gendered scripts of respectability.

We do not know how young women of Arab–Australian backgrounds feel about such flexibility or casualisation and it is important that future research address such issues to enhance our understanding of the social mobility projects in which ethnic minority youth engage. Melissa Gregg's groundbreaking ethnography of contemporary working practices revealed that many women, especially mothers, preferred working irregular hours and from the home office as it suited their domestic responsibilities (2011). This might be the case for Arab–Australian young women as they develop creative careers, but we simply do not yet have the data to develop a comparative analysis between young men and women's creative vocational aspirations.

A distinctive angle of this research is that I not only looked at the conditions of creative labour that work against my informants, but also addressed the ways in which working experiences are shaped by forces outside of formal employment, namely family and friendship networks in the local community. One of the most important findings is that these young men imagine their individual lifestyles and vocational identities outside the parameters defined for them within the local ethnic community. This kind of intergenerational tension within ethnic communities has been explored in several studies but these tensions are often framed as problems arising from language barriers. Here, I have shown how creativity is evaluated in normative communal terms and that *this* is the source of intergenerational tensions between these young men and the older members of their migrant communities.

Tied into creativity is the language of passion, which, as I have suggested, refers to the personal investments these young men make in their own creative talents or skill and is thus an integral part of their social mobility project. Research that has examined the features of knowledge economies, post-industrialisation, and processes of urban regeneration have all reiterated that there is now little separation between work and lifestyles, or formal employment and leisure. Informants use the language of passion in a way that resonates with the discourse that the ability to integrate one's life passion into a paid role is liberating. By framing their aspirations in this way – as ones that are built on passion and not economic gain – a central tension emerges within their family dynamics. I have shown that Arab–Australian men must engage in negotiating their involvement in knowledge economies with parents who fail to comprehend. In turn, they become forced to renegotiate localised masculine templates for work and adulthood because of the many ways that creativity and creative labour undermine these templates.

Communities and belonging

Giddens (1991) suggests that in a postmodern world, communities develop outside of or distinct from the traditional institutions of family, church, or school. He argues that today we have fleeting attachments to various communities at different moments in our lives. In this study, I found that Arab–Australian young men from Bankstown look forward to pursuing creative courses in higher education institutions as well as working in creative fields, regardless of the pay packet, because they seek to belong to the kind of community Giddens refers to; one that is based on shared creative lifestyles and youthful subcultural interests rather than on a shared migrant history. This particular aspiration among many of the informants, to find a space to belong within the nation that is separate from a pre-existing migrant category, was a key finding in this study.

I dealt with this theme most specifically in Chapters 2 and 3 where I looked at peer relations within local Bankstown schools and youth cultures in higher education spaces. As I have shown however, these aspirations are rarely consummated. University is instead a moment of reckoning whereby my interviewees were filtered out of creative subcultural scenes for not adhering to highly specific codes of style and realise that those who most easily adapt to creative lifestyles are the young people who are already privileged. Youthful fantasies of escaping to bohemia are thus never realised and notions of creativity are instead discursively reconstructed at various points of the life-history interview in order to deal with this kind of rejection.

I would argue that the kind of rejection experienced by these young men from the youthful creative scenes during university was the experience that most dramatically altered the vocational directions of many informants. In Chapter 5, I detailed the work that some young men go on to do, as community arts workers and as 'ethno-political brokers'. We can conclude that this vocational identity is directly tied in to the discomfort that Arab–Australian young men are made to feel at university.

Thus, the challenge of creative work is twofold for these young men. First, to pursue a creative passion in the way they originally conceive during adolescence is to disconnect with their local ethnic community which they do not want to do. Second, the riskiness of pursuing a creative vocational aspiration is, as they realise in university, unlikely to pay off because they are not fully welcomed in the inner city creative tribe nor are they comfortable with the 'pretensions' associated with such scenes. The narratives explored in this book are a distinctive take on working in creative industries because they impress upon us the various ways that communal dynamics and growing up in predominantly working-class pockets of Western Sydney have lasting effects for the formations of vocational identities within youth and early adulthood.

Using a narrative analysis approach, I have also sought to show how informants attempt to establish a sense of uniformity and linearity across their life histories. I have suggested that by making links throughout various moments of their lives, these young men were seeking recognition as creative people in local communities where there are few precedents for such recognition. For instance, it was revealed throughout this book that creativity is often used by informants to refer to their 'unorthodox' youthful identities and establish hierarchies among Arab–Australian young men within their schools and extended social networks. While some studies have looked at the educational experiences of Arab–Australian or Muslim youth, peer relations are often glossed over. Here, we saw that youthful divisions operate along the lines of style and leisure interests, around different attitudes towards education and vocational options. These distinctions, I suggested, are indicative of the ways these young men understand creative identities. That is, creative vocational aspirations are not only formulated with the aim of pursuing a particular youthful interest and trying to develop this into a career, but also in order to distinguish the creative youth from the problematic 'Leb' youth in their local communities who display the markers of limited futures; ones that potentially keep them 'stuck' in Bankstown.

Research that focuses on ethnic minority youth and multiculturalism tends to pay most attention to the ways that various groups of young people establish a sense of belonging in local spaces in relation to youth from different ethnic backgrounds (Harris 2009; Wise 2009). That research makes important contributions to our understanding of how young people construct local spaces of belonging outside of the official, adult discourse of social cohesion. However, the narratives I explored in Chapter 2 reveal some of the limitations of this literature in Australia. The subcultural practices and youth style of ethnic minority youth are less often discussed. The discussion in this book, that creativity creates divisions among Arab–Australian young men from Bankstown, revealed that some young men work hard to establish their disconnection from the localised migrant community in which they are assumed to automatically feel a sense of belonging. As such, the articulation of a creative identity can be understood as the active rejection of the categories of difference ascribed to these youth in a multicultural state.

Notes

1 http://www.economist.com/blogs/graphicdetail/2016/03/daily-chart-20
2 http://www.smh.com.au/federal-politics/political-news/australians-want-boat-arrivals-treated-more-harshly-poll-20140107-30g97
3 http://www.smh.com.au/federal-politics/political-news/in-a-rare-disclosure-abbott-government-admits-turning-back-633-asylum-seekers-20150806-gist50.html
4 https://www.theguardian.com/australia-news/2016/aug/10/the-nauru-files-2000-leaked-reports-reveal-scale-of-abuse-of-children-in-australian-offshore-detention?
5 http://www.sbs.com.au/topics/life/culture/article/2016/07/22/why-it-so-much-worse-be-called-racist-actually-be-one
6 http://www.independent.co.uk/news/uk/crime/brexit-hate-crime-racism-stats-spike-police-england-wales-eu-referendum-a7126706.html
7 http://www.sbs.com.au/news/article/2015/03/25/violent-attack-sydney-muslim-woman-highlights-reports-islamophobia
8 https://www.ag.gov.au/NationalSecurity/Counteringviolentextremism/Pages/LivingSafeTogetherGrantsProgramme.aspx
9 http://www.dazeddigital.com/artsandculture/article/24579/1/how-a-new-wave-of-poc-artists-are-challenging-britishness
10 http://www.dazeddigital.com/artsandculture/article/24579/1/how-a-new-wave-of-poc-artists-are-challenging-britishness

References

Archer, L. (2003) *Race, Masculinity and Schooling: Muslim Boys and Education*, Buckingham, Open University.

Beck, U. (2000) *Risk Society: Towards a New Modernity*, London, Sage Publications.

Cuthill, M. and S. Scull (2011) 'Going to university: Pacific island migrant perspectives. Underlying factors constraining access to higher education for young people from low socioeconomic backgrounds in Australia: Pacific Island migrant perspectives', *Australian Universities Review*, 53(1): 5–13.

Florida, R. (2003) *The Rise of the Creative Class: And How it's Transforming Work, Leisure, Community and Everyday Life*, North Melbourne, Vic Pluto Press.

Giddens, A. (1991) *Modernity and Self-Identity*, Cambridge, Polity.

Gregg, M. (2011) *Work's Intimacy*, Cambridge, Polity Press.

Harris, A. (2009) 'Shifting the boundaries of cultural spaces: Young people and everyday multiculturalism', *Social Identities*, 15(2): 187–205.

Haukka, S. (2011) 'Education-to-work transitions of aspiring creatives', *Cultural Trends*, 20(1): 41–64.

Idriss, S. and Morgan G. (2017) 'Longue duree masculinity: Conserving the craft ethic in the new economy', in *Masculinity, Labour and Neoliberalism*, Eds. Walker, C and Roberts, S, London, Palgrave.

Kelly, P. and J. Kenway (2001) 'Managing youth transitions in the network society', in *British Journal of Sociology of Education*, 22(1): 19–33.

Lahire, B. (2003) 'From the habitus to an individual heritage of dispositions. Towards a sociology at the level of the individual', *Poetics* 31: 329–355.

Modood, T. (1993) 'The number of ethnic minority students in British higher education: Some grounds for optimism', *Oxford Review of Education*, 19(2): 167–182.

Nayak, A. (2003) *Race, Place and Globalisation: Youth Cultures in a Changing World*, London, Berg Publishers.

Roberts, K. (2007) 'Youth transitions and generations: A response to Wyn and Woodman', *Journal of Youth Studies*, 10(2): 263–269.

Roberts, K. (2009) 'Opportunities structures then and now', *Journal of Education and Work*, 22(5): 355–368.

Said, E. (2004) *Power, Politics and Culture: Interviews with Edward Said*, London, Bloomsbury.

Wise, A. (2009) '"Its just an attitude that you feel": Inter-ethnic habitus before the Cronulla Riots', in *Lines in the Sand: The Cronulla Riots and the Limits of Australian Multiculturalism*, Ed. G. Noble, Sydney, Institute of Criminology Press.

Wyn, J. (2005) 'Youth, Risk and Education', in *No Time to Lose: The Well-being of Australia's Children*, Eds. S. Richardson and M. R. Prior, Carlton, Vic, Melbourne University Publishing, pp. 255–280.

Wyn, J., S. Lantz, and A. Harris (2012) 'Beyond the transitions metaphor: Family relations and young people in late modernity', *Journal of Sociology*, 48(1): 3–22.

Index